Assessing Service Quality

Satisfying the Expectations of Library Customers

Peter Hernon and Ellen Altman

AMERICAN LIBRARY ASSOCIATION
Chicago and London
1998

Project editor: Louise D. Howe

Cover design: Tessing Design

Text design by Dianne M. Rooney

Composition in Janson Text and Univers using QuarkXpress 3.32 by the dotted i

Printed on 50-pound Victor Offset, a pH-neutral stock, and bound in 10-point coated cover stock by Victor Graphics

The paper used in this publication meets the minimum requirements of American National Standard for Information Sciences—Permanence of Paper for Printed Library Materials, ANSI Z39.48-1992. ∞

Library of Congress Cataloging-in-Publication Data

Hernon, Peter.
    Assessing service quality : satisfying the expectations of library customers / Peter Hernon, Ellen Altman.
       p.   cm.
    Includes bibliographical references (p.   ) and index.
    ISBN 0-8389-3489-7 (alk. paper)
    1. Libraries and readers—Evaluation. 2. Libraries and readers—United States—Evaluation. I. Altman, Ellen. II. Title.
Z711.H45   1998
025.5—DC21   98-8815

Printed in the United States of America.

02 01 00 99 98   5 4 3 2 1

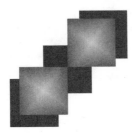

For Elinor and Allan

Contents

Figures

Preface

At a time when librarians are trying to cope with fast-paced technological change, shrinking budgets, massive reorganization, downsizing, and depressing predictions about the future of libraries, why should they be interested in yet another book about the assessment of library services? We will address this question by offering a new approach. Instead of presenting a cookbook of measures to apply to various services, we identify some touchstones critical to the well-being of libraries: customers, satisfaction, loyalty, and reputation. The concepts of loyalty and reputation are relatively new in the professional literature; a number of librarians dispute the notion that library users are customers. Furthermore, we distinguish between satisfaction and service quality; much of the literature confuses or ignores the distinction between the two.

Many in the profession strongly believe that only they, the professionals, have the expertise to assess the quality of library service. Such a belief may have validity in the abstract, but it fails to acknowledge reality. Every customer evaluates the quality of service received and decides when (and if) she or he will seek further interactions with the library. Behaviors and attitudes toward the library over time influence both customer perceptions about the library and the views of stakeholders who make decisions affecting the library's funding.

Service quality, as presented here, views the service provided by an organization from the perspective of the customer. It encourages the organization to meet specific customer expectations and to increase the number of customers who are loyal and delighted with the services provided.

Assessing Service Quality complements, but does not duplicate, our *Service Quality in Academic Libraries.*[1] The purposes of this new book are to:

- Suggest new ways to think about library services
- Explain service quality and further the development of its theoretical base

- Clarify the distinction between service quality and customer satisfaction
- Identify strategies for developing a customer service plan that meets the library's customer-focused mission, vision, and goals
- Identify procedures for measuring service quality and satisfaction
- Challenge conventional thinking about the utility of input, output, and performance measures, as well as public library role adoption or service response
- Suggest possible customer-related indicators that provide insights useful for library planning and decision making
- Encourage libraries to take action—action leading to improved service and accountability

Although the book focuses on academic and public libraries, the basic principles, strategies, and assessment procedures presented apply in other settings.

Traditionally, the amount of resources and productivity counts have been (and still are) used to assess the quality of libraries. Performance and output measures were developed as better indicators of service delivery, but they have been more discussed than widely used, as is confirmed by the small number of public libraries reporting them. Although performance and output measures have served an important purpose, the current cross-disciplinary evaluation literature lacks a standard nomenclature for such terms as "performance measures" and "outputs." Given that different people use the same terms but with widely varying meanings, it is time to replace such terms with new ones, and to explore other ways of evaluating and benchmarking library services. In effect, it is time to develop new ways to look at service.

Because technology offers new methods of information delivery, traditional counts of productivity underestimate the actual volume of business performed. New issues, such as those related to distance education, use of library World Wide Web sites, and partnership and consortium arrangements for gaining access to "virtual library" collections, make it clear that volumes of business are deceptive measures—ones becoming more complex to gauge. The library community needs to shift its focus from measures reporting volume of business, such as for circulation, to more meaningful indicators of customer loyalty, expectations, preferences, and satisfaction. The new indicators should report information about present and potential customers, their needs, expectations, and preferences, as well as the problems they encounter and how library staff handle those problems. Such information is useful for promoting customer loyalty, enhancing the service reputation of libraries, and for planning and decision making.

Customers are more than a source for data collection; they are the reason for libraries' existence. It is important (if not essential) to listen to, and learn from, customers and to use the insights gained to improve services. A number of libraries have ignored customers because they perceive customers as a captive audience. Chapter 12 dispels that notion as it enumerates the many competitors poised to challenge the library's perceived monopoly.

As the new millennium is about to unfold, librarians need new ways of thinking and alternatives for applying a customer-centered model of service quality. We regard this work as one in progress, because it provides a base upon which others can build. The approach presented here recognizes that holistic evaluation involves the use of both quantitative and qualitative data, as each type complements the other. The methods described in this book are not intended as a package to be adopted in their entirety, as, say, *Output Measures for Public Libraries* was intended.[2] The approach presented here is too large and too complex for any library to undertake at one time. Rather, our intention has been to present some new ways to think about service, along with some methods for evaluating and improving service. Libraries can select, from among the methods discussed, those most appropriate to their particular situation, and implement them at a pace that suits their needs.

Most people who become librarians do so from a desire to connect people with books and information—a concept that is the cornerstone of service quality. But, somehow, along the way, the profession has gotten caught up in bean-counting: how many of this and how much of that, as though the items counted exist in a universe totally unto themselves. It is our hope that the ideas presented here will encourage librarians to remember the ideals that attracted them to the profession and to abandon such misperceptions as "customers cannot judge quality," "customers do not know what they want," "library customers are a captive audience," and "professional hegemony will be undermined by kowtowing to customers."

If libraries do not want to be as service-centered as Nordstrom, Inc., or L. L. Bean, what are they willing to commit to? What is the source of their service inspiration? What service reputation do they generate? The answers to such questions will have a definite impact on the extent to which customers are loyal to the library, and on the number of customers who are delighted or completely satisfied—not merely appeased.

Peter Hernon and Ellen Altman

NOTES

1. Peter Hernon and Ellen Altman, *Service Quality in Academic Libraries* (Norwood, N.J.: Ablex, 1996).
2. See Nancy A. Van House, Mary Jo Lynch, Charles R. McClure, et al., *Output Measures for Public Libraries* (Chicago: American Library Association, 1987).

Acknowledgments

We wish to thank Allan D. Pratt for his patient reading of various drafts, his helpful comments, and his diligent preparation of figures. We also appreciate the copyediting of Timothy Jones, School of Communications and Information Management, Victoria University of Wellington, Wellington, New Zealand. Danuta A. Nitecki critiqued the manuscript for us, and we appreciate her helpful suggestions. As she so correctly reminded us, an extended discussion of service quality involves a combination of theory, attitude building, and practical guidance. Needless to say, any errors in this book are ours.

1

Understanding Ends and Means

. . . [T]he ethos of collection over customers has guided libraries since at least World War II.

—Peter Hernon and Ellen Altman[1]

Too many libraries, locked into the mind-set of size over service, are lumbering toward obsolescence.

—Robert Schwarzwalder[2]

Historically, the quality of a library has been measured by the size of its collection. The acquisition of the millionth volume was cause for celebration, and press releases flooded local and national news media. The millionth volume or a million-dollar "book" budget gave bragging rights to the library's director. "For decades, library directors, upon retirement, had wanted to be known for the number of titles added . . . during their tenure."[3] Collection size is the determining factor for membership in the prestigious Association of Research Libraries (ARL). The *Chronicle of Higher Education*, the major publication for news of academia, publishes a list of the largest academic libraries—the criterion is still collection size. State library agencies, in establishing systems for public libraries, used collection size to designate regional centers—a status that brought both statewide prestige and money to the chosen library.

Such thinking focused both resources and attention on the processes and functions associated with collection growth. Title-by-title selection and acquisition gave way to approval plans that facilitated the arrival of titles in bulk. Cooperative cataloging, especially through bibliographic networks, facilitated recording these titles in the library's catalog and moving them quickly to the shelves. With one order to a subscription agent, thousands of serials could be purchased and paid for with an annual check.

During the 1970s, many academic libraries were regarded by university administrators as "bottomless pits" because of constant entreaties for more money to "keep up with the publishing output." In the 1980s and 1990s, the pleas for more money centered around the large annual increases in the prices of scholarly and professional journal subscriptions and the need for electronically delivered resources and their requisite infrastructure.

Some critics noted the fallacy of equating collection size with quality —not all the libraries were counting items in the same way, while others kept outdated and unwanted books to boost their volume count. Obviously, the sheer number of volumes does not necessarily mean that the library collection matches readers' interests, and many titles go unused—they do not even circulate. Nevertheless, collection size has been firmly equated with status and library quality. The collection in many libraries became an entity in its own right, devoid of any implications about its usefulness to the library's community. Indeed, a 1997 book about libraries as gateways to electronic information contains the following statement about Harvard University Libraries: "The collection is, as it has always been, paramount."[4]

Service Quality

Because of this historical focus, library quality has been synonymous with collection size—an assessment of what the library *has*—rather than with what the library *does*. Yet, *library* quality and *service* quality are very different measures. A parallel can be drawn with the observations made by Raymond F. Zammuto and others, who studied student services offices in universities: "The idea of service quality as opposed to educational quality has not received much attention in higher education."[5] That situation is changing as most academic institutions now strive to attract and retain students. Service quality has become a topic of considerable interest for many service units on campus.

In the past several decades, as budgets for the purchase of materials have shrunk, the phrase "access not ownership" has become common. The means to achieve that access—interlibrary loan—did not change radically until recently, when the Internet became widely available to educational institutions. The result has been a major shift in resources, attention, and interest from the library "collection" to the information superhighway. The Internet and the World Wide Web (WWW)—how to use them, what sites are good, how to catalog WWW pages, and a myriad of associated topics—fill the pages of the professional literature and now seem the prime preoccupation of the library community. In all likelihood, access to Internet and associated resources will equal, if not surpass, physical volumes in the collection as the new standard of library quality. Yet, such a focus still says nothing about the quality of service provided and received.

For a library, service quality encompasses the interactive relationship between the library and the people whom it is supposed to serve. A library that adheres to all the professionally approved rules and procedures for acquiring, organizing, managing, and preserving material but has no customers cannot claim quality because a major element is missing—satisfying people's needs, requests, and desires for information. Maurice B. Line defined librarianship as "managing information resources for people."[6] How the library sees and interacts with those people—customers—clearly affects the quality and nature of the service rendered. As Françoise Hébert notes, "When library and customer measures of quality are not congruent, the library may be meeting its internal standards of performance but may not be performing well in the eyes of its customers."[7]

Patrons, Users, Clients, or Customers?

The name we use to describe the individuals we serve affects how well we do our jobs.

—John H. Sandy[8]

Organizations refer to the people they serve by many different terms: *clients, patients, students, readers, passengers, visitors, guests.* Such terms make these individuals seem something other than customers. Librarians often prefer the terms *patron* or *user,* perhaps to avoid the implication of an exchange occurring between the library and the people using the service. Yet, both words have rather negative connotations, as Darlene E. Weingand points out:

> The word *patron* is associated with the act of giving support and protection, such as occurred in the Renaissance between royalty and artists. The impression here is one of unequal status, of the powerful protecting the less powerful. This is not the type of relationship that puts libraries on an equal level of partnership with their communities. Further, while *user* accurately describes someone who uses the library, the term is quite unspecific and is widely associated with the drug culture.[9]

Special librarians and subject specialists in university libraries probably come closest to treating their users as clients. In the case of subject specialists, faculty and doctoral students who are repeat users become clients. These librarians know their clientele personally and have insights into their research and related interests. Yet, being a client does not preclude one from being treated like a customer.

Public libraries have different types of customers with different types of interests. These range from the preschooler who comes to a story hour, to the homeless man who wants to read the newspaper, to the businesswoman who needs tax regulation guidelines. All have different interests, but most want materials, information, or a place to sit and use library resources. A customer is the recipient of any product or service provided by the organization. That recipient might be either internal, such as a coworker in the same or another unit, or external—someone in the community wanting materials or information.

Research reporting some initiatives by government agencies to focus on customers noted that "the use of language can be pivotal in getting people to recognize that those they serve are their customers."[10] That research elaborated on how language influenced behavior in several instances. The Internal Revenue Service (IRS) regional center in Utah referred to tax filers in good standing as *compliers* and individuals not in good standing as *noncompliers*. The term *noncompliers* soon evolved into *deadbeats*, and those so called were treated accordingly. The Madison, Wisconsin, police department "now refers to all citizens as customers, including those who break the law. The police chief encourages officers to know their customers better."[11]

Some academic librarians argue that students cannot and should not be regarded as customers. Yet, students surely are potential customers when they select a school to attend. During high school, they are bombarded with advertising from colleges eager to enroll them. They are customers in the bookstore and food courts on campus, and when they purchase tickets to college sporting and entertainment events.

Only in the classroom can the status of students as customers be questioned. Only the teaching faculty have the expertise and the responsibility to set curricular requirements and to evaluate the students' performance. Even then, students have the right to appeal unfavorable decisions, evaluations, or treatment. Only other teaching faculty, however, decide the merits of the appeal. Yet, faculty may feel competition from within their own department and from other departments to attract students, as administrators and legislators determine which academic units to eliminate, restructure, or combine. Clearly, for this and many other reasons, faculty should be committed to continuous improvement.[12]

Another interesting notion, now widely accepted, is that organizations have *internal* as well as *external* customers. Internal customers depend on or receive work from another unit of the library. Such work can include information or reports, or processes and activities to be performed. Outsourcing may be one way to meet the needs of internal customers in a more timely manner. Public service staff are customers of the various units that acquire, catalog, process, and shelve materials.

It is interesting to note that in organizations that do not specifically call attention to meeting the needs of internal customers, turf wars break out. Joseph A. Boissé notes that the establishment of teams may actually exacerbate the warfare: "Since the teams enjoy great independence of action and decision making, whoever coordinates or facilitates cooperation becomes a key player in the new organization."[13]

Weingand notes that:

> the word customer, which implies payment for a product or service, is a better reflection of what actually transpires between the library and people in the community. With this term the mythology of the "free" library is dispelled, and a more accurate metaphor for service is substituted.[14]

Whatever the term, the people who interact with the service are the *reason* for the organization's existence. Therefore, their needs and desires should *drive* the service. Although the total quality management (TQM) movement has recently focused attention on customer service, the idea is not new.

As Arnold Hirshon notes, "Customer service was not a concept invented by total quality management experts."[15] The concept dates to the nineteenth and early twentieth centuries and to practices found in retail trade and hotel management. Other chapters in this book offer further evidence of why the concepts of *customer* and *customer service* are applicable to library and information science.

Although Lizabeth A. Wilson, associate director for Public Services at the University of Washington, does not use the word *customer*, she recognizes the basic elements of service quality:

> We need to acknowledge that taking care of the user is a priority. Second, we have to turn that acknowledgement into action. We have to not only talk the talk, but walk the talk [*sic*]. In the user-connected library, quality services and user satisfaction are goals shared by all staff, not just the director.[16]

Brian Quinn, like some other authors, argues that nonprofit organizations, such as libraries, have many customers—including, for instance, faculty, parents of students, academic administrators, members of governing boards, and state legislators—whose interests compete or conflict.[17] Obviously, he confuses customers with stakeholders; the distinction between the two is not always well understood. Customers are the people who actually *use*, or are likely to use, the library's services. The U.S. Department of Defense finally decided that its true customers were the military personnel who had to use the weapons that the department purchased, not members of Congress, the weapons companies, nor the taxpayers.[18] These others who have an interest in the organization, usually related to funding, are *stakeholders*. Stakeholders may exert influence, primarily through funding or legislation, but they are not customers.

Other authors have expressed concern about library service being equated with "customer and commodity."[19] They perceive libraries and their activities to be on a higher plane than their retail or commercial counterparts, and decry the assessment of rather basic processes, functions, and services as pedestrian and unsuitable. Indeed, one such author has criticized suggestions for measures that reflect the percentage of students and faculty who check out library materials or the number of courses requiring use of library resources as having "no direct connection to learning, research or intellectual activities in general. Rather they deal with the handling of things."[20] What that author fails to understand is that the library's contributions to facilitating education, promoting a love of learning, and aiding research very much depend on how well the library "handles things." None of these higher-order conditions can occur unless the library "handles things" in such a way that individuals find and are able to use the materials and information they seek.

We also want to nip in the bud the idea that higher-order conditions occur by some sort of intellectual osmosis. The truth is: *Unless customers and the collection come together in a way both interesting and meaningful to customers, the library is nothing more than an expensive warehouse.* Hard work, much of it "pedestrian," must be performed before this coming together can occur—even in the Magic Kingdom. "As Walt Disney once said, 'there is no magic to magic. It's in the details.'"[21]

It should be clear by now that the library as a vast collection, a warehouse filled with books and other printed materials, can no longer be justified as either a concept or a reality. The economic pressures on higher education and local government are causing both academic administrators and elected officials to question long-standing assumptions about many of their units. These units are now being scrutinized for their actual value to the sponsoring organization. Many are increasingly expected to fund their operating costs from revenue they raise. For example, the parks department in Maricopa County, Arizona, now raises 70 percent of its operating budget. "And the pressure is on for the parks to bring in even more. . . . Parks that pay their own way [is] the goal of many counties across the nation as they struggle with dwindling government support."[22]

Obviously, adding value, service quality, and customer satisfaction are new and pressing concepts for libraries, but they are concepts vital to libraries' continued well-being. After all, "the consequences of unquality are customers who leave disappointed, who tell others about how they feel, and who may never return to the library."[23]

It is not our intention here to delve into the reasons for these pressures to improve service quality, but rather to concentrate on *how* libraries can assess and improve customer satisfaction, enhance service quality, and add value in ways meaningful to their sponsoring organizations. The first principle is to focus on the purpose of librarianship— "managing information resources in ways that will serve people."[24] This purpose incorporates Ranganathan's five laws[25] and allows people who seek material or information to receive it—that is, to obtain certain types of materials within certain parameters.

The Library Customer Is Still the Customer

Some librarians resist the notions of *customer* and *service quality* because they equate them with the principle that "the customer is always right." Customers are *not* always right, but they do have a right to express their opinions and to learn about the library's service parameters.

Most customers have *expectations* about the service, though sometimes those expectations are unrealistic or unreasonable. (There will always be customers like the woman in an Oregon public library, in 1997, who was outraged when she could not obtain a 1991 North Carolina state income tax form.) Nor are we referring here to problem patrons who engage in irrational, prohibited, and, in some cases, illegal behaviors. Customers, as defined here, are individuals who want some assistance or some materials that the library might or might not hold. Customers might not know, however, what is unrealistic or unreasonable unless and until the library tells them. This requires some thinking on the part of library administrators to distinguish between core and peripheral services and to identify those that will not be offered. This also requires notifying the community of those decisions and perhaps even gaining support for them.

One library offers an excellent example of thinking through its service priorities. The primary customers for New Zealand's Department of Courts Library are judges—people who are accustomed to having all their demands quickly gratified. The library developed a strategic plan for information service for courts in six regions covering the entire country. The plan, approved by a committee that included judges, specified what the library would and would not do for customers in light of its budget. Before adoption of the strategic plan, judges were constantly asking library personnel to photocopy materials, sometimes the judges' own rather than library materials. Armed with the strategic plan, the library administration has made it clear that the staff do not photocopy any materials for judges. Nor do the staff perform any online searches. The judges or their assistants are expected to do these tasks. On the other hand, the library has developed and maintains a database of prison sentences given for each crime, which judges frequently consult in determining sentences for their own cases.

Details of the Department of Courts Library's budget are disseminated to customers so that they may understand the constraints under which the library operates. This is a novel but creative way to explain why some things cannot be done or why some materials cannot be purchased. Sharing this information with customers also allows them to comment about library priorities. Sometimes the priorities of the library and those of its customers are not the same. However, if the library is to serve the interests of its customers, their preferences deserve serious consideration.

Customer Satisfaction and Service Quality

Many library surveys ask about customer satisfaction, sometimes in a general context and sometimes in relation to specific services. Usually the questions about satisfaction allow for scaled responses (e.g., ranging from "not satisfied at all" through "partially satisfied" to "satisfied" and "completely satisfied"). Too often, satisfaction surveys are really intended as library report cards. In fact, some surveys actually ask participants to assign the library a grade from A to F. There is usually no intent to take any remedial action based on replies to these questions, but rather to use the responses in negotiations with administrators in the sponsoring institution.

That librarians have truly not been much concerned with satisfaction among customers is confirmed by Rachel Applegate, who notes the absence of a subject heading for "customer satisfaction" or any related term in *Library Literature* and who characterizes the literature as "overwhelmingly, even oppressively, behaviorally based: uses, not users, system performance, not patron perception."[26] Also, the terms *satisfaction* and *service quality* are frequently used interchangeably; this mistake has led to more confusion.

According to Kevin Elliott, who cites a number of marketing experts, *satisfaction* is "the emotional reaction to a specific transaction or service encounter."[27] That definition is consistent with one cited by Applegate, which says that "satisfaction is ultimately a state experienced inside the user's head."[28] Satisfaction may or may not be directly related to the performance of the library on a specific occasion. A customer can receive an answer to a query but be unsatisfied because of an upsetting or angry encounter. Conversely, although the query might remain unanswered, another customer might feel satisfied because the encounter was pleasant and the helper interested and polite.

Service quality, on the other hand, "has been described as a global judgment, or attitude, relating to the superiority of a service."[29] The inference is that the satisfaction levels from a number of transactions or encounters that an individual experiences with a particular organization fuse to form an *impression* of service quality for that person. The *collective* experiences of many persons create an organization's reputation for service quality.

Service Quality—Perception Is Reality

When consumers purchase a service, they purchase an experience.

—John E. G. Bateson[30]

Every organization's service has a quality dimension—ranging from wonderful to awful. Service and quality cannot be disconnected. Quality is the manner in which the service is delivered, or, in some cases, not delivered.

Service quality is multidimensional. Two critical dimensions are content and context. *Content* refers to obtaining what prompted the visit—particular materials or information, study space, or an acceptable substitute. *Context* covers the experience itself: interactions with staff, ease or difficulty in navigating the system, and the comfort of the physical environment.

Customers who come into the library as well as those who "visit" through an electronic highway experience both the content and context of the service. From these interactions, customers form opinions and attitudes about the library. Customer expectations can influence satisfaction with both content and context. These expectations may or may not match what the library thinks appropriate, but nevertheless *they represent reality for the customer.*

Expectations change according to what customers want and how urgently they want it. Sometimes they are seeking a quiet place to read, sometimes just a book for enjoyment, and sometimes a vital bit of information. Importance and urgency, though seldom considered, are likely to have a strong influence on customers' satisfaction with a service. The prevailing custom has been to treat all searches or inquiries with equal priority, except those from persons of special importance to the library, such as an administrator in the sponsoring organization. The concept of equal treatment should be reconsidered because of its impact on consequences to the customer. If the level of service for all is high, exceptions become detrimental, costly, distractive, and unnecessary.

Service quality is a complex concept: It has several dimensions beyond the content/context and the performance/performance-expectations gap. Service quality is both personal to individuals and collective among many customers. Each individual who interacts with the library forms an opinion about the quality of services provided, ranging from highly positive to highly negative. When the collective opinions of many customers become known and seem to agree, those opinions create a *reputation* for the library and for the quality of its service.

Impressions of service quality, in a number of instances, can also be changed; perceptions move up with positive experiences and down as a result of negative ones. Chapters 6, 7, 8, and 10 will present some techniques for assessing service quality and satisfaction so that libraries can review their mission and vision statements, and assess their service reputation and image, while adapting goals and objectives to cope better with customer expectations.

Why Assess Quality?

If an organization cannot effectively measure quality performance, it will not be able to manage it.

—Kevin M. Elliott[31]

Libraries have gathered and reported statistics about their collections, funds, and staff for decades. These statistics have, however, concentrated primarily on finances, the resources purchased with those finances, and workloads. Nevertheless, an information gap remains. These traditional statistics lack relevance. Most of the traditional statistics do not measure the library's performance in terms of elements important to customers. They do not really describe performance or indicate whether service quality is good, indifferent, or bad. Even worse, they do not indicate any action that the administration or any team could or should take to improve performance.

Libraries need measures to assess service quality on a much broader scale than resources held, resources acquired, and activities completed. The current statistics for both academic and public libraries emphasize expenditures. Focusing on money can be dangerous, because it emphasizes the cost of the library to the sponsoring organization at a time when top administrators are looking closely at costs and how to contain them. Even businesses that have relied on financial data as the ultimate indicator of performance now recognize the need for broader measures.

The Balanced Scorecard

Profit, which accountants call *return on investment (ROI)*, has been the traditional measure of business success. Yet, these days, ROI is no longer considered the only or the ultimate measure of performance. Many businesses have adopted the concept of the balanced scorecard as an assessment method. The *balanced scorecard* is a "matrix of measures that can show the performance of the organization from the perspective of each of its stakeholders."[32] The scorecard asks questions about four key areas common to most organizations:

1. How do customers see us?
2. How do we look to decision makers and the community? (financial perspective)
3. What must we excel at? (This question looks to the internal working of the organization.)
4. Can we continue to improve and create value?[33]

The balanced scorecard is essentially a tool for strategic management. Implementing the balanced scorecard requires that the administration answer the four preceding questions in terms of the present situation and desired outcomes for the future. The next step is to define the factors critical for success and then to identify measures that indicate success.

Measures relating to customers might indicate, for instance, the percentage of repeat customers, the percentage of customer complaints, and the number of new registered borrowers. Internal measures might focus on cycle times and employee productivity and skills. At the end of the specified time period, all the measures are combined to produce an overall score. Although we are not advocating adoption of the balanced scorecard, its principles have merit in that they encompass a wider variety of factors than do the traditional counts reported by both public and academic libraries in their annual reports and in national compilations of library statistics.

Other Dimensions of Service Quality

George E. Kroon, a marketing consultant, offers four other ways to look at service quality: conformance, expectation, market, and strategic.[34] Because the last of these measures, strategic, applies only to commercial establishments, we will not consider it here.

Conformance requires that standards for quality be set for many processes and functions. The intent is to reduce mistakes (shelving errors), streamline work flow (cut backlogs), and establish required behaviors on the part of staff (ask if the customer got what was desired). Setting standards for service quality, as opposed to targets for work productivity in technical services or restrictions on the time allowed to answer reference questions, is rather a novel idea for libraries, but one whose time has come. The library has considerable control over quality as conformance to standards that it can use to improve service in many areas.

The idea of conformance standards leads to consideration of three kinds of situations that might negatively affect service quality: predictable, foreseeable, and unpredictable. *Predictable* situations are those over which the library has considerable control, and, thus, can take action to prevent or at least minimize. *Foreseeable* situations are those that are likely to happen, but for which the time frame between occurrences is longer and incidences are fewer than for the predictable ones. To some extent, it is possible to plan for even *unpredictable* and unlikely situations. For example, staff trained to respond to certain disasters or crises, such as fire, bomb threats, and tornadoes, can greatly ameliorate the situation. Following are examples of each type of library situation.

Predictable situations
    Equipment failures (paper jams, burnt-out bulbs)
    Network crashes
    No paper in photocopiers and printers
    Staff absences
    Patron ignorance
Foreseeable situations
    Power failures
    Weather problems
    Budget cuts and recisions
Unpredictable situations
    Natural disasters
    Fire
    Psychopaths

The downside of concentrating solely on conformance quality is that the focus is internal and may not match customer expectations or preferences. Kroon cites the Swiss watch industry as an example; it set high standards for mechanical timepieces while customer preferences had moved on to digital watches. Although conformance standards are desirable, they should not be used in isolation.

The second dimension is customer *expectations*. Expectations will be influenced by factors outside management's control: customers' prior experience, word-of-mouth, and competitor behavior. Performance that repeatedly, or in some particular way, fails to meet customers' expectations is a clear signal to management that performance needs improvement. Such improvement can be facilitated by training, technology, or conformance standards. Sometimes, however, customers have erroneous or unrealistic ideas about the service. For example, customers who dislike the online public access catalog (OPAC) and want the card catalog returned should be helped to overcome their fear of the technology. In other cases, customers should be told *why* their expectations cannot be met.

The third dimension of service quality is *market perception*—evaluation against competitors. Libraries have not really thought about competitors; usually they look at the market in terms of peer institutions. Nevertheless, competition from super bookstores, online suppliers of journal articles, the WWW, and nontraditional colleges and universities, including the virtual university, may become more serious in the future (see Chapter 12). Even other libraries can be competitors if customers have the option of using them. Figure 1.1, adapted from one presented by Kroon, depicts the differences in quality dimensions.

FIGURE 1.1
Differences in Quality Dimensions

	Dimension		
	Conformance	**Expectation**	**Market**
Viewpoint	Internal	External	Peers and competitors
Key terms	Service quality	Expectations Performance gap	Peer performance
Focus of effort	Processes Functions Services	Service Customer	Peer comparisons
What to assess	Transactions Performance Context	Customer expectations vs. performance and vs. importance	Rankings/ratios with peer data
Superior quality results in:	Stakeholder satisfaction	Performance exceeding expectations Loyalty	Good reputation
Inferior quality results in:	Errors Higher costs Delays Lost customers	Bad word-of-mouth Dissatisfaction	Unfavorable reputation compared to peers

Adapted from George Kroon, "Improving Quality in Service Marketing," *Journal of Customer Service in Marketing and Management* 1, no. 2 (1995): 13–28. Copyright 1995, The Haworth Press, Inc., Binghamton, New York.

The Payoff for the Library

In an information rich world where human attention is the scarce commodity, the library's business is orchestrating human attention structures.

—Richard A. Lanham[35]

With all the recent techniques for better management (e.g., Total Quality Management, reengineering, and empowerment) and the new technologies that have been adopted, many organizations, including libraries, are suffering from what Tony Hope and Jeremy Hope characterize as "improvement fatigue."[36] These techniques hold out the promise of increased profits for business, but what can they offer to nonprofit organizations like libraries?

Most librarians are not consciously aware of the two things that are basic to the success of their libraries—the attention they get from individual customers, and their reputation. People have many choices about how to spend their unstructured time—they can watch TV or a movie, surf the Web, attend a ball game, or shop at the mall. In addition, as Ralph Norman describes it,

> for a wide and complicated series of reasons, we are producing a much greater volume of text than anybody is reading or able to read. The intellectual sensorium is clogged, glutted, surfeited, full, overstuffed, bloated, teeming, overabundant, overflowing.[37]

Everybody is bombarded with messages and stimuli. Therefore, *attention* and *time* are two of the most valuable assets that individuals have. Those who choose to spend these assets in the library or using library resources should be regarded as precious customers.

Domino's Pizza no longer considers the delivery of a pie as merely a one-time ten-dollar transaction. Instead, the firm's management stresses the potential lifetime value of that customer if service quality can secure loyalty. The long-term value of each customer might amount to many thousands of dollars. Recognizing the value of *repeat customers* is important for the success of most organizations. Repeat customers, especially the more frequent ones, tend to be loyal. The library's repeat customers already have proven their interest in reading and seeking information. Loyalty means that the customers return repeatedly; they recommend the library to their friends and colleagues, and may be more forgiving when the system makes a mistake. Some of them will actively campaign for library bond issues or protest library budget cuts.

Libraries need to create more loyal customers, yet many public librarians seem to talk more about attracting nonusers than keeping present customers happy or finding out why previous customers no longer return. Academic librarians may take the short-term view—it is four years and gone for the largest number of students. Such an attitude fails to consider the ripple effect as former students tell friends and family about their experiences with higher education. Moreover, as these alumni prosper, the college or university will approach them as potential donors or contributors, but may encounter resentment for their past treatment. Research indicates that only completely satisfied customers can be reasonably classified as loyal (see Chapters 9 and 10).

This is a major reason why paying close attention to library service quality is critical.

A new trend in the nonprofit sector is to allow customers more choice.[38] For example, Pell grants, food stamps, and vouchers for school choice have personal preference components. Charges for use of campus computing facilities have become widespread since the 1980s. Now, some academic institutions are flirting with the idea of having departments purchase information from the campus library. In essence, the library would have to earn all or part of its operating funds from the academic departments. The theory is that "customer-driven systems waste less, because they match supply to demand."[39]

The collective experience of customers creates a reputation for the library. That reputation will become known to the administrators who fund the library and to the library community—the students, the faculty, the public, and the taxpayers. What kind of reputation does a library have? How well does that reputation match the one that library staff desire? If the library wants a better reputation, what is it doing to improve it? These questions need serious consideration in every library. Librarians need to consider how to describe the benefits of their service better to the administrators who fund them. Otherwise, some other agency will set mandatory indicators of performance, as the Audit Commission did for Britain and Wales. In both places, all public libraries are now required to publish the following performance indicators in the local newspaper at the end of the calendar year:

- Number of items issued
- Number of hours open
- Number of visitors
- Total pounds spent per capita
- Materials per capita
- Cost per issue (circulation)

Cost per issue has become a rather contentious measure, as some elected officials and local officials perceive it to be a measure of efficiency and may use it to challenge libraries where cost per circulation seems high. Obviously, letting others decide how to measure library quality poses its own problems.

Summary

Each year the Malcolm Baldrige National Quality Award recognizes outstanding American companies. "Of the seven categories on which this award is based, the most highly weighted is 'customer satisfaction.'" In this category, companies are judged on the following elements: knowledge of customer requirements and expectations, determination of customer satisfaction, ability to summarize satisfaction results, and comparisons to other companies.[40]

Companies that have won this award, given since 1987, have enjoyed considerable success. In December 1996, the National Institute of Standards and Technology (NIST), a unit of the U.S. Department of Commerce, examined the stock market performance of the winners. "It found that from 1988 to 1996, the [stock prices of the] fourteen publicly traded Baldrige winners . . . gained 325% vs. 112% for the S&P Index."[41] Clearly, service quality has a significant payoff.

The time has come to stop confusing means—process and functions related to the collection or to technology—with ends (i.e., purpose), or managing information resources for people. People are the reason for having a library—without them there is no need for any library. Service is basic to the customers' satisfaction or delight with the library:

> A service can be an idea, entertainment, . . . information, knowledge, . . . social innovation, circumstance, convenience, food, security, or any number of other things. Service may also be defined as a deed, a performance, a social event or an effort and output that is consumed where it is produced.[42]

The collective opinion of customers creates the library's reputation for service quality. Service quality, a complex phenomenon, is composed of the content of the service itself and the context in which the service is rendered. It is also affected by the quality of the information supplied and used, and the expectations that customers have for the service. All managers should want to avoid situations in which library performance is poor and expectations are low, but customers appear indifferent or satisfied. Service quality is both individual and collective. The collective assessment of service quality creates the library's reputation in the community and for the administrators who fund the library.

Traditional library performance measures do not reflect service quality. Their focus is primarily on expenditures for resources rather than on delivery of service. For these and other reasons, library managers must look for better ways to measure and describe the quality of their services, and, in effect, demonstrate that the organization deserves the type of recognition bestowed on the Baldrige Award winners.

NOTES

1. Peter Hernon and Ellen Altman, *Service Quality in Academic Libraries* (Norwood, N.J.: Ablex, 1996), 157.
2. Robert Schwarzwalder, "Building the Digital Sci/Tech Library. Part 1: The Revolutionaries Handbook," *Database* 20, no. 3 (June/July 1997): 63.
3. Hernon and Altman, *Service Quality in Academic Libraries*, 157.
4. Richard De Gennaro, foreword to *Gateways to Knowledge: The Role of Academic Librarians in Teaching, Learning and Research*, edited by Lawrence Dowler (Cambridge, Mass.: MIT Press, 1997), vii.

5. Raymond F. Zammuto, Susan M. Keaveney, and Edward J. O'Connor, "Rethinking Student Services: Assessing and Improving Service Quality," *Journal of Marketing for Higher Education* 7, no. 1 (1996): 46.

6. Maurice B. Line, "What Do People Need of Libraries, and How Can We Find Out?" *Australian Academic & Research Libraries* 27, no. 2 (June 1996): 77.

7. Françoise Hébert, "Service Quality: An Unobtrusive Investigation of Interlibrary Loan in Large Public Libraries in Canada," *Library & Information Science Research* 16, no. 1 (1994): 20.

8. John H. Sandy, "By Any Other Name, They're Still Our Customers," *American Libraries* 28, no. 7 (August 1997): 43.

9. Darlene E. Weingand, *Customer Service Excellence: A Guide for Librarians* (Chicago: American Library Association, 1997), 2.

10. Carolyn R. Farquhar, *Focusing on the Customer: A Catalyst for Change in the Public Sector. Lessons from the North American Study Tour on Total Quality in the Public Sector* (Ottawa, Canada: The Conference Board of Canada, 1993), 12.

11. Ibid.

12. Jann E. Freed and Marie R. Klugman, *Quality Principles and Practices in Higher Education* (Phoenix, Ariz.: Oryx Press, 1997), 150–52.

13. Joseph A. Boissé, "Adjusting the Horizontal Hold: Flattening the Organization," *Library Administration & Management* 10, no. 2 (spring 1996): 81.

14. Weingand, *Customer Service Excellence*, 2.

15. Arnold Hirshon, "Running with the Red Queen: Breaking New Habits to Survive in the Virtual World," in *Advances in Librarianship*, vol. 20, edited by Irene Godden (San Diego: Academic Press, 1996), 5–6.

16. Lizabeth A. Wilson, "Glacier or Avalanche? Shifts in the Electronic, Education, and Library Landscape," in *LOEX of the West: Teaching and Learning in a "Climate of Change,"* edited by Thomas W. Leonhardt (Greenwich, Conn.: JAI Press, 1996), 9.

17. Brian Quinn, "Adapting Service Quality Concepts to Academic Libraries," *Journal of Academic Librarianship* 23, no. 5 (September 1997): 362.

18. David Osborne and Ted Gaebler, *Reinventing Government: How the Entrepreneurial Spirit Is Transforming the Public Sector* (Reading, Mass.: Addison-Wesley, 1992), 166.

19. John M. Budd, "A Critique of Customer and Commodity," *College & Research Libraries* 58, no. 4 (July 1997): 317.

20. Ibid., 318.

21. Laura A. Liswood, *Serving Them Right: Innovation and Powerful Customer Retention Strategies* (New York: Harper Business, 1990), 17.

22. Kathleen Ingley, "Pressure's on for Parks to Be Self-Supporting," *Arizona Republic*, August 31, 1997, A1.

23. Hébert, "Service Quality," 20.

24. Maurice B. Line, "Line's Five Laws of Librarianship . . . and One All-Embracing Law," *Library Association Record* 98, no. 3 (March 1996): 144.

25. S. R. Ranganathan's Five Laws of Library Science are: (1) books are for use; (2) every book its reader; (3) every reader his [or her] book; (4) save the time of the reader; and (5) a library is a growing organism. See also Maurice B. Line, "Use of Library Materials" [book review], *College & Research Libraries* 40, no. 6 (November 1979): 557–58.

26. Rachel Applegate, "Models of Satisfaction," in *Encyclopedia of Library and Information Science* 60, Supplement 23 (New York: Marcel Dekker, 1997), 200.

27. Kevin M. Elliott, "A Comparison of Alternative Measures of Service Quality," *Journal of Customer Service in Marketing and Management* 1, no. 1 (1995): 35.

28. Applegate, "Models of Satisfaction," 201.

29. Elliott, "A Comparison of Alternative Measures," 35.

30. John E. G. Bateson, "Evaluating the Role and Place of Marketing in Service Firms," in *Service Management Effectiveness*, edited by David E. Bowen, Richard B. Chase, Thomas G. Cummings, and Associates (San Francisco: Jossey-Bass, 1990), 325.

31. Elliott, "A Comparison of Alternative Measures," 42.

32. Tony Hope and Jeremy Hope, *Transforming the Bottom Line: Managing Performance with the Real Numbers* (Boston: Harvard Business School Press, 1996), 96.

33. Robert S. Kaplan and David P. Norton, "The Balanced Scorecard—Measures That Drive Performance," *Harvard Business Review* 70, no. 1 (January/February 1992): 72.

34. George E. Kroon, "Improving Quality in Service Marketing," *Journal of Customer Service in Marketing and Management* 1, no. 2 (1995): 13–28.

35. Richard A. Lanham, "A Computer-Based Harvard Red Book," in Dowler, ed., *Gateways to Knowledge*, 165.

36. Hope and Hope, *Transforming the Bottom Line*, 2.

37. Ralph Norman, "The Scholarly Journal and the Intellectual Sensorium," in *The Politics and Processes of Scholarship*, edited by Joseph M. Moxley and Lagretta T. Lenker (Westport, Conn.: Greenwood Press, 1995), 80.

38. Osborne and Gaebler, *Reinventing Government*.

39. Ibid., 184.

40. Bob Hayes, *Measuring Customer Satisfaction* (Milwaukee, Wisc.: ASQC Quality Press, 1992), 2.

41. Lani Luciano, "Money Helps: Answers to Your Questions," *Money* 26, no. 4 (April 1997): 175.

42. David A. Collier, "Measuring and Managing Service Quality," in Bowen et al., eds., *Service Management Effectiveness*, 237.

2

A Look in the Library Mirror

Libraries say they support user self-sufficiency. I challenge you to go into any of our libraries and see if you don't experience anxiety and heart palpitations when you have to use the library as a user.

—Lizabeth A. Wilson[1]

In the 1991 film *The Doctor*, John McKee (played by William Hurt) gets to experience the hospital where he is an esteemed heart surgeon from the perspective of a patient when he is diagnosed with throat cancer.[2] His long waits to see the doctors, canceled appointments, and indifferent and sometimes rude treatment from both staff and physicians first anger him and then awaken him to the fact that all patients, including his own, are more than just sick bodies. The situations depicted in the film are familiar to many people who have interacted with medical facilities in recent years. Customer problems with banks, stores, airlines, and many other service organizations stem from one source—failure to view policies and procedures from the perspective of the customers.

United Airlines, after 30 years of advertisements inviting would-be passengers to experience the "friendly skies," recently embarked on an advertising campaign designed to show an understanding of passengers' frustrations and the airline's attempts to relieve them. One television commercial shows United employees annoyed because the speaker for a scheduled meeting is half an hour late, but no one seems to know why.

Suddenly, in walks the speaker, who compares their annoyance with those of delayed and uninformed passengers. Get the message? All new customer service employees at Greyhound Bus Company get to ride on a dirty, smelly bus that arrives far behind schedule. The intent is to make these new employees aware that passengers do not like such conditions either. It is worthwhile to consider some situations and experiences in libraries that might negatively affect service quality. From the customers' perspective, libraries have their unexplained delays and dirty buses, too.

Self-Sufficiency

Because of stagnant or declining budget allocations, many libraries have made conscious attempts to foster customers' self-sufficiency. Sometimes this self-sufficiency is euphemistically called *empowering* customers. Whatever term is used, the result is that customers are expected to do more and more for themselves. Now there is nothing inherently wrong in trying to promote customer self-sufficiency. Most people are used to fending for themselves in supermarkets, department stores, and gas stations. In fact, many customers like to be able to peruse the merchandise without sales personnel hovering in the background or actively trying to induce purchases. Within the next few years, customers in self-service shopping emporiums may well be expected to register their purchases with portable optical scanners.

Self-sufficiency works well in supermarkets and department stores because the experience is rather predictable. Most supermarkets have similar floor plans; even though the particular items in aisle 7 may differ from store to store, the layout is familiar enough for a new customer to understand how the system works. The same is true of the chain department stores. *Predictability* promotes self-sufficiency.

However, unlike the large rectangle common to retail shopping, the structure of most libraries is not predictable; indeed library buildings are intended to be unique. That means that each first-time customer has to navigate the floor plan and decipher the system. Whether that navigation and deciphering are easy or frustrating depends on decisions made by architects, library administrators, staff, and others. Libraries can do many things to make the experience easy and successful. On the other hand, certain practices or policies make the experience confusing and frustrating. *How the library helps or hinders navigating and deciphering the system alters customers' perceptions of the quality of service provided and their attitudes about librarians and libraries generally.*

Despite efforts to stamp out the popular stereotype of the librarian, it remains strong because people *can identify that image with their own experiences*. Many people find the library an arcane and frightening place.[3] Indeed, a number of articles in professional journals have described the condition called "library anxiety." Many customers are confused about how to locate what they want. It is much easier to find a bag of flour in a supermarket than to find a particular book in a library, or, worse, a specific fact among all those books. Nor are call numbers and catalogs, whether card or electronic, easily understood by the uninitiated. In addition, customers are frequently unsure of the appropriateness of asking for help, especially when staff seem occupied with other tasks. Reports of unpleasant experiences by those who do ask are not uncommon.[4]

Moreover, as George D'Elia and Eleanor Jo Rodger found,

> fewer than half (42 percent) of the users of the Free Library of Philadelphia asked a librarian for assistance. Often, the only contact with the staff is at the circulation desk; the rest of the user's visit amounts to self-service.[5]

"Self-service," as Thomas Childers and Nancy Van House note, "limits both the library's ability to serve and its ability to assess and represent its service."[6] All this underscores the importance of customer contact with library staff, and the role this contact plays in service quality.

To promote self-sufficiency or "coproduction," where customers participate in the service delivery process,[7] it is first necessary to make the organization welcoming and transparent, not hindering customers in their pursuit of materials or information. Following are nine practices that hinder customer coproduction and perhaps induce frustration.

1. Permitting long delays in reshelving items (i.e., books, periodicals, and videos)
2. Requiring customers to bring in items for renewal
3. Failing to monitor or restrict use of the online public access catalog (OPAC) and other workstations for receiving and sending e-mail messages, thus making queuing a problem as customers wait to use the computers
4. Having multiple interfaces for using online resources and electronic texts, thereby confusing customers
5. Providing poor quality printers for computer workstations
6. Sending library notices by mail, rather than e-mail
7. Not posting directions for obtaining a photocopy card on or near the copiers
8. Filling paper trays for copiers and printers only once a day, no matter how much the machines are used. The schedule, not the need, is paramount.
9. Failing to post instructions on the photocopier indicating how to position the item to be copied. Sometimes the paper tray is in the portrait position, other times it is in the landscape position. Customers must guess. Half the time they guess wrong, and waste their first copy.

By the way, the last three examples relate to photocopying, a service that more libraries are outsourcing. Many libraries may not regard photocopying as a core service, but customers might.

To summarize:

Library operations don't occur in a vacuum. They take place within an institutional culture and environment. This institutional milieu creates the service atmosphere and significantly influences the approach that staff members take when performing routine tasks. In libraries where a commitment to service is present but at a minimum level, the institutional culture may be task-oriented; administrative and staff concerns are directed toward the successful, efficient completion of routine duties.

At the opposite end of the continuum the library culture regards customer satisfaction as the primary goal, and both administrators and staff direct their energies and activities toward that goal.[8]

Peculiarities of Placement

[P]eculiarities in placement of materials . . . cause problems for browsers—these peculiarities do not bother librarians, who are so used to dealing with these quirks they no longer see them.

—Sheila Intner and
Elizabeth Futas[9]

Staff members at one public library are beset with numerous questions about where to find books even though the customers have the call numbers and the OPAC claims the items are "in." This library has many separate shelving areas that are not indicated on the catalog record: old fiction, new fiction, old mysteries, new mysteries, old large-print items, new large-print items—all are simply noted as "fiction" or "large print" in the OPAC record.

In this same library, juvenile titles are not indicated as such in the OPAC record. Yet customers are expected to "know" that the title is a juvenile and, therefore, is shelved in the juvenile collection. Confusing? You bet.

A large sign identifies the "Fiction and Biography" area, while nearby a section of shelves contains biographies but no fiction. Browsers may be puzzled that the books seem so dated. Puzzlement could be mitigated by a notice that more recent biographies are now classified in the nonfiction collection. The classification of biography under the career of the biographee or historical period seems a recent trend in many public libraries. For libraries intending to reclassify the materials now housed in a separate "biography" collection, some notice to customers about the change in classification seems appropriate.

Separating genre titles—mystery, romance, science fiction, westerns —seems like a good idea. Yet, many libraries deal inconsistently with genre books, and this leads to customer confusion. Some titles in the same series, such as Sue Grafton's Kinsey Milhone books or the cases investigated by Archie McNally in the series by Lawrence Sanders, are placed in the genre collection while others are shelved in the fiction collection—although the distinction between the two collections is not readily apparent. Sometimes, copies of the same title appear in both collections. One library shelves titles in the mystery collection if the book or series has a detective as the main character. How customers are to fathom this arrangement is itself a mystery, because the policy has never been conveyed to them. Even stranger, the library does not adhere to its own policy, in that titles having no detective also appear in the mystery section. No wonder customers might be confused.

Signage

We need to look at space through the user's eyes.

—Lizabeth A. Wilson[10]

The intelligent placement of well-designed signs ought to reduce customer frustration and enhance customer self-sufficiency. When signage is poor or limited, the library becomes a maze for many of its customers. One multilevel academic library has a sign only on the ground floor indicating which floors house certain classification numbers. Even though OPAC terminals are conveniently located on each floor, someone unfamiliar with the library's arrangement has to return to the ground floor from as far away as the fourteenth floor to determine the location of call numbers. In this same library, oversized books are housed together on each floor. Although the OPAC records indicate volumes as oversized, they do not indicate the special shelving. That information is found in a pamphlet—available only on the ground floor.

Signs indicating the classification numbers posted flat at the ends of stack ranges are another annoyance. In some libraries, these signs have been removed or need updating, as redoing them each time books are moved from range to range is considered too much trouble. In large, multistoried libraries, a map on each floor showing layout empowers customers and answers many of their questions about location.

Staff

[The librarian behaved] as if to get rid of me; as if she had other things to do and resented spending so much time.

—Catherine Sheldrick Ross and Patricia Dewdney[11]

Because of financial stringency, students and support staff are now assigned to do work formerly handled by librarians or paraprofessionals. Some of the newer staff do a fine job. It is, however, disconcerting to encounter staff at public service desks too engrossed in checking collection order slips, performing clerical tasks, or playing solitaire or other games on computer terminals to answer customer questions.

Circulation staff who ignore reports of malfunctioning self-issue machines are another example of indifference to customers who are trying to be self-sufficient. A sign that the machine is not functioning and the problem is being addressed would alleviate multiple reports and complaints to the staff as well as the frustration and annoyance of customers.

The self-issue machine in one public library does not handle some transactions. Customers then must queue for checkout by a circulation attendant. The attendants tell customers that the bar codes were not properly placed for the self-issue machine to read, because "we didn't know that we would get this machine." The self-issue machine in a nearby city, however, has no problems reading all bar codes. In addition, some circulation systems allow customers to check the status of items charged to them, whereas other systems do not. These examples illustrate that customers cannot necessarily predict the level or type of service that a library will provide.

Staff have been expected to learn a lot about information technology these past few years. Unfortunately, some have not received sufficient training to enable them to be *helpful* to customers who want to use electronic resources. When customers ask for help or complain that the system is not working properly, the behaviors displayed by untrained staff may range from ignorance and fear to frustration and hostility. Technologically savvy customers consider these responses to be indications of ineptness. Customers who are technologically uninformed or timid have their uneasiness about computers reaffirmed by these encounters.

Reducing "Dumb" Questions

Customers would not ask so many "dumb" questions if libraries informed them better in the first place. For example, placing bound periodical volumes on reserve with no notice either on the shelf or in the OPAC is likely to prompt a question from customers who expect to find the volume for 1994 between those for 1993 and 1995.

Taking issues from shelves for binding—and the length of time they remain at the bindery—are a mystery to most customers, even knowledgeable ones. One library shelves all bound periodical volumes by classification number, but unbound issues are held in a "current" periodical section on the ground floor and shelved by title. "Current" can range from the most recent issue to the last three years. Adding to the confusion, some titles are bound with issues for two or three years under the same cover, but this can be determined only by examining the bound volumes.

Frustration

People like systems that are easy to use, and they tend to give up when confronted by confusing or forbidding systems.

—Maurice B. Line[12]

Customer frustration is a topic seldom encountered in the professional literature or mentioned by librarians. Nevertheless, it is a rather common occurrence in both academic and public libraries. A customer's frustration increases with the time and effort expended in an unsuccessful search for information or materials. Usually, time spent in a library is considered positive, but time spent looking for missing items or trying unsuccessfully to locate a specific piece of information is both unproductive and discouraging. This frustration has several causes. A principal one, inherent in the nature of libraries, is that demand for particular items frequently exceeds supply. Other causes of frustration are the customers' inability to understand the system, library practices that hinder customers from obtaining what they want, and staff members who neglect to ascertain if customers found the information or the items desired. Because most frustrated customers simply leave without complaining, the library has no indication of the magnitude of this frustration.

Frustration is the obverse of service quality. Many frustrated customers never return, or, if they do, it is infrequently, especially if they find no improvement in the situation. Worse still, they tell friends, family, and colleagues of their experiences, and word of mouth is a powerful factor in shaping the reputation of the library in its community.

As a result, librarians face a difficult task—providing a system that meets multiple needs, perspectives, and expectations. As Maurice B. Line has noted,

> A maxim that should be displayed prominently in every library is "It is better and easier to design systems around human beings than to re-design human beings to fit systems." An ideal system is one that is de-signed to serve the majority of needs in the most effective and efficient way possible, but that also allows non-standard needs to be met and non-standard people to be served.[13]

Summary

Many notable examples of unhelpful service provided by libraries could easily be rectified. For instance, the circulation desk staff at a major research library are not allowed to accept fine money; it has to be paid to the fines office. However, that office, which employs two full-time assistants, is closed evenings, weekends, and Wednesday afternoons. The library does not provide a dropbox for depositing payments. For students with full-time jobs off campus who come to classes only in the evening and use the library on weekends, this situation creates considerable frustration.

Some libraries have erected high counters between staff and customers. Staff can either stand or sit on high stools. The intent probably was to allow eye contact between staff and customers, which seems perfectly reasonable, but high counters might make customers feel disadvantaged or feel that asking questions is always part of a formal process. A high counter can be a formidable barrier to customers who are short or to those in wheelchairs, who are considerably disadvantaged both by the arrangement and by the reluctance of staff to come from behind the counter to assist.

A far too common practice among reference staff is to consult the OPAC terminal mounted on the countertop and show the record by turning the screen toward the customer. One customer commented that the librarian "seemed hesitant to move beyond using her terminal to an-swer the question."[14]

Weingand makes an important observation by noting that "customer service excellence begins with a restless dissatisfaction with the status quo and the belief that one can do better."[15] The examples noted in this chapter are only intended as a reminder that library staff can always do better. Figure 2.1 offers further evidence that libraries and library staff might do things that confuse, hinder, or frustrate customers.

The system should be designed for the convenience of the customer, not the staff. Remember *The Doctor* and Weingand's reminder that

> "Libraries are service organizations." This is a statement that most li-brarians believe in and would ratify. Yet, if it were true all the time in every library, there would be little or no need for this book.[16]

FIGURE 2.1
Customer Frustration List

1. Customer is unable to locate materials or information.
2. Telephone is not answered promptly when customer calls.
3. Length of time until a reserved material is available seems too long.
4. Library staff are not friendly or helpful.
5. Library staff appear to be busy or unapproachable.
6. Parking is not available nearby.
7. Line at checkout is too long.
8. Librarian is not available to assist in locating material or information.
9. Customers are notified at inopportune times that requested items have arrived.
10. Library staff interpret policies literally and display a lack of flexibility.
11. Library hours are not convenient.
12. Customer must wait at the service desk while staff answer telephone.

Source: Darlene E. Weingand, *Customer Service Excellence* (Chicago: American Library Association, 1997), 73.

Libraries, like any service organization, should seek to improve their performance and not be satisfied with the status quo. It is always possible to improve.

NOTES

1. Lizabeth A. Wilson, "Glacier or Avalanche? Shifts in the Electronic, Education, and Library Landscape," in *LOEX of the West: Teaching and Learning in a "Climate of Change,"* edited by Thomas W. Leonhardt (Greenwich, Conn.: JAI Press, 1996), 14.
2. *The Doctor,* directed by Randa Haines. Touchstone Pictures, 1991. The film was based on the book, *A Taste of My Own Medicine,* by Ed Rosenbaum, M.D. (New York: Ballantine Books, 1991).
3. Marie L. Radford and Gary P. Radford, "Power, Knowledge, and Fear: Feminism, Foucault, and the Stereotype of the Female Librarian," *Library Quarterly* 67, no. 3 (July 1997): 250–66.
4. Patricia Dewdney and Catherine Sheldrick Ross, "Flying a Light Aircraft: Reference Service Evaluation from a User's Viewpoint," *RQ* 34, no. 2 (winter 1994): 217–29; Catherine Sheldrick Ross and Patricia Dewdney, "Best Practices: An Analysis of the Best (and Worst) in Fifty-Two Public Library Reference Transactions," *Public Libraries* 33, no. 5 (September/October 1994): 261–66.
5. George D'Elia and Eleanor Jo Rodger, *Free Library of Philadelphia Patron*

Survey: Final Report (Philadelphia, Pa.: Free Library of Philadelphia, 1991), quoted in Thomas A. Childers and Nancy A. Van House, *What's Good? Describing Your Public Library's Effectiveness* (Chicago: American Library Association, 1993), 26.

6. Childers and Van House, *What's Good?*, 27.

7. Ibid.

8. Darlene E. Weingand, *Customer Service Excellence: A Guide for Librarians* (Chicago: American Library Association, 1997), 13.

9. Sheila Intner and Elizabeth Futas, "Evaluating Public Library Collections," in *The Whole Library Handbook 2*, compiled by George M. Eberhart (Chicago: American Library Association, 1995), 304.

10. Wilson, "Glacier or Avalanche?," 9.

11. Ross and Dewdney, "Best Practices," 264.

12. Maurice B. Line, "What Do People Need of Libraries, and How Can We Find Out?," *Australian Academic & Research Libraries* 27, no. 2 (June 1996): 79–80.

13. Ibid., 79.

14. Ross and Dewdney, "Best Practices," 264.

15. Weingand, *Customer Service Excellence*, 9.

16. Ibid., 2.

3

"Your Mission, Should You Choose to Accept It . . ."

A well-defined mission serves as a constant reminder of the need to look outside the organization not only for "customers" but also for measures of success. The temptation to content oneself with the "goodness of our cause"—and to substitute good intentions for results—always exists in nonprofit organizations.

—Peter Drucker[1]

Any discussion of meeting or exceeding customers' expectations must occur within a context—that of the organizational mission, goals, and objectives. As libraries explore and adopt pledges about meeting expectations and customer service standards or plans, they must do so within a larger context. The purpose of this chapter is to provide a context against which libraries can assess service quality and customer satisfaction. The information gathered can then be used to revisit mission statements, goals, and objectives to ensure that they meet the needs of a dynamic organization entering a new century and coping with change. It is essential to mitigate the perception of the library as a bottomless financial pit, especially where expenditures for technology are concerned.

The phrase "Your mission, should you choose to accept it . . ." was always spoken in the first minutes of *Mission Impossible*, a television program popular in the 1970s. The voice on the tape specified clearly and unambiguously what the team of daring adventurers was to accomplish to complete the assignment successfully.

Unfortunately, most missions are not so precisely defined and, even worse, become muddled over time. This is especially true of public libraries. Perhaps once, early on, the mission givers (local officials or trustees) instructed their public library (mission taker) about its purpose and the accomplishments expected. Unfortunately, there are few instances of public libraries being so explicitly instructed. Mission implied by the givers is inferred by the takers.

Consequently, public libraries have had difficulty in articulating a mission because of the diversity among clientele and the lack of direction from local officials. To fill the void, the public library community itself articulated a mission or set of purposes for the library: information, education, and recreation. Many public libraries, however, wrote their own mission statements and emphasized their purpose as the promotion of such conditions as "creative use of leisure time," "good citizenship," and "democracy." Curiously, most of these statements neglected to mention who was to be affected or who was the focus of these lofty statements—the customers. Fortunately, most local officials never asked for proof of mission fulfillment.

In the 1980s, the Public Library Association (PLA) promulgated the idea that local libraries, in consultation with members of the community, select and adopt roles (i.e., purposes) from a prepared list. These roles, along with planning instructions, were described in a monograph published by the American Library Association (ALA).[2] Curiously, role adoption shifted the focus from users and the community to the library itself. From 1989 through 1995, the PLA's annual *Statistical Report* carried information on the role(s) selected by libraries participating in the survey. In the 1995 survey, 816 libraries, whose community sizes ranged from approximately 800 to over 3.5 million, participated. Among those reporting role selections, the one most often chosen as primary among both large and small libraries was "popular materials center."[3] These participants represent about one-tenth of total U.S. libraries; however, they are also, on average, the larger and better libraries. (A two-part package that substantially revises the original planning and role-setting process to encompass service responses was recently released by ALA.)[4]

Increasingly, however, local officials are questioning the propriety of supporting private recreation with public funds by purchasing such materials as mystery and romance novels. Some local officials expect that the Internet will supplant the library as the preferred information resource. Clearly, some rethinking of the activities performed by public libraries is occurring.

In the case of academic libraries, mission statements usually revolve around the libraries' support for teaching, service, and research, for specific constituent groups—students, faculty, staff, and administrative personnel. However, as academe, especially the large universities, has shifted emphasis from teaching to learning and from research to grantsmanship, the missions of the libraries should reflect the changes.

The library needs vision and mission statements showing its role and responsibility in supporting the vision and mission of the institution.[5] According to Jann E. Freed and Marie R. Klugman, "a vision statement is a philosophy about values; it is futuristic and optimistic. . . .

[It] answers the question: Where do we want to be in five to 10 years and what do we want to be doing?"[6] A mission statement, in contrast, describes the library's purpose, specifies what the library contributes to the overall institution's mission, and "differentiates the institution from other institutions."[7] It does not merely explain what the library does. A statement focusing on providing access to those print and electronic information resources and services required to support the college's or university's teaching and research—or, in the case of public libraries, to meet all the information needs of the public—may create an impression of the budget for building the collection as a "bottomless pit" draining precious financial resources. Institution administrators and faculty, or city/town managers, need direction about spending priorities, especially those relating to technology, and the library's vision and service plans.

Larry Hardesty, Jamie Hastreiter, and David Henderson,[8] Charles R. McClure et al.,[9] and Glen E. Holt[10] provide examples of library mission statements but do not link them to service quality and customer-based service. Mary E. Clack reproduces the mission statement of Harvard College Library and offers a "working document on values."[11] This document has seven short sections, only one of which concerns the service the library provides. The first value, "access/service and collections/scholarship," affirms the library's responsibility to its user community.[12] The other sections discuss staff development, the physical/psychological work environment, cooperation/teamwork, respect (for colleagues), communication (primarily within the organization), and change and innovation (initiative and flexibility, and visionary leadership). Clearly, the values expressed in this statement are primarily about relationships within the library rather than about the quality of service to library customers or to the college community.

The typical mission statement confirms the characterization of cartoonist and humorist Scott Adams that the statement is "a long, awkward sentence [paragraph, or page] that demonstrates management's inability to think clearly."[13] The statement probably also states the obvious, does not issue a challenge to the library, and is not framed within the context of a vision likely to appeal to businesspeople sitting on boards of regents or serving as trustees, or to state legislators trying to gain a sense of the direction and purpose of the college or university and eager to hold academe to the type of accountability commonly used in business. "Once a vision or mission statement has been developed, it is vital that the statement is communicated to all members of the institution and that members understand the statement and refer to it in their day-to-day work."[14]

According to Betsy Sanders, former vice president and general manager of Nordstrom, Inc.,

> Unfortunately, well-wrought words, even when etched in concrete do not make a mission statement. That statement is made by the constant, shared redefining of the *why* of the business. For others to share in your success, they, too, must be able to internalize the significance of what it is you are about. The answer to this question ["Why are we in business?"] must be clear, candid, constantly communicated, and dynamic.[15]

Sanders also encourages businesses to develop a vision that articulates where they are going: "Encouraging everyone to share the vision and to become involved in its ongoing refinement is the essence of truly empowering the organization."[16]

Peter Brophy and Kate Coulling appear supportive of the distinction made by Sanders. They see a "danger" to mission statements providing a "starting point" for total quality management (TQM) or customer-based service. They point out that

> [t]he organization may start to define quality purely as the achievement of the corporate mission. In other words a service is fit for [its] purpose if it aligns with the corporate mission, rather than if it is fit for the customer's purposes. Equally, customers' requirements may be perceived as legitimate only if they fit in with the organizational mission.[17]

As a result, Brophy and Coulling recommend that libraries constantly revisit their mission statements, compare them "with the real needs of all customers," and recognize customers as "the major stakeholders."[18]

Access and Assistance[19]

No matter the type of library, most librarians can agree with G. Edward Evans and Sandra M. Heft that the primary responsibilities of a library are "to provide access to information in all its many forms and formats . . . [and] to provide assistance in locating specific pieces of information sought by individuals in the service population."[20] These responsibilities—*access* and *assistance*—are constant over time and over all types of libraries and information centers.[21]

Most mission statements, however, do not explain who gets access and/or assistance, and what is to be accessed. In reality, access might be limited to certain categories of people—for instance, residents, students, faculty, and registered borrowers. Access has become more restrictive because of licensing agreements for electronic information, and is limited to particular types of informational or recreational items—those that can be purchased from certain types of distributors. The issues of quantity or quality relating to either access or assistance are ignored. Another important point is that these primary purposes represent the consensus of librarians, and not that of the community to be served, nor that of the community's decision makers.

Both access and assistance are concepts open to wide interpretation. Access can mean entry into the library building, or use of an item owned by a far-distant library. Assistance can mean pointing out the location of an atlas or preparing a long bibliography. The *way* that those responsibilities are carried out distinguishes one organization or information unit from another. The repeated and successful *fulfillment* of these responsibilities constitutes mission accomplishment for the organization.

Access and assistance are basic to the missions of libraries. Without access, none of these other conditions—supporting teaching and research, providing information, education, and recreation, or any role specified in the PLA planning process—can be achieved. Access to the materials and information desired is a first step that must be satisfied before any higher-level conditions can occur.

If an academic library accepts a mission to support teaching and research, then customers' expectations about accessing materials for courses and research have validity. Customers of libraries that claim the role of popular materials center should be able to gain access to such materials without difficulty or undue delay. All customers have a right to expect staff to be courteous and knowledgeable and to serve them reasonably promptly.

A Mission Is More Than Good Intentions

Frame the mission statement in terms of what you contribute, not what you do.

—Benjamin Schneider and David E. Bowen[22]

The central part of a mission tends to be highly stable, even though the environment in which the organization operates may change rather dramatically. For example, despite the transition from one-room schools in which students wrote on personal slates to the modern buildings in which students write on personal computers, the mission of schools remains the same—to teach students to read, write, compute, understand, and think well enough to function in contemporary society. The means to accomplish the mission, however, vary depending on local conditions and changes over time.

Continuous improvement in process or product to carry out the mission is essential for organizational well-being. Therefore, plans or concepts on how to accomplish the mission, or how to accomplish it "better," are needed. All plans (activities, whether ongoing or proposed) and decisions need to be scrutinized to determine how they contribute to the library mission—access and assistance.

Guy A. Marco puts library activities and functions into four classes that should be helpful in considering whether or how library activities and practices contribute to access and assistance. These classifications are:

Ideal—essential to accomplishment of a given mission

Useful—supportive of mission accomplishment, but not essential

Useless—irrelevant to mission accomplishment

Counterproductive—obstructs mission accomplishment[23]

It may seem strange to list *useless* and *counterproductive* as considerations, but organizations regularly make decisions and plans and take actions that are useless and counterproductive.

Let us consider three rather common library practices or services and relate them to Marco's classification. Academic librarians might receive release time to work on a research project and to publish the results but might not relate that research to library planning and decision making. This is counterproductive. In effect, no follow-through occurs between the doing and reporting of research and the use of that research for improving library services and management.

On the other hand, flagging serial titles that the library owns in an electronic index such as *Lexis-Nexis* is useful. The flagging helps prevent customers from wasting their time looking for unfindable articles. In addition, acquiring indexes that cover as many of the serials owned by the library as possible can be classified as ideal because it is essential to access.

Goals and Objectives

Missions are actualized by goals and objectives. *Goals* are "general descriptions of conditions intended to exist at a future time,"[24] whereas *objectives* are

> descriptions of specific conditions that are intended to exist by certain points in the future, the conditions being measurably different from those conditions that existed when the objectives were set or made. . . . An objective differs from a goal by having measurability: at a certain time (its deadline or expiry date) the objective can be assessed by any rational observer and judged to have succeeded or failed.[25]

Libraries can develop goals and objectives related, for instance, to improving bibliographic accessibility, physical availability, and professional service. Not only should the library have organizational goals and objectives, but each unit within the library should have its own goals and objectives that facilitate the achievement of librarywide goals.

Assuming a goal of "providing high-quality reference and referral services to library clientele," objectives might be to:

- Increase, by 10 percent, the number of hours that staff members provide public service at the main reference desk within the next six months
- Increase, by 5 percent, the accuracy of answers given to library customers within the next fiscal year
- Include access to the World Wide Web (WWW) on all the computers in the reference department within the next six months
- Purchase three CD-ROM products dealing with familiar quotations for placement in the reference area by the end of the fiscal year
- Permit customers to download files from the WWW by the end of the fiscal year

For both the library and its composite units, the adoption of goals and objectives is necessary, but they should be accompanied by action and by some way to evaluate the extent of accomplishment. In retail trade, sales personnel have monthly quotas to reach. In some instances,

"Your Mission, Should You Choose to Accept It . . ."

consistent inability to reach these targets results in probation or termination. Department heads or team leaders may work with employees to set targets to be achieved weekly, monthly, annually, and so forth. Thus, managers measure the extent to which agreed-upon objectives are met while employees know which objectives are most important and can focus time and effort on their achievement.

Sanders encourages businesses to set and maintain high standards, through their goals, by demanding the best from their employees. "The expectation of excellence causes everyone to stretch, and the customer is well served in the process."[26] For this reason, it is critical that everyone be involved in: (1) understanding why the organization is in business, and (2) "planning how to move that business forward."[27]

Goals and objectives, in summary, reflect the perspective of the organization and what it wants to achieve. Extrapolating from the work of Sanders, and Brophy and Coulling, four key questions are:

1. To what extent do customers shape the planning framework, including the direction or focus of goals and objectives?
2. To what extent should they shape the framework?
3. Is this framework important to them?
4. How will the organization adopt a systems approach in which all departments work together and are responsive to the information-seeking behavior and requirements of the customers?

An example from the retail industry illustrates how an organization can actively decide to focus on service quality and build customer satisfaction. Nordstrom's department store is renowned for its customer service. Sales associates, who can earn over $100,000 a year, specialize in personal service and, even without a customer making a request, will search the store to assemble a selection of items from which to choose. Because of the strong service orientation, customers remember how they were treated and how the organization stands behind its promises and the quality of the products purchased. Nordstrom has been known to accept as returned merchandise items that the store never stocked.[28] The reason is to create or keep a loyal Nordstrom customer. The company maintains a large in-store inventory to ensure that customers find a suitable item. Nordstrom's catalogs facilitate mail-order purchases. The intent is that, when customers think about purchasing clothes, they automatically associate their need with one department store—Nordstrom.

Keeping shoes properly paired is important to most shoe stores. Nordstrom recognizes, however, that the size of each foot may differ so much that a person might need two different sizes of the same shoe. The store allows customers to pair shoes of different sizes as one purchase for one price. Of course, the store ends up with unmatched pairs of shoes, but expects the difference to balance out over time. Clearly, the needs of the customer are paramount to the service provided.

Such customer-driven practices should not be interpreted to mean that the customer is always right. The organization chooses which expectations it wants to meet as part of its service plan (see Figure 7.8).

(Nordstrom probably goes farther than others with the expectations that it chooses to meet.) There will be situations in which library staff clearly realize that the expectations of the particular person they are helping are not in the best interest of either the library or other customers.[29]

Philosophy and Values

Every organization is shaped by both a philosophy and a set of values. These are not necessarily high-minded or erudite. They may not be articulated or even perceived consciously by the people who work in the organization. Philosophy and values are absorbed into organizations in various ways: by the vision articulated by the organization's founder, by a set of widely accepted professional values, by the actions of long-tenured managers, or by the accretion of habits over time. The organization's philosophy and values are revealed by the manner in which it operates, by its interactions with customers or clients, and by the attitudes of the employees toward the organization's work, its customers, and its management.

In essence, the organizational *culture*, shaped by the organization's philosophy and values, largely determines the quality of its service. The Nordstrom examples clearly show that customers are *valued*, whereas some other organizations seem unresponsive or actually hostile to customers.

For example, how should customers respond to the public library that does not permit downloading of files or documents from the WWW because of fear that customers may use contaminated disks that will spread a virus throughout the system? Or, what if that library does not have the Adobe Acrobat for reading documents in Portable Document Format (PDF) from the WWW, because it does not want to provide paper gratis and is concerned about the expense of replacing toner cartridges frequently? Although the answers to these questions may be complex, should not the library find solutions that are in the best interests of customers?

The Library as a System

A library is composed of a set of units or departments, or teams in the case of some restructured libraries, theoretically working toward a common purpose—accomplishment of the library's and institution's mission. The library is more than the mere sum of these units and teams; it is a system in which the interaction of the parts affects the well-being of the whole, just as one organ affects the overall health of the body, or one mechanism can affect a car's driveability or safety.

The *general systems model*, also called an open or dynamic system, provides an important framework for understanding how problems can transcend individual parts and affect many other activities and units.[30]

"Your Mission, Should You Choose to Accept It . . ."

For example, the availability of resources affects an organization positively and negatively, just as the availability of food can affect a human body. How those resources are transformed into products and services, and how well the library meets the information needs and expectations of its customers, are analogous to how a human body might be affected by the nutrients consumed.

General systems theory views organizations as being composed of three parts: input, feedback, and reality.[31] The inputs, of course, strongly influence both feedback and reality. These parts provide "a way to evaluate the relationship among the components of the organization and between the organization and its environment."[32]

Resources are the most commonly considered input. A definite connection exists between the adequacy of resources (personnel, equipment, and physical surroundings) and services, and between services and effectiveness (either good or bad), as viewed from both the organization's and the customers' perspectives. Inputs, however, do not have to be tangible. Attitudes and behaviors can also be inputs that produce positive or negative feedback and, hence, have an impact on reality for both the customers and the organization. For example, a backlog created by one unit or team (input) can create havoc for internal customers throughout the system (feedback) and disrupt service for customers (reality). More positively, a new WWW page allows customers to pose reference questions and request interlibrary loans via modem (input). This greatly increases the number of transactions (feedback), while creating the impression that the library is customer oriented and technologically advanced (reality).

All parts of the organization need to recognize their interdependence and to overcome the belief that one part is more important than the others. Dependence can be recognized by looking at the organization through the eyes of customers and asking "What can the customer expect from the library, regardless of the collection or service used?" and "How can all parts of the library work together to improve the utility of each collection and the quality of each service?"

The key to quality service is that each part, unit, or team discharges its responsibilities so well that the organization creates what some authors have called *seamless service:*

> The service in all of its dimensions and characteristics is delivered without a hitch. It is simultaneously reliable, responsive, competent, courteous, and so forth, and the facilities and tools necessary for it are all put into play smoothly and without glitches, interruptions, or delay.[33]

In essence, the customers are not aware that the process of delivering the service might be complex. In fact, they do not care. "Seamless service is something all customers expect."[34]

The general systems model and open systems characteristics offer a "coarsegrained" view of effectiveness.[35] The approach taken here and in the other literature of service quality presents "a finer grained framework," one focusing on what is really important to both customers and the organization: that *the organization should be in harmony with its customers.*[36]

Customer Service Plans

According to Arnold Hirshon,

> if an organization expects to deliver high-quality services, it is important to establish a shared benchmark for the library staff and customers to judge what constitutes quality service. To do this, the library must clearly articulate and publicize its service standards.[37]

The analogy is that buyers expect the products they purchase to perform as expected for a reasonable period of time. The product's manufacturer frequently stands by product quality by offering a warranty or guarantee. For libraries, the question becomes: What are service organizations, such as libraries, willing to pledge or guarantee concerning the quality of their services? A service plan offers one answer.

A *service plan* is a promise to live up to the library's mission and goals in a way that is considerate of customers. In some ways, the plan is a vision statement of the type of service or product that the organization considers its highest priority. The plan not only articulates a philosophy of service, but also makes explicit promises to library customers. Adopting a plan is a serious undertaking in that the document, once adopted, cannot be filed and forgotten, as so many mission and goals statements have been.

Hirshon notes:

> There are certain principles that should underlie a customer service statement. The statement should be written from the perspective of the customer, not the staff. The focus should be on frequently used customer-apparent services, not on background operations that may be important for effective function, but of which customers are unaware. The statements should be clear and concise, and avoid the use of jargon. Statements should be unambiguous and phrased positively. Equivocating words or phrases, such as "generally," "usually," or "whenever possible," should be eliminated.[38]

A service plan declares:

- A commitment to high-quality programs and operations
- Openness to the concept of change
- Responsiveness to the needs and priorities of customers
- A commitment to providing equitable access to library resources and systems
- A willingness to work together as a team
- The availability of training and development opportunities for all staff

A service plan might also contain a declaration that every staff member is accountable for doing effective and efficient work in pursuit of the provision of high-quality services, and recognize that each staff member contributes to the fulfillment of the library's service mission.

The plan might contain a "commitment to excellence" that conveys a set of service promises that apply to all service areas within the library:

- Respond to customer needs and priorities in a professional, timely, courteous, and helpful manner
- Offer programs and services that are responsive to culturally diverse customers and foster an appreciation of diversity among staff
- Offer programs and services that are responsive to physically challenged customers, and promote a better understanding of their information-gathering behavior
- Maintain open lines of communication and consultation regarding library policies and programs among library management, staff, and customers

Such promises identify a diverse set of responsibilities, many of which might be equated to goals, and serve as a reminder that a library is a customer-focused system, whose whole is greater than the sum of its parts. Where the focus is on activities rather than results, performing an activity—not achieving a result—becomes the standard.

Hirshon reminds us that the service plan should contain a second part: "specific quality measures for each customer service."[39] This part corresponds to objectives and should be measurable; for example, "we will respond personally to your signed suggestions within five working days" or "we will acknowledge you immediately at any service desk and serve you within three minutes or call additional staff."[40] Such examples do not require a survey to measure the extent of compliance. Instead, staff members can check a random sample of signed suggestions and measure the turnaround and outcome (i.e., how satisfied was the customer with the response), or, at random times, they can use a stopwatch to determine how well staff members complied with the three-minute requirement. The library, however, must set the time frame, such as three minutes or five days. A key question is: How do the library's administration and staff agree on that time frame and convey the policy to customers?

Library Service Plans

Wright State University Libraries, in Dayton, Ohio, produced a service plan that lends itself to group consensus and measurement—not all of which results in subjective judgments. The library staff identified what is important to their customers and which expectations they regard as highest priority and will consistently meet from year to year.

Released as a brochure and also available at the University's Web site, the customer service plan—"Our Commitment to Customer Service" —contains a Commitment to Excellence and a pledge covering General Services, Collections and Electronic Information Services, Reference and Research Services, Information Delivery Services, and Special Collections Services.[41] Most of the statements in the pledge can be easily monitored as to their fulfillment. Only 10 of the 40 promises lack the specificity for direct measurement. For the points that specify a time frame or speak in terms of absolutes, it would be possible to compute a corresponding ratio. For example,

$$\frac{\text{Number of new periodicals shelved within 24 hours of receipt}}{\text{Number of new periodicals received in the past 24 hours}} = \underline{\hspace{1cm}} \times 100 = \underline{\hspace{1cm}} \%$$

$$\frac{\text{Number of current periodicals reshelved within 24 hours of use}}{\text{Number of current periodicals needing reshelving}} = \underline{\hspace{1cm}} \times 100 = \underline{\hspace{1cm}} \%$$

$$\frac{\text{Number of telephone questions answered within 24 hours of receipt}}{\text{Number of telephone questions received in the past 24 hours}} = \underline{\hspace{1cm}} \times 100 = \underline{\hspace{1cm}} \%$$

Obviously, to assess how well such promises are being met, the library staff do not need to survey customers or rely on self-reports of staff members. Rather, both the numerators and denominators can be counted objectively.

Lehigh University Information Resources, which is responsible for both the libraries and university computing and communications, has developed service standards that cover the following areas within the context of a mission statement: general services; client assistance services; computing and communication systems; electronic information and library collections; and classroom, media, duplication, and report services (see Figure 3.1). Modeled after the Wright State University pledge, these service standards (or customer pledge), in general, permit quantitative assessment by stressing a time frame and reliablility percentages, and indicate that the "success" of technological and other services can be approached from the "quality of service we deliver to you."

"Your Mission, Should You Choose to Accept It . . ."

FIGURE 3.1
Lehigh University Information Resources Service Standards

The mission of Lehigh University Information Resources (LUIR) is to support the university mission facilitating the access, collection, management, and analysis of academic and enterprise-wide information. LUIR strives to be an agile organization that enables learning and research through the application of state-of-the-art technologies and methods to fulfill and anticipate client needs.

Lehigh University Information Resources is firmly committed to providing the highest level of resources and services for Lehigh students, faculty, and staff. Inside this brochure you will find our general and specific standards of excellence for each service area.

LUIR will measure our success by the quality of service we deliver to you. We have specific, measurable goals in place for every service unit, many of which are described in this brochure. We will make every effort to meet or exceed these service goals. We will continually evaluate and update these standards. We value your opinions.

If you have suggestions to improve this service statement or our operations, suggestion boxes are available on the IR Web page and at the help desks at the Fairchild-Martindale Library, Linderman Library, and the Computing Center. In addition, all IR group and team leaders (listed in this brochure) will gratefully accept your compliments, questions, or complaints.

General Services

Make service to you our top priority. We will:

- Acknowledge you immediately at public service desks and assist you within five minutes. We will expeditiously make special arrangements if you have a complex request, a consulting need, or research problem that cannot be resolved immediately.

- Answer phones immediately and offer to call you back if we must put your call on hold for more than three minutes. Respond to voice mail or electronic mail messages within 1 business day.

- Provide reasonable seating capacity and maximum availability to basic library and computing services at the Information Commons at Fairchild-Martindale.

- Provide services on a most-needed basis for all other IR staffed facilities. Display hours of operation prominently at all sites, on voice mail, and online.

- Provide clean, comfortable, and quiet environments for work and study.

- Engage in effective two-way communication by: regularly publishing newsletters and guides; meeting with faculty liaisons and department chairs at least once a semester; sponsoring colloquia to advance learning; and soliciting feed-back through surveys and focus groups.

- Respond to signed comments, suggestions, or complaints within 5 business days. Widely publicize changes in our services or resources, and provide opportunities for training for new services.

Client Assistance Services

Assist you in the use of information resources (computing and communications systems, library collections, and related services) and provide you with the training you need to use them on your own. We will:

- Provide customized and in-depth consulting services, which will be scheduled within 1 business day of the request.

- Respond to online inquiries within 1 business day.

- Offer instruction geared to your needs, including scheduling customized course-based instruction within two weeks of a faculty request, and a regular series of seminars about any supported service or system to any individual or group that requests it.

- Make available comprehensive, easy to follow, and up-to-date instructions and guides for our services at all IR help desks and online.

(Continued)

- Publish standards and guidelines for the software and hardware that we support, and that are essential for network and database compatibility.

- Aid in the assessment of your information needs, develop and evaluate potential solutions, and implement agreed upon solutions.

Computing and Communication Systems

Provide excellent computing and communication systems to meet your needs. We will:

- Ensure the reliability and at least 99% average availability of all electronic information systems, including central servers and networks.

- Ensure reliability and at least 90% average availability of computers, workstations, and printers at all public sites.

- Provide efficient and reliable telephone service, with system availability of greater than 99%, and requested changes to telephone services processed within 5 business days.

- Guarantee that operating systems and key applications supported by IR are current and network compatible.

- Provide at least two months notice for planned operating systems or software changes at public sites and on IR servers.

- Provide you with an initial repair assessment within 1 business day when supported computing equipment is dropped off for repair, or within 2 business days if a site visit is required.

- Announce planned downtime at least 48 hours in advance, and schedule maintenance and downtime during low use hours.

- Maintain back up files on all campus-wide systems so we can restore or reload lost or corrupted files within 1 business day in case of system failure.

- Respond to reported or potential security violations on the same day.

- Maintain strict confidentiality at all times for all centrally stored files and e-mail messages.

- Provide reliable off-campus, high-speed modem access to the campus network and to the Internet with system availability and no busy signals at peak hours on average 90% of the time.

- Investigate immediately any reports of a suspected virus or hacker.

Electronic Information and Library Collections

Provide excellent library collections and electronic information resources to meet your needs. We will:

- Work collaboratively with faculty to ensure that our library, media, and software collections support the instructional and research mission of Lehigh University and meet the needs of students, faculty, and staff.

- Order or report back to faculty on book order requests within 5 business days.

- Catalog new library materials accurately and within 3 weeks of receipt.

- Check out and in all library materials with 99% accuracy and within 1 business day.

- Shelve new issues of journals within 1 business day of receipt and keep current with the reshelving of all current periodicals.

- Reshelve books and bound journals within 24 hours of use, and maintain the shelves in the proper shelving order with at least 98% accuracy.

- Process interlibrary loan requests within 1 business day of receipt.

- Make available newly received material that is requested "rush" within 1 business day.

- Fill in-house photocopy requests within 2 business days.

- Retrieve library material from the remote Library Materials Center within 1 business day.

Classroom, Media, Duplication, and Report Services

Provide well-maintained computer classrooms and media and computer labs, and support audio-visual instruction in designated classrooms throughout the campus. We will:

- Respond immediately to problems in classrooms with instructor stations, projection equipment, or any other malfunctions that interfere with the progress of a scheduled class, and respond to all other such problems within 1 business day.

- Deliver and set up a computer and media display equipment in classrooms when scheduled 3 business days in advance.

- Provide well-maintained, highly accessible basic and advanced media production facilities for faculty, staff, and students to produce presentation and other media materials of the highest quality, with staff and documentation available to provide expert assistance.

- Provide general purpose printing at all public computing sites, with specialized printing capabilities available at the Computing Center.

- Offer reasonably priced and highly reliable self-service photocopiers at Linderman and Fairchild-Martindale Libraries, with equipment repaired within 4 hours and machines fully stocked every day.

- Produce and deliver regular reports in support of the business needs of the university within 2 business days.

Information Resources Leadership

[This section contains the name of the leader, the group or team with which the leader is affiliated, and that person's e-mail address and phone number]

IR Commitment To Excellence

Our facilities and resources will be conducive to study and research. We will offer courteous, prompt, and accurate client services that provide the assistance you need, or we will put you in direct contact with someone who can.

IR Clients

LUIR primarily serves the students, faculty, and staff involved in academic, research or administrative activities of the University. Limited services are available to faculty and students of other academic institutions. Cognizant of a special relationship with Lehigh alumni, LUIR offers selected services to graduates at a reduced rate. Members of the general public are welcome in the government documents library, open stack areas in the libraries, and special collections, but most computing resources are not available. Non-Lehigh individuals and corporations may purchase selected services on a fee-based arrangement.

Reprinted with Permission of Arnold Hirshon, Vice Provost for Information Resources, Lehigh University, E.W. Fairchild-Martindale Library & Computing Center, Bethlehem, PA.

The Camden County Library System in New Jersey has created "Our Promise to You . . . ," a brochure for customers. Although less explicit than the service plan of Wright State University, it nevertheless describes the kind of service that the community is entitled to receive (see Figure 3.2). Statements cover personal service from the staff, materials, information, and upkeep of the buildings.

FIGURE 3.2
"Our Promise to You . . . from the People of the
Camden County Library System"

This is a publicly funded library system and you are entitled to:

- Polite, knowledgeable, friendly, and helpful service
  from well-trained staff.

- Quality service at all facilities and on the telephone.

- Personal attention.

- The direction or assistance you need to insure full benefit
  from library services.

- Confidentiality concerning your borrowing records within the confines
  of the law.

- A wide range of materials to fulfill the needs of adults and children.

    Books, magazines, newspapers, audio and video cassettes. When
      we do not own an item you want, we will try to get it from
      another library in the area, the state or the nation.

- Information provided quickly and accurately.

    Our many information resources include a large reference
      collection, computer searching, business services and
      periodicals indexes.

    LibraryLink enables you to access our online catalog from your
      home or office.

- Easy access to library services.

    Libraries are open during business hours, evenings and weekends.
      The main branch is open Sundays from Labor Day to mid-
      June.

    The online catalog directs you to library materials in all formats.
      We are here to help you make the best use of the catalog.

    All facilities are handicapped accessible. Assistive listening devices
      are available to the hearing impaired at library meetings.

    Telephone renewal is offered for materials that are not overdue
      or on request.

    Library buildings that are safe, clean, well-maintained and
      smoke-free.

Source: Camden County Library System, "Our Promise to You . . . from the
People of the Camden County Library System" (Voorhees, N.J.: The Library, August 23, 1994).

"Your Mission, Should You Choose to Accept It . . ."

Summary

Mission and vision statements about the importance of customers are only as good as their impact on behavior from the board room to the mail room.

—National Performance Review[42]

"In the corporate sector, a customer service strategy has become a vital component of business success," and companies have "engineered their success through formal plans to ensure customer satisfaction."[43] There is no reason that libraries, even those in the nonprofit sector, cannot develop customer service strategies that recognize that "good service adds value to library resources."[44] These strategies must be linked to the mission, vision, philosophy, values, goals, and objectives of the library and the organization within which the library resides.

The emerging plan must be acceptable to and empower all library staff members, as customers learn which of their expectations are highest priority to the library. The results of meeting the promises of the service plan can and should be measured on a regular basis. Customer-related performance indicators, discussed in the next chapter, provide an excellent framework for measuring the extent to which a library meets its service commitment.

NOTES

1. Peter Drucker, *Peter Drucker on the Profession of Management*, edited by Nan Stone (Cambridge: Harvard Business School Press, 1998), 134.

2. Charles R. McClure, Amy Owen, Douglas L. Zweizig, Mary J. Lynch, and Nancy A. Van House, *Planning and Role Setting for Public Libraries: A Manual of Options and Procedures*, 2d ed. (Chicago: American Library Association, 1987).

3. Public Library Data Service, *Statistical Report '95* (Chicago: American Library Association, 1995).

4. Edith Himmel and William J. Wilson, with ReVision Committee of the Public Library Association, *Planning for Results: A Public Library Transformation Process*. Part 1: "How-to Manual"; Part 2: "Guidebook" (Chicago: American Library Association, 1998).

5. See Guy St. Clair, *Customer Service in the Information Environment* (London: Bowker Saur, 1993); Wilma Reed Cipolla, "The Mission of a University Undergraduate Library: Draft Model Statement," *College & Research Libraries News* 48, no. 4 (April 1987): 192–194.

6. Jann E. Freed and Marie R. Klugman, *Quality Principles and Practices in Higher Education: Different Questions for Different Times* (Phoenix, Ariz.: Oryx Press, 1997), 59.

7. Ibid. "A mission statement is most useful when it articulates why a particular college or university education would be less than distinctive if its academic library was not perceived to be an essential organizational culture." Stephanie Rogers Bangert, "Values in College and University Library Mission Statements: A Search for Distinctive Beliefs, Meaning, and Organizational Culture," in *Advances in Librarianship*, vol. 21, edited by Irene Godden (San Diego, Calif.: Academic Press, 1997), 104.

8. Larry Hardesty, Jamie Hastreiter, and David Henderson, *Mission Statements for College Libraries* (Chicago: American Library Association, Col-

lege Libraries Section, College Library Information Packet Committee, 1985).

9. McClure et al., *Planning and Role Setting for Public Libraries*.

10. Glen E. Holt, "On Becoming Essential: An Agenda for Quality in Twenty-First Century Public Libraries," *Library Trends* 44, no. 3 (winter 1996): 550–53.

11. Mary Elizabeth Clack, "Values, a Process of Discovery: The Harvard College Library's Organizational Values Process," *Library Administration & Management* 9, no. 3 (summer 1995): 146–52.

12. Ibid., 150–151.

13. "Making Team Work Like Roman Orchard Slaves: A Dilbert's-eye View of the Modern Office," *Newsweek* 129, no. 19 (May 6, 1996): 50.

14. Freed and Klugman, *Quality Principles and Practices in Higher Education*, 63.

15. Betsy Sanders, *Fabled Service: Ordinary Acts, Extraordinary Outcomes* (San Diego, Calif.: Pfeiffer, 1995), 69.

16. Ibid., 71.

17. Peter Brophy and Kate Coulling, *Quality Management for Information and Library Managers* (Hampshire, England: Aslib/Gower, 1996), 76.

18. Ibid.

19. The term was taken from an advertisement by AT&T WorldNet Service.

20. Edward Evans and Sandra M. Heft, *Introduction to Technical Services*, 6th ed. (Littleton, Colo.: Libraries Unlimited, 1995), 4.

21. Some libraries prefer mission statements that focus on process issues—for instance, "to collect . . . ," "to organize . . . ," and "to preserve. . . ." Such issues do not reflect the library as a service organization.

22. Benjamin Schneider and David E. Bowen, *Winning the Service Game* (Boston: Harvard Business School Press, 1995), 252.

23. Guy A. Marco, "The Terminology of Planning: Part 1," *Library Management* 17, no. 2 (1996): 21.

24. Ibid., 20.

25. Guy A. Marco, "The Terminology of Planning: Part 2," *Library Management* 17, no. 7 (1996): 18.

26. Sanders, *Fabled Service*, 73.

27. Ibid., 72.

28. Robert Spector, *The Nordstrom Way: The Inside Story of America's #1 Customer Service Company* (New York: Wiley, 1995).

29. Ibid., 38.

30. Peter Hernon and Ellen Altman, *Service Quality in Academic Libraries* (Norwood, N.J.: Ablex, 1996), 23–26; Thomas A. Childers and Nancy A. Van House, *What's Good? Describing Your Public Library's Effectiveness* (Chicago: American Library Association, 1993), 12–14.

31. Joan Koob Cannie, with Donald Caplin, *Keeping Customers for Life* (New York: AMACOM, 1991), 19.

32. Childers and Van House, *What's Good?*, 14.

33. Schneider and Bowen, *Winning the Service Game*, 8.

34. Ibid.

35. Childers and Van House, *What's Good?*, 13

36. Ibid.

37. Arnold Hirshon, "Running with the Red Queen: Breaking New Habits to Survive in the Virtual World," in *Advances in Librarianship*, vol. 20, edited by Irene Godden (San Diego, Calif.: Academic Press, 1996), 5.

38. Ibid., 7.

39. Ibid.

40. Ibid.

41. See Hernon and Altman, *Service Quality in Academic Libraries*, 59–60; Susan Wehmeyer, Dorothy Auchter, and Arnold Hirshon, "Saying What We Will Do, and Doing What We Say: Implementing a Customer Service Plan," *Journal of Academic Librarianship* 22, no. 3 (May 1996): 179–80; "Our Commitment to Excellence," Wright State University Libraries, http://www.libraries.wright.edu/services/Customers_Services.html.

42. See National Performance Review, *Serving the American Public: Best Practices in Resolving Customer Complaints* (Washington, D.C.: Government Printing Office, 1996).

43. Wehmeyer, Auchter, and Hirshon, "Saying What We Will Do," 173.

44. Ibid.

4

Measuring and Assessing the Components of Service Quality

Nonprofit institutions tend not to give priority to performance and results. Yet, performance and results are far more important and far more difficult to measure and control in the nonprofit [institution] than in a business.

—Peter Drucker[1]

A library and its services, much like a contoured landscape, can be viewed and assessed from a multitude of perspectives. Perspectives commonly referred to in the literature of library and information science (LIS) include inputs, outputs, outcomes, performance measures, effectiveness, and efficiency. Because a number of authors within and outside LIS have, over the past 10 or 15 years, defined and used these terms in different ways, we believe that these terms now confuse, rather than clarify the ways to judge and manage the results obtained from an assessment. When referring to inputs, outputs, and performance measures, the U.S. Office of Management and Budget (OMB) concurs with our conclusion and notes that "no standard definitions currently exist" and that "the nomenclature of measures cannot be rigidly applied."[2]

Thomas A. Childers and Nancy A. Van House view "effectiveness very broadly" and believe it deals with "goodness, achieving success, and the quality of performance." They define "effectiveness as impact on the consumer or user and efficiency as the economy with which 'effect' is achieved."[3] When assessing an organization's effectiveness, they suggest the following critical questions:

To what extent does the organization achieve its goals (input, process, output, or outcome goals)?

To what extent is the organization a *healthy operating unit?*

To what extent can the organization capture from the external environment the *resources* needed to survive or thrive?

To what extent are the various *stakeholders'* priorities met?[4]

Childers and Van House see effectiveness "largely [as] a point of view" and as defying a single definition. They note that "there are multiple groups to be satisfied"; a multiple constituency approach defines effectiveness in terms of meeting "the needs and expectations of strategic constituencies, such as certain user groups or leaders in the community."[5]

Drawing on the work of Kim S. Cameron, Joseph A. McDonald and Lynda Basney Micikas declare that "no conceptualization of an effective organization is comprehensive."[6] They define effectiveness in terms of "successful organizational transactions," which, they explain, "include the interaction among all activities and people in the library, as well as those transactions between the library and its environment."[7]

Like Cameron, and Childers and Van House, McDonald and Micikas encourage a multiple constituency approach to assessment. Libraries serve different constituencies and should not treat them as a monolith. The same applies to assessment or evaluation. Although there are multiple perspectives and approaches to assessment, no single one has gained universal or general acceptance, and no single one will accomplish everything that librarians would like. Equally as important, research in such areas as service quality and satisfaction, calls for some reconceptualization and determination about the priorities for assessment.

This chapter cannot avoid adding some descriptive terms while simultaneously presenting different ways to look at the library landscape. Our intent is to offer a broad overview of some of the possibilities for assessment for readers to consider and to choose those most pertinent to their particular situations and priorities.

All assessment is composed of three parts:

1. The thing to be measured.
2. The means by which the measurement is taken.
3. A judgment about the sufficiency or goodness of the thing being measured.

These are analogous to a piece of cloth and a yardstick. The cloth is the *what* to measure and the yardstick represents the *how* to measure. Assessment is a judgment about the sufficiency and suitability of the cloth for the purpose desired.

According to F. W. Lancaster, "an evaluation [assessment] is performed not as an intellectual exercise but to gather data useful in problem solving or decision making activities."[8] First, however, a decision must be made about *what* to assess. Childers and Van House offer similar insight into goodness:

We are fundamentally evaluative animals and, just as we evaluate all things, we evaluate organizations. They are supposed to accomplish something, to be in some way good for something, and someone has always been there to ask the question, "How good?"[9]

Who answers the question "How good?" when it comes to the library, from what perspective, and using what information and data? What is the quality of that information and those data? Are the information and data interpreted objectively or subjectively, and do they match the question being asked?

What to Measure

When librarians do not characterize their work in terms of products and services designed to meet information needs, they fail to clarify the parameters of their knowledge work for themselves or their information-seeking clients.

—Valerie Florance and Nina W. Matheson[10]

It has been stated that almost everything can be the subject of assessment and measurement, and, as Peter H. Rossi and Howard E. Freeman observe, "systematic evaluations of both existing and new . . . [human services] programs are now commonplace."[11] This book, however, focuses on library and information services and on the factors that reflect different dimensions of those services. Some of these factors are quite traditional and straightforward, whereas others are less common or very complex. Clearly, librarians can assess or evaluate many things about which they can make judgments relevant to planning, decision making, accountability, and documenting their accomplishments.

Measurement Choices

Library staff and other evaluators can examine the following elements:

Resources

The dollars available to pay for personnel, collections, and equipment are vitally important to any library. Without staff or collections, libraries could not maintain the functions common to all information services. Resources include not only dollars, but also the staff time, materials, services, and supplies that those dollars can buy. Increases and decreases in purchasing power can also affect resources, sometimes quite significantly.

Physical Environment

The library facility must provide a level of comfort acceptable to most customers and to staff. Lighting, temperature, humidity, noise level, seating, and cleanliness influence comfort. Personal safety is another factor necessary for comfort. Discomfort on any of these factors may negatively affect staff performance.

Team or Unit

Although individuals comprise the work group, the focus here is on the group and its effectiveness and efficiency. The monographic cataloging team, the reference department, or the systems unit are examples.

Functions

These are major activities common to all libraries. G. Edward Evans and Sandra M. Heft describe nine library functions, which can be assessed separately or in some combination:[12]

Identification—locating pertinent items

Selection—deciding which identified items to purchase

Acquisition—securing the items selected

Organization—cataloging and indexing the items for ease in retrieval

Preparation—making the material ready for use

Storage—placing the items in an accessible location

Interpretation—helping customers to identify items pertinent to their information needs

Utilization—providing equipment and space for customers to use materials in the library, and time open (hours of service)

Dissemination—maintaining a system that allows customers to take materials from the library

To their list, we add *management*, providing the coordination for all the other functions and thereby facilitating service. Management also secures the resources and makes assessments and decisions about their deployment.

Processes

These are the separate steps that comprise a function. For example, the *preparation* function involves placing the call number on the item, sometimes putting on a plastic jacket, stamping the item for library ownership, and, in some cases, pasting in slips or pockets, and/or inserting the bar code.

Customers

These are the recipients of library service. Faculty members and students are the primary customers for academic libraries. By their assignments and course requirements, faculty members directly influence students' use of the library. For a public library, customers encompass community residents, those for whom the library receives outside funding (e.g., from the state), and anyone benefitting from the "open-door" policy. Customer attributes, such as age, gender, occupation, student status, location of residency, and preferences in materials or services, are examples of elements for analysis.

Community

Members of the library's community, both customers and noncustomers, can be the focus of assessment. In essence, everyone who qualifies for borrowing privileges is a member of the library's community. Data about community members' demographic characteristics, their respective attitudes toward or perceptions of the library, and their reasons for use or nonuse can be explored.

Use

The ways that customers interact with the library constitute use. Use applies not only to circulation but also to interactions, for instance, with the online public access catalog (OPAC), electronic resources, equipment, furniture, and staff. The focus is on activities directly generated by library customers. Traditionally gathered measures reflect the volume of business but not perceptions about the quality of the service or customers' satisfaction with the service.

Service

Service represents the sum of functions and their related processes. Typically, services have been specific, and called information service, technical service, children's service, and so forth. However, such terms focus on organizational groupings or isolated activities rather than on what the library is supposed to do for all its customers. Library customers want answers and help, not "reference service." Or, as a former president of the hardware manufacturer Black & Decker supposedly told his employees, "Customers do not want quarter-inch drills, they want quarter-inch holes." Expressing a similar sentiment, Glenn Miller, former director of the Orange County Library System in Orlando, Florida, wrote, "If the public library is to continue to exist, then the library will necessarily have to develop and serve its customers in the ways they desire."[13]

In order to encourage librarians to think about service in the larger context, we have adopted Evans and Heft's view of service as bibliographic, physical, and intellectual access to library materials.[14] Access and assistance for gaining access are the essence of library and information services because they represent the fundamental requirements that must be fulfilled before any benefits can be derived from the library's efforts, such as support of education, intellectual enlightenment, or knowledge.

Consequence

The focus here is on what happens to customers as a result of interaction with the library. Consequences are sometimes referred to as benefits. Joanne Marshall found that people did things differently if they were given more information: Physicians changed treatments and financial services personnel altered business decisions.[15] A key question becomes: Have the resources and services of the academic library, for instance, contributed to the granting of a patent, the publication of a monograph or scholarly article, or the achievement of a particular grade on an assignment? For public library customers, consequences might include enjoyment or enlightenment resulting from reading or viewing library material, resolving a problem with a company by being able to locate the name and address of the chief executive officer (CEO), or using recipes from the library for a party. These examples show benefits. Not all interactions with the library, however, are beneficial—sometimes, if the information cannot be obtained, the result to the customer is negative. Therefore, the results of interactions with library services are consequences, rather than benefits.

Impact

Impact relates to mission. The academic institution that funds the academic library expects the library to have a positive and continuous effect on teaching, learning, and research. Local government expects the public library to contribute positively to the educational, intellectual, and cultural life of the community, as well as to support business and economic growth through the services provided.

Most of the 11 elements identified are somewhat interrelated. In particular, resources, or the lack of them, influence many of the elements. Processes are required for the completion of functions that contribute to service. Use is a subset of service. Consequence and impact are dependent on use and service.

How to Measure

What library managers want to know about any of the 11 elements determines how the measurement should be made. Measurement, a tool in the assessment or evaluation process, "is the collection and analysis of objective data describing library performance on which evaluation judgments can be based. Measurement results are not in themselves 'good' or 'bad'; they simply describe what is."[16] The meaning of the data depends on the goals, objectives, and other expectations of the library and those to whom the library director reports (e.g., provost, mayor/city manager, or board of trustees).

Eleven questions outline the different "hows" of measurement and, in effect, encompass input, output, performance, and outcome measures. The questions can be used singly or in groups. In fact, some of the "hows" are calculated by using data derived from other "hows." This list of measuring rods progresses from the highly quantitative to the highly qualitative. The focus also shifts from a library or internal perspective to a customer or external perspective. The questions are as follows:

1. How much? Cost is the focus. Local government officials and academic administrators, along with tax and tuition payers, are interested in costs. Library personnel are interested in both budget allocations and costs. The amounts designated or spent for personnel, collection, purchased services, and equipment *presume*, rather than demonstrate, the quality of service. In one sense, the resources allocated, coupled with the cost of operation, indicate the importance of the library to the parent institution in higher education or local government. Resources also indicate the confidence that the parent institution has in the library's wise use of those resources to provide good service.

"How much?" can also be used to assess the physical facility by measuring the lighting, temperature, humidity, and noise levels, using equipment designed for such measurement and relying on acceptable standards endorsed by the respective professional associations.

2. How many?   Such questions relate to workload. The numbers of items processed in cataloging, classifying, shelving, and checking-in new items are easily counted. Staff members are interested in how busy their team or unit is, as well as in how much work the organization accomplishes. Workloads are one of the most commonly used perspectives in describing libraries. Workload measures are used primarily to justify to decision makers, both those inside the library and those who fund it, the need for resources—staff, equipment, or dollars. Workload measures imply the provision of service, but tell nothing about the actual service delivered.

It is possible to calculate the number of customers that the library encounters during any specified time period. The number of registered customers in relation to the size of the library community reflects what businesses call *market penetration*. It is a credible indicator for public libraries, since registration is a conscious, voluntary action. Two important questions are: (1) How many must be counted in order to generalize the results to a population? and (2) How many customers in the sample are counted more than once?

It is possible to assess building security, in part, by the number of incidents reported by category—that is, thefts of customer property, assaults, and so forth.

3. How economical?   Thrift is the focus. This perspective relates *how much* a service or an activity costs in terms of staff time or materials to *how many* are processed or handled. Efficiency is inferred from the calculation.

4. How prompt?   This question assesses *speed* in completing processes or functions. Average times to completion for reference questions, interlibrary loans, or cataloging of materials indicate how promptly the library responds. The data for this assessment are total time (minutes, hours, days, or months) taken and the number of items completed for any one process or function. Because keeping track of times for every process of interest can be cumbersome, promptness can be calculated by using samples.

5. How accurate?   This is not a question much asked about libraries, with the possible exception being vendor profiles for approval plans, the outsourcing of services, and unobtrusive testing of library reference services.[17] Yet it can be extremely important. "How accurate?" can be asked about cataloging in relation to Library of Congress (LC) standards and *Anglo-American Cataloguing Rules*, about some answers to reference questions in relation to current or historical events, about the completeness of information provided for certain factual or bibliographic inquiries, and about the shelving of materials. Misshelved items and items that the OPAC designates as "in library" but that are not on the shelves are major sources of customer frustration in many libraries. Sampling is the least cumbersome way to collect data for determining *how accurate*.

6. How responsive?   The focus here is on how well the library anticipates customer questions and problems and works to eliminate or ameliorate them. Responsiveness, which assesses such functions as management and services, can be examined by counting the number of things that management and staff anticipate customers want (e.g., photocopy machines that take coins as well as cards). Data about responsiveness are usually binary, in that the element or service is either available or not, and these service elements are also countable in terms of the numbers available.

Helpfulness is another indication of responsiveness. Customers perceive staff members who actively assist them, rather than pointing or shrugging, as responsive. Even if a customer does not obtain what was sought, her or his perception of staff responsiveness might be quite positive. Library failure to be responsive usually causes customer frustration.

7. How well?   Library staff members might focus on how successfully a function or a service accomplishes its stated objectives and furthers library goals. The comparison is made against established criteria; perhaps the library tracks its performance over time. Users might characterize *how well* in terms of *how promptly, how courteously,* and *how accurately* their requests for information were handled. Customer and staff perceptions may differ sharply about how well a function or a service performs. These perceptions are subjective, but have validity because they influence perceptions and attitudes about the library.

8. How valuable?   For a customer, measuring the experience against the cost (time, effort, or money) of going to the library instead of doing something else is an assessment of value; for instance, was the trip worth the effort? Tefko Saracevic and Paul B. Kantor examine value in the context of "value-in-use of library and information services based on user assessments."[18] Value, therefore, looks at the customer and how that person approaches a library service. Among other things, this approach addresses such consequences as: (1) the "reasons why a customer came to the library or accessed the given library service at this time"; (2) "what the customer got out of the use; what benefits did he/she receive"; (3) "what would a customer do otherwise, if the service were not available at that library"; and (4) "elaboration on why did the customer give a particular score on the Likert scales."[19]

Another indication of value is willingness to pay for the service. An increasing number of public libraries now provide rental collections of best-sellers and videos. How heavily these collections are used indicates the *value* that customers place on being able to get these items quickly. Individuals who make decisions about budgets also have their own impressions about which library elements are valuable and which are not. "Value for money" is becoming a commonly heard statement among public librarians. Some local government officials think that popular fiction should not be provided at taxpayer expense, and others consider the library to be an important cultural asset. Library staff have ideas about the value of certain functions that may or may not match those of most external library customers. Service priorities among the library's customers ought to be a major consideration.

Within the business community, value has another meaning, one that might be useful to a public library if members of the board of trustees or city council, or the mayor or city manager, are businesspersons. There might be a desire to increase "the value that technology provides to the business while maximizing IT [information technology] effectiveness and efficiency."[20] Value, as a result, relates to spending on technology and to such questions as "What value are we getting for our money? Are we spending the right amount on technology? Where is the money going?"[21]

9. How reliable? Although librarians would like to believe that all customers leave the library with the information or materials they came to obtain, that does not always occur. Although customers know this, they form impressions about how consistently a library's service provides what they want in terms of physical and intellectual access to items or subjects desired. Dependability in terms of bibliographic, physical, and intellectual access is a major component of reliability. Reliability has another dimension: the consistency of treatment received by customers. Do they receive similar treatment over time and from different members of the staff?

10. How courteous? Service quality has two parts: the service actually delivered, and the transaction between the customer and the service organization. When the transaction involves staff members, then the personal interaction becomes important. If the transaction is frustrating or unpleasant, the customer will assess it negatively. The typical experience for customers becomes, in their minds, the standard of performance for the library.

11. How satisfied? "Consumer researchers have moved from the *literal* meaning of fulfillment or satisfaction and now pursue the concept as the consumer [or customer] experiences and describes it."[22] The issue of satisfaction is linked to the concept of service quality and the ever-growing literature on that topic. The focus of service quality is on the match between customer expectations and the service delivered. Expectations, however, have to be confined to those that the library is prepared to meet. Although customers might like to order library materials as they order pizzas for home delivery, such service is infrequently offered; some libraries, however, do provide home or office delivery of books and articles.

Users form perceptions and attitudes about service quality based on their experiences with the library's materials, services, staff, and physical environment, or on the stories told about transactions with the library by people they trust.

Indicators of satisfaction include the willingness to return or to use a service repeatedly, to recommend a service to others, to support a service, or to advocate its support to others. Furthermore, "completely satisfied" customers are much more likely to repeat their business than are those who are "merely satisfied."[23] Thus, a measure of willingness to return might distinguish between those "completely satisfied" and those displaying lesser degrees of satisfaction.

The Range of Assessment

Figure 4.1, which outlines the elements pertinent for each of the 11 "How . . . ?" questions, serves as a reminder that there is no "one-stop shopping" for assessment. Depending on what they want to know, library managers have choices. Furthermore, some of the questions focus more on the organization and its perceptions about the services offered, whereas others directly take customer perspectives into account and do not infer customer satisfaction. Viewed from another perspective, does the library assume it knows what customers want and need, as well as knowing what their preferences are, or does it ascertain the information directly from the customers and respond accordingly? Needs, wants, preferences, and satisfaction represent different perspectives and elements. It merits repeating that no one-stop approach encompasses all these perspectives.

Who Decides What Is Important?

Ford and GM are very proud of the fact that when their cars come off the line they are "better" in quality terms than the Japanese. The trouble is that management and union people alike define quality as what is IN the car when they deliver it. But it is the customer who defines quality, not the manufacturer.

—Peter Drucker[24]

A number of stakeholders, besides the staff and library administrators, have an interest in the library. These include customers, decision makers who oversee and fund the library (e.g., academic administrators or local government officials), and the community at large, whether the library is academic or public. Taxpayers and those who pay tuition fees have a stake even though they may never enter the library.

Library staff can best address issues related to economy, workload, and volume of use, since these matters are of considerable interest to them. Customers, however, determine issues of consequences, expectations, and satisfaction. Both the library and its customers have an interest in and opinions about issues relating to responsiveness, value, and reliability; these may not be congruent. The library and the customers also may not have the same opinions about the qualities of promptness, accuracy, and courtesy. Each has a different perspective and a differing interest.

The Q Words: Quantity and Quality

Because libraries engage in many activities that can be easily counted, librarians have tended to focus on *quantities* of use as indicators of the goodness of the service. Even though the prevailing professional philoso-

FIGURE 4.1

Components of the "How . . . ?" Questions from the Library and Customer Perspectives

Library Control					Library and Customers Decide			Customers Decide		
How much?	How many?	How economical?	How prompt?	How valuable?	How reliable?	How accurate?	How well?	How courteous?	How responsive?	How satisfied?
Magnitude	Magnitude	Resources used	Cycle times	Effort expended	Dependability	Completeness	Accuracy	Attentive	Anticipatory	Expectations met
Percent of change last year	Change	Units processed	Turnaround time	Cost	Access	Comprehensiveness	Promptness	Welcoming	Helpful	Materials obtained
Percent of overall change			Anticipatory	Benefit obtained	Accuracy	Currency	Courtesy		Empathetic	Personal interaction
Costs							Expertise			Ease of use
										Equipment used
										Environment
										Comfort
										Willingness to return

phy asserts that interaction with library materials (i.e., reading) has a beneficial effect upon people, the emphasis has remained on quantity. Nevertheless, quantity alone is seldom of concern to customers. Rather, they judge the library by how well it meets their particular expectations. Customer expectations can be quite different form those of the librarians.

It is becoming increasingly important to have measures that reflect some aspects of quality, that is, service quality, and indicate how customers respond to services or functions. Customer-based assessments can also address another aspect of quality—*excellence*.

A common concern is the value that different units provide to the sponsoring institution. Many special libraries are increasingly concerned with proving their value to avoid closure or outsourcing. Now, questions about value are being raised in higher education and local government. Some measures need to be adopted solely for the library that place the library within the broader context of issues—beyond cost—important to the parent organization. Unlike measures for resources or use, they need to examine other facets of the picture, those of primary concern to the parent institution grappling with determining and demonstrating quality. In the case of academic libraries, the focus might be on the quality of teaching and learning and the role of the library in enhancing critical thinking, information literacy, or the educational agenda of classroom faculty, or in assisting the institution in retaining students—avoiding their transfer to other institutions and the consequent loss of revenue.

Figure 4.2 offers examples of measures that are of considerable interest to both the academic library and the institution's administrators. These examples reflect important issues. Clearly, there is a need for indicators relating to customer loyalty (translated into donations and fund-raising, and the amount of money received), student retention, and student learning. Some of these issues (e.g., loyalty) have a direct relationship to the library and can provide a highly visible means for

FIGURE 4.2
Measures of Interest to Academic Libraries and Central Administration

1. Number of graduates donating money for the library in relation to the total number of graduates. (The number of graduates must reflect those for whom the institution has current addresses and those who, of course, are still alive.)

2. Amount of donations for the library in relation to total donations (not grants) for parent institution.

3. Number of graduating students who are library borrowers in relation to number enrolled.

4. Number of graduating seniors who get into the graduate program of first choice in relation to the number of graduating seniors wanting to attend graduate school. (Regarding this measure, the library could factor in the number who were extensive library borrowers.)

5. Number of transferring students who are active or extensive library borrowers in relation to the number of students who transfer to other academic institutions.

6. Number of community users of the library who are "completely satisfied" with the library and its services in relation to the number expressing lesser degrees of satisfaction.

FIGURE 4.3

Stakeholder Interest in Certain Questions about the Library

Stakeholder Group	How Much?	How Economical?	How Well?	How Valuable?	How Satisfied?
Library Staff	High	High	High	High	High
Customers	Low	Low	High	High	High
Decision Makers	High	Medium	Medium	Medium	Medium
Community	Medium	Medium	Low	Low	Low

demonstrating the value of the library to the overall institution (see Chapters 9 and 12).

Given the amount of time that a number of library directors are devoting to fund-raising,[25] it would seem that more library services might pattern themselves after the private sector and encourage customer loyalty, willingness to return or reuse, and satisfaction. Such a focus on quality might have some ultimate relationship to donations and financial support for the library after students graduate.

Judgments about the library may vary among and within stakeholder groups, and certain interests important to one may conflict with the interests of another. For staff, those interests include job security and salary issues. For decision makers, the interests may be staying well within the budget or cutting costs, including those related to personnel. Customers want their service expectations to be met, while taxpayers and those who write tuition checks prefer that costs either do not increase or, if they must, do so minimally. Figure 4.3 shows the level of interest each stakeholder group has in some of the "How . . . ?" questions. Note that the figure moves from quantitative questions on the left to qualitative questions on the right. The qualitative assessments are based on opinions, experiences, and expectations.

Both the library and its customers should be interested in the intersection between "How well?" and "How valuable?" The library has some control over "How well?" but customers really decide about service performance and its value.

Relating "What" to Measure with "How" to Measure

It is important that library managers understand the ways that the elements in the things to measure can relate to the different "hows" of measurement. Figure 4.4 shows these relationships. It is not necessary to answer all the "How . . . ?" questions related to any particular thing that can be measured.

FIGURE 4.4

Relating "What" to Measure with "How" to Measure

WHAT TO MEASURE

Question	Internal Perspective								External Perspective		
	Resources	Physical	Team/Unit	Process	Function	Customer	Use	Service	Consequences	Community	Impact
How much?	×	×	×							×	
How many?	×	×	×	×	×	×	×			×	
How economical?			×	×							
How prompt?			×	×							
How accurate?			×	×							
How responsive?			×		×		×	×			
How well?			×	×	×		×	×	×	×	×
How valuable?			×	×	×		×	×	×	×	
How reliable?						×	×	×			
How courteous?						×		×			
How satisfied?									×		×

Some, indeed many, library activities can be assessed in several ways and from different perspectives. Bibliographic instruction (BI), for example, can be assessed by the number of sessions offered ("How many?"), number of students attending ("How many?"), and cost per session and per student ("How economical?"). The library might assess value by comments from faculty about the BI program or by an increase in the number of faculty members requesting BI for their students. Faculty might assess "How well?" by an increase in the number of references cited in students' papers or by a perceived improvement in the quality of completed assignments. For students, the grade achieved from the assignment related to the BI program influences the perception of value.

Compared to What?

Absolute numbers—"How much?" or "How many?"—represent data collected by librarians in many categories—circulation, serials received, and expenditures for certain items. The "How much?" or "How many?" question is usually followed by a desire for a comparison that places the numbers in some context and makes them more meaningful. The comparison can be against past years, peer institutions, or past procedures, or it can be on a per capita basis.

Although absolute numbers can be compared, usually the magnitude of the numbers is greater than most people can comprehend. A simple way to understand the data is to use *rankings*, comparing such similar factors as budget, staff, collections, and subsets of each of these. The Association of Research Libraries (ARL) has published rankings for decades to compare its member libraries on various factors.

Another way to simplify understanding is to compare one year's data with those of another. The annual *Statistical Report* from the American Library Association's Public Library Data Service has a category indicating the percentage of increase or decrease in local funding for each library compared with the previous year. Percentage measurement requires two absolute numbers, because one is dependent on the other. *Ratios*, which are simply variants of percentages, are another means of making numbers more relevant.

Figure 4.5 identifies 30 ratios that primarily reflect resources. These "input measures" indicate what libraries "put-in" to the system. Three measures suggest "gross" quantity of borrowing (items 28–30) and two indicators convey "gross" quantities of volumes added to the collection (items 13 and 21), but there is no coverage of other aspects of the quantity of service provided.[26] There is no mention of the quality of any aspect of service. Twenty-seven measures reflect the capacity for service—similar to the resources in a warehouse awaiting orders from customers. They are all based on expenditures—25 from the current year and 2 (items 14 and 22) from both current and past expenditures.

FIGURE 4.5
ARL Selected Ratios

1. Professional staff as a percentage of total staff
2. Support staff as a percentage of total staff
3. Student assistants as a percentage of total staff
4. Ratio of professional staff to support staff
5. Serials expenditures as a percentage of library materials expenditures
6. Library materials expenditures as a percentage of total expenditures
7. Binding expenditures as a percentage of total library expenditures
8. Salary expenditures as a percentage of total library expenditures
9. Operating expenditures as a percentage of total library expenditures
10. Unit price of monographs
11. Unit price of serials
12. Total library expenditures per faculty
13. Volumes added (gross) per faculty
14. Volumes held per faculty
15. Paid serial subscriptions per faculty
16. Monographs purchased per faculty
17. Total library staff per faculty
18. Library materials expenditures per faculty
19. Serials expenditures per faculty
20. Total library expenditures per student
21. Volumes added (gross) per student
22. Volumes held per student
23. Paid serial subscriptions per student
24. Monographs purchased per student
25. Total [library] staff per student
26. Library materials expenditures per student
27. Serials expenditures per student
28. Items loaned over items borrowed
29. Items borrowed per faculty
30. Items borrowed per student

See Martha Kyrillidou, *Developing Indicators for Academic Library Performance: Ratios from the ARL Statistics, 1994–95 and 1995–96* (Washington, D.C.: Association of Research Libraries, 1997). (For the interactive edition of ARL statistics, see http://www.lib.virginia.edu/socsci/newarl/).

The percentages relating expenditures on staff, serials, library materials, binding, and operations to the total spent are slices in a pie called *expenditures*. The measures relating to faculty and students (e.g., monographs purchased per . . .) are specious in that they count the same dollars twice. The true ratio should be computed using the campus population actively involved in teaching and research, not the subsets thereof. In essence, the first 27 measures could be replaced by one—total annual expenditures. In the absence of profit or other financial indicators, the ability to obtain resources has been perceived as an indicator of success of the library's chief administrator.

The Academic Library Survey (ALS), which the National Center for Education Statistics (NCES), U.S. Department of Education, conducts periodically, reports data similar to those from ARL. The most recent report—covering 1992—concentrates on seven indicators:

1. Total full-time equivalent (FTE) library staff
2. Total FTE library staff per 1,000 FTE students and per 100 full-time instructional faculty members (i.e., total instructional faculty on 9–10- and 11–12-month contracts)
3. Total volumes held
4. Total volumes held per FTE student
5. Total library operating expenditures
6. Total library operating expenditures as a percentage of total education and general expenditures
7. Total library operating expenditures per FTE student

The survey reported these indicators because:

(1) they provide information in key areas to the status of academic libraries; (2) data were available for these indicators for both 1990 and 1992; and (3) response rates for these indicators in 1992 exceeded the NCES standard of 70 percent. Full-time equivalent (FTE) library staff persons, rather than librarians specifically, were chosen to describe personnel resources since FTE library staff is a more inclusive indicator (and, in fact, includes librarians). In addition, it should be noted that as of 1992, the ALS did not collect data on some of the electronic technologies that now play major roles in the delivery of academic library services.[27]

These measures have the same weaknesses as the ARL measures. Furthermore, libraries may develop a defensive posture toward such data. They might want to protect their existing ranking—ensuring that it does not decline and that of a peer institution does not increase. Such a posture does not lead to or encourage improved quality.

Using the Information about "What" and "How"

Change, uncertainty, and complexity are endemic to the 1990s. Only the most nimble organizations have prospered. In addition to their ability to adapt to the changing climate, these organizations are aware of the need to concentrate on continuous quality improvement in products and/or services. Libraries have certainly concentrated on information technology and electronic resources. Perhaps it is time to focus on other areas needing improvement.

Benchmarking

Continuous quality improvement requires that organizations address such questions as:

- Are we performing better than we did in the past?
- Are we performing as well as, or better than, other units on campus or in local government?
- Are we performing better than our competitors?
- Are there other libraries or organizations that are performing well and from which we can learn?

These questions are not new to the thoughtful library manager. The process of gathering information to make such types of comparisons has, however, acquired a trendy name: benchmarking. Benchmarking comparisons are usually based on time, cost, and quality as measured against previous performance, others in the organization or profession, or the best in that class. These focuses are called: *internal, competitive,* and *functional* or *comparative*.

Internal Benchmarking

The most common way to begin is with internal benchmarking done within the library. New processes can be compared with old; closely related teams or units using common or shared performance parameters can be matched. Teams divided by subject, whose other duties are similar, could be compared according to *how many, how much, how economical, how prompt, how responsive,* and/or *how well.* The best-performing team or unit sets the benchmark (standard) for the others to attain. Relying only on internal analysis, however, reinforces an inward focus that can engender complacency or set up rivalries within the organization that become counterproductive.

Competitive Benchmarking

Competitive benchmarking generally focuses on *direct* (so-called peer libraries and institutions) or *indirect* (related organizations, such as bookstores) competitors. Historically, comparisons involved resources and workload measures. The ARL rankings are an example. Staff, in a library ranked 32nd on "library materials expenditures per faculty," might assume that their library is "better" on this factor than the library ranked 38th. This is a highly dubious assumption, because the ranking does not indicate anything about the appropriateness of the expenditure for the community, the interests to be served, or other factors related to Figures 4.1 and 4.3. On the other hand, externally oriented benchmarking, especially with a best-in-class organization, makes staff aware of improvements that are many times greater than they would have thought possible.[28] Nonetheless, before embarking on such benchmarking, it is essential to determine the degree of comparability—comparing like, not unlike, items.

Functional or Comparative Benchmarking

Benchmarking might also be functional—targeted at organizations in other fields to see how a particular function is carried out—or generic—going beyond a particular function and identifying the ways in which other organizations, libraries or otherwise, operate. For example, Xerox had a problem with its warehousing operations that caused customer dissatisfaction. For solutions, Xerox managers looked to the L. L. Bean Company, which sells clothing by mail. L. L. Bean is noted for its high customer satisfaction, which largely depends on the efficiency and effectiveness of its warehousing operation. Many of the Bean techniques were applicable to Xerox's situation.[29]

Areas of Benchmarking

Benchmarking can be undertaken in almost any area of organizational endeavor. The basic requirements are that key performance variables be identified, measured, analyzed, and compared to provide a basis for planned performance improvement. As well, benchmarking can be applied internally to reflect change over time and changes in processes in order to determine whether or not the services to customers are improving. Businesses commonly identify their core services—those expected to provide high degrees of customer satisfaction—and set benchmarks for other services that they intend to develop as core services. Thus, they target the areas to benchmark as they improve the quality of service provided. The key is to be clear about the organization's needs and the areas and processes to improve. The general aim should be to keep it simple by concentrating on a few chosen measures and following through on needed changes.[30]

Using internal benchmarking, library managers, together with the staff, can set the baseline for service performance as reflected through a particular measure—for example, the time to respond to an information request sent on e-mail. Initially, performance might be set at "75 percent of all e-mail reference questions will be answered within 24 hours"; once that target has been achieved consistently, the expectation level might be raised.

Benchmarking that is well done has been characterized as an attitude that emphasizes excellence in performance, not simply improvement. As a first step, however, the key is to improve, and continue to do so, rather than to be satisfied with the status quo. Should resources decline, the approach is to look for ways to do the right things smarter, rather than to continue routine processes that contribute little to service quality or customer satisfaction. A caution about internal benchmarking is necessary. Library managers should first ask if a process needs to be done at all or if every step is necessary. Clearly, the value of such benchmarking and the instances in which it is used must be reviewed.

FIGURE 4.6
Steps in Benchmarking

1. Select activity for benchmarking.
2. Determine what to compare (internal or external).
3. Select the measure and the target to achieve.
4. Determine how to gather the data—quantitative and/or qualitative.
5. Collect, analyze, and interpret the data.
6. Implement change (in context of goals, objectives, or other expectations).
7. Revisit the expectations and decide whether to set new targets.
8. Revisit steps 5 through 7.

Figure 4.6 identifies the steps in benchmarking. A key is to set targets and measure achievement against them. Based on the data gathered, library managers can introduce change as needed and set new targets to improve service. They should not, however, expect staff simply to work harder!

A Question of Balance

Leaner, meaner, and *flatter* aptly describe what has happened to many organizations in the 1990s. The drive to cut costs and obtain "value for money" is as pervasive in higher education and government as it is in large corporations. Reductions of resources have a systemic effect on an organization—the goodness or badness of the effect has to be acknowledged and considered in the light of its impact on the library's quality and its ability to fulfill its mission.

As Roswitha Poll and Peter te Boekhorst note,

> The library should not be content to know that . . . [it] is producing services in a cost-effective way, but also [it should know] that those services are chosen, designed and delivered in a way that offers the greatest benefit to the primary user group.
>
> For example: "Cost per Enquiry Answered" should be set in relation to the performance indicator "Correct Answer Fill Rate" [number of questions answered correctly over number of questions asked] and perhaps also to "User Satisfaction with Reference Staff."
>
> In this way, the library will be able to escape the danger of being one-sided, of stressing service quality while neglecting needful economy, or of ignoring users' needs in the bliss of being thrifty. Knowledge of both the quality and the cost of library services is needed for management decisions in setting priorities and allocating resources.[31]

Qualitative Analysis: The Missing Portion of the Picture

Most measures tell only a part of the story; that part may involve a minor storyline or be unimportant in meeting the organization's mission. Rankings, percentages, and ratios are useful for things that are countable, but they all need some context to make the meaning more understandable. As well, certain measures might be used in combination. For example, Allan D. Pratt and Ellen Altman tested the relationship between certain Public Library Association (PLA) designated "output measures." In essence, little correlation existed among any of the output measures.[32]

On the other hand, not everything worth knowing can be counted precisely and reduced to a rank, percentage, or ratio. Many aspects of information service are intangible, and must be assessed in other ways. Herein is the value of qualitative analysis. Satisfaction, like service quality, is subjective, and certain attitudes or opinions cannot necessarily be reduced meaningfully to a quantitative measure.

No local government ever agreed to fund a public library merely to circulate books. The intent was always something more edifying, and the edifying part was used to convince local officials that the library would be a community asset. Even golf courses and swimming pools are established and maintained partly because of the health benefits—fresh air and exercise—accruing to golfers and swimmers. The expectation for the library has been, and continues to be, the *opportunity* for education and self-improvement as well as the economic benefits both to individuals and to the community derived from an educated, well-informed, and employed citizenry.

Taxpayers who never use the library have been willing to fund libraries for the same reasons, and also for the *opportunity* of possible benefits to their children and grandchildren. Clearly, something more than the mere number of items circulated is expected.

Such perspectives are important, but they underscore that impact is separate from the other types of assessments. Impacts are important to the sponsoring organization because they relate to the purpose (mission) of the library and to the direct or indirect effects or consequences resulting from achieving program or service goals and objectives. Impacts, which are outside the scope of this book, are extremely difficult to measure.

What Now?

Counting and measuring are useful, but another element is needed to assess service quality—*judgment*. It is necessary, but insufficient, to know that a library has 60 percent of the items that customers need and that it takes three weeks for a book loaned by another library to arrive. The real question should be: Is such performance acceptable to both the library and the customer?

Because there are no universally accepted standards or norms for performance on any aspect of library processes, functions, or service, senior staff in each library have to decide on the acceptable level of performance. The next step is to communicate the standard to the staff whose work directly influences performance. Unless these steps to set standards are taken, each staff member determines his or her own standard for acceptable service. That standard may be unacceptable or insufficient to customers.

It is neither necessary nor desirable to set standards for every process, function, or service all at once, or even within a short period of time. Indeed, that would be counterproductive. It is important to set a standard for one area or for each team to work on achieving a common standard. Slow and steady improvement will be more readily accepted and better implemented than swift and large-scale changes.

Organizations can adopt more than one perspective. They can pick and choose those that meet their particular needs. For instance, library managers might want to determine how effective (including cost-effective) a particular service is. They might also want to judge it in the context of customer expectations and satisfaction, knowing that the insights gained will help to reshape and revitalize that service.

The intention of this book is not to advocate one perspective over another, but rather to explain customer-driven perspectives and show how librarians can gather useful data for meeting customers' expectations and ensuring their satisfaction. They might even create a customer value chain, "defined as moving from customer satisfaction to customer loyalty."[33]

Measures of Consequences

Consequences are the results of interactions with the library service. Interactions with library materials can and do affect individuals' lives—both positively and negatively. Academic librarians, for example, might like to believe that: (1) students who are frequent borrowers earn higher grades than students who seldom come to the library, and (2) students who cannot obtain materials when they need them receive poor grades. Consequences can also be affected by components of service quality, in particular promptness and reliability. If the customer's deadline for receipt of the information is not met, or if the answer given to an important question is incorrect, then consequences are likely to be negative.

The library may gain some indication of negative consequences by tracking unsatisfactory transactions—materials desired but not obtainable, interlibrary loan items that arrive too late for course or research deadlines, and reference questions that the library was unable to answer.

To determine the positive consequences, librarians can ask the customers. Joanne Marshall[34] and José-Marie Griffiths and Donald W. King[35] asked special library customers about the consequences of using library materials. Although their lists of consequences relate primarily to special libraries and particular occupations, there is no reason why public and academic libraries cannot ask their customers about the consequences of library use.

Such information is of great interest to the decision makers who fund the library. Those who think that the public library is merely a recreational outlet for genre readers might be surprised by the range of consequences for customers.

Summary

"Library use is largely self-service."[36] For this reason (if not for others), it is important to review the issues discussed in this chapter as well as the types of assessment depicted in Figure 4.7. Such a review should lead to judgments and actions that will improve the organization's service performance and image. Other chapters will build on this foundation and indicate how to examine both service quality and satisfaction. As a result, librarians will gain better insights about customers' wants and needs as well as the gap between service expected and service provided.

The library community has embraced such terms as *input, output, performance,* and *outcome* measures, and explored impact measures—how a service has made a difference to learning, to job or classroom performance, to scholarly production, and so on. These terms, however, lack universal acceptance and have been defined in various ways. Input, output, and performance measures present the organizational or library perspective and what that entity considers important: often, resource allocation and volume of business. Outcome measures might examine outputs or quality assurance, but the term also implies results and perhaps even impacts.

Clearly, libraries need to adopt a customer focus and to concentrate on what is important to customers (see Figure 4.8). Instead of adding to the definitional and conceptual confusion by selecting a term such as *outcome measures,* we refer to the types of indicators discussed in this book as *customer-related indicators.* Such indicators provide insights into:

FIGURE 4.7
Countables and Assessables

How Much?	{ Resources Market Penetration	
How Many?	{ Workload Amount of Use Number of Customers	Countable
How Well?	{ Customer Expectations	
How Valuable?	{ Consequences of Use	Assessable
How Satisfied?	{ Customer Interaction	

Measuring and Assessing the Components of Service Quality

- Effectiveness
- Attributes of timeliness and accuracy
- Customer satisfaction
- Quality (customer perceptions and expectations)
- Complaint analysis
- Processes (queuing, making contact with service personnel, and performance of tasks essential for producing satisfied and delighted customers)

Later chapters will offer examples of customer-related measures and present new ways of looking at and assessing library services.

FIGURE 4.8
Conceptual Framework for Measures Relating to Library Service

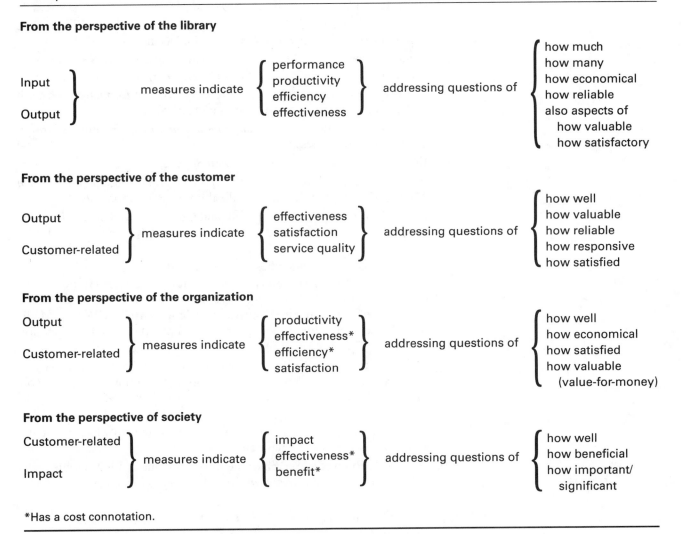

From the perspective of the library

Input / Output } measures indicate { performance / productivity / efficiency / effectiveness } addressing questions of { how much / how many / how economical / how reliable / also aspects of / how valuable / how satisfactory

From the perspective of the customer

Output / Customer-related } measures indicate { effectiveness / satisfaction / service quality } addressing questions of { how well / how valuable / how reliable / how responsive / how satisfied

From the perspective of the organization

Output / Customer-related } measures indicate { productivity / effectiveness* / efficiency* / satisfaction } addressing questions of { how well / how economical / how satisfied / how valuable / (value-for-money)

From the perspective of society

Customer-related / Impact } measures indicate { impact / effectiveness* / benefit* } addressing questions of { how well / how beneficial / how important/ / significant

*Has a cost connotation.

NOTES

1. Peter Drucker, *Managing the Nonprofit Organization: Principles and Practices* (New York: HarperCollins, 1990), 107.

2. U.S. Office of Management and Budget, "Primer on Performance Measurement" (revised February 28, 1995), 1 (ftp://ftp.fedworld.gov/pub/results/primer0.1.txt).

3. Thomas A. Childers and Nancy A. Van House, *What's Good? Describing Your Public Library's Effectiveness* (Chicago: ALA, 1993), 5.

4. Ibid., 7.

5. Ibid.

6. Joseph A. McDonald and Lynda Basney Micikas, *Academic Libraries: The Dimensions of Their Effectiveness* (Westport, Conn.: Greenwood Press, 1994), 30.

7. Ibid., 36.

8. F. W. Lancaster, *If You Want to Evaluate Your Library . . .* (Champaign, Ill.: University of Illinois, Graduate School of Library and Information Science, 1988), 1.

9. Childers and Van House, *What's Good?*, 5.

10. Valerie Florance and Nina W. Matheson, "Health Science Librarian as Knowledge Worker," *Library Trends* 42, no. 1 (summer 1993): 199.

11. Peter H. Rossi and Howard E. Freeman, *Evaluation: A Systematic Approach*, 5th ed. (Newbury Park, Calif.: Sage, 1993), 4.

12. G. Edward Evans and Sandra M. Heft, *Introduction to Technical Services*, 6th ed. (Littleton, Colo.: Libraries Unlimited, 1995), 4.

13. Glenn Miller, *Customer Service and Innovation in Libraries* (Fort Atkinson, Wisc.: Highsmith Press, 1996), 9.

14. Evans and Heft, *Introduction to Technical Services*, 4.

15. Joanne Marshall, *The Impact of the Special Library on Corporate Decision Making* (Washington, D.C.: Special Libraries Association, 1993).

16. Nancy A. Van House, Beth T. Weil, and Charles R. McClure, *Measuring Academic Library Performance: A Practical Approach* (Chicago: ALA, 1990), 4.

17. To date, more than 90 studies have examined the accuracy of reference staff when answering certain types of questions. See Peter Hernon, "Unobtrusive Testing," in *Evaluating Library Programs and Services: TELL IT! Training Manual*, edited by Douglas Zweizig with Michele Besant (Madison, Wisc.: University of Wisconsin, School of Library and Information Studies, 1993), 71–80.

18. Tefko Saracevic and Paul B. Kantor, "Studying the Value of Library and Information Services. Part II. Methodology and Taxonomy," *Journal of the American Society for Information Science* 48, no. 6 (1997): 543.

19. Ibid., 545. A Likert scale consists of a series of items to which the subject responds by marking on an intensity scale the extent to which he or she agrees or disagrees with each item.

20. Howard A. Rubin, "In Search of the Business Value of Information Technology," *Application Development Trends* 1, no. 12 (November 1994): 24.

21. Ibid., 23.

22. Roland T. Rust and Richard L. Oliver, *Service Quality: New Directions in Theory and Practice* (Thousand Oaks, Calif.: Sage, 1994), 4.

23. Pat L. Weaver-Myers and Wilbur A. Stolt, "Delivery Speed, Timeliness, and Satisfaction: Patrons' Perceptions about ILL Service," *Journal of Library Administration* 23, nos. 1 and 2 (1996): 39.

24. Peter Drucker, *Managing for the Future: The 1990s and Beyond* (New York: Truman Tally Books, 1992), 346.

25. See Susan K. Martin, "The Changing Role of the Library Director: Fund-Raising and the Academic Library," *Journal of Academic Librarianship* 24, no. 1 (January 1998): 3–10.

26. In recent years, ARL has treated such items as the number of reference questions asked as a service indicator.

27. National Center for Education Statistics, *The Status of Academic Libraries in the United States: Results from the 1990 and 1992 Academic Library Surveys*, NCES 97-413 (Washington, D.C.: Government Printing Office, 1997), 3, or http://nces.ed.gov/pubd97/97413.html.

28. Robert G. Eccles, "The Performance Measurement Manifesto," in *Performance Measurement and Evaluation*, edited by Jacky Holloway, Jenny Lewis, and Geoff Mallory (London: Sage, 1995), 7.

29. Tony Hope and Jeremy Hope, *Transforming the Bottom Line* (Boston: Harvard Business School Press, 1996), 102–3.

30. See Joy Tillotson, Janice Adlington, and Cynthia Holt, "Benchmarking Waiting Times," *College & Research Libraries News* 58, no. 10 (November 1997): 693–694, 700. The researchers "measured the length of time users had to wait at the Information Desk before speaking to a librarian, the length of time the librarians spent with each user, and the number of users who left the desk without speaking to a librarian." Furthermore, they "counted the total number of users arriving at the desk, whether they spoke to a librarian or not." They also monitored the amount of time spent in helping users with CD-ROM questions (p. 693).

31. Roswitha Poll and Peter te Boekhorst, *Measuring Quality: International Guidelines for Performance Measurement in Academic Libraries*, IFLA Publication 76 (New Providence, N.J.: K.G. Saur/Reed Publishing, 1996), 40.

32. Allan D. Pratt and Ellen Altman, "Live by the Numbers; Die by the Numbers," *Library Journal* 122, no. 7 (April 15, 1997): 48–49.

33. National Performance Review, *Serving the American Public: Best Practices in Customer-Driven Strategic Planning* (Washington, D.C.: Government Printing Office, 1997), 38.

34. Marshall, *Impact of the Special Library.*

35. José-Marie Griffiths and Donald W. King, *Increasing the Information Edge* (Washington, D.C.: Special Libraries Association, 1993).

36. Childers and Van House, *What's Good?*, 26.

5 What Can Go Wrong with Numbers

A very indignant city council member has phoned . . . demanding an explanation. . . . You spend over $85 per capita while the others comparable to your library spend about $55; other libraries circulate about 25,000 items per employee per year; yours, just over 19,000.

—Allan D. Pratt and Ellen Altman[1]

Measuring and assessing service elements in the library can be highly useful to management, but must be done with care and foresight about what might go wrong. The purpose of this chapter is to provide a cautionary note about the use of any performance indicator, especially measures of input (reflects those resources essential to providing library services) and output (conveys the amount of service provided).

Any measure, including customer-related ones, should be linked to performance targets and outcomes, which monitor, and are intended to improve, the quality of service over time. Nonetheless, any data reported as performance indicators might be used for political purposes, purposes not always aimed at developing and improving library services. As Peter Hernon and Charles R. McClure note, "Information is a tool useful for acquiring and retaining power. Information may enable an organization to advance its image and role as dynamic and meeting its mission, goals, and objectives."[2]

Do More Resources Mean Better Service?

A widespread assumption exists that resources equate with quality service and, ergo, with more resources, the library automatically provides more and better service. Library directors have been using that argument for years. That assumption has now been severely tested in a study that correlated expenditures with services provided in the 24 libraries serving over one million population in the *1996 Statistical Report* of the Public Library Data Service.[3] No direct linear relationship occurred between resources and number or quality of any output measure—circulation per capita, reference transactions, holdings, registrations as a percentage of population, or collection turnover. In fact, there was little, if any, meaningful correlation on any of these measures. This result shows that more resources do not necessarily translate into better service. "Better" assumes quality and, from the perspective of this book, customers will make their own determination about quality. That perspective must become central to the assessment process.

Rankings Can Be Not Only Misleading but Also Dangerous

Most library directors would be delighted to announce that they presided over the best-funded library in the area, the state, the region, or the country. But the city councilors who funded one such library were horrified to learn that they were supporting the most expensive public library in New Zealand. The reaction was not pride, but determination to cut the library's resources. These councilors did not want to have the best-supported library in the country. For them, one slightly-better-than-average library would be just fine. As a result, the library's budget was slashed and the full-time staff was cut by one-third. This case is a good example of how rankings and resource statistics can be more harmful than helpful. (In today's fiscal environment, this example may not be extreme. Look at the number of administrators—outside the library—who firmly believe that the Internet is a viable substitute for a library and its collections and services.)

Information about the New Zealand library's high level of financial support was included in statistical reports that compared the largest public libraries in the country on a number of factors, including cost per circulation, circulations per staff member, and volumes per capita. In comparison with the other libraries mentioned in the report, this library had a higher cost per circulation and a lower number of circulations per staff member. Upon external review, these ratios were taken as indicators of excess and waste in the system and low productivity on the part of staff. The city councilors used volumes per capita as an indication of the materials budget being overgenerous.

The real situation is somewhat different. The city in this example used a total charge-back approach in calculating the library's expenditures. The library was charged more than $1 million for depreciation on its central building and over $3 million for debt service on the building, and had many other charges that the other cities did not assign to their libraries. In fact, because the charges to the libraries differed from city to city, the comparison of expenditures among this group of libraries was faulty. Nonetheless, using noncomparable data, other comparisons were made. Of course, costs per circulation were higher for the library in the example; all expenses were higher because of the charge-backs.

Another misleading statistic was the high volume count per capita. This library had not weeded its collection for many years. When it moved into a new central building, the staff moved books from storage to fill the empty space. These books were still in the collection some years later, although, because of their age and poor physical condition, few circulated.

Some Statistics Become Double-Edged Swords

The number of volumes in the collection has been presumed to indicate quality. In some cases, it may. This number, however, can be interpreted as reflecting a collection so extensive that few new materials are needed.

The preceding example about books per capita shows how some statistics can be double-edged swords. If the library described earlier now gets rid of all those titles that should have been discarded long ago, the city government is likely to accuse it of manipulating the number of volumes to make a case for an increase in the materials budget.

Another library placed a bar code on each serial issue received because it circulated serials. The city council hired a consultant to evaluate the library, and he asked the systems librarian for the number of titles that had not circulated in the past five years. The number was obtained by matching bar codes to circulation records using the online public access catalog (OPAC). The number was quite high—over 500,000—because each issue of a serial had been bar coded and, thus, recorded as a separate item. Yet, only the number—500,000—not the explanation, appeared in news reports about the need to streamline the library.

The amount of time spent in the library is sometimes considered an indication of use on the part of the customers. Time spent certainly can imply reading and using materials, but time can also be spent trying to find materials and having other frustrating experiences. On the other hand, a library whose system is transparent, one that makes it easy for customers to find what they are looking for quickly and to leave the building perfectly satisfied—or even not have to come in for every transaction—will come out low on time spent. Time alone as an indicator can also be a double-edged sword, and should be used very carefully.

All Activities Are Not Equal

When activities are lumped together in one report, it is difficult for the reader to understand that these are not necessarily comparable in terms of staff used, time expended, or impact on customers. For example, it takes only a few seconds to charge or discharge an item, whereas making a presentation to a class or visiting a school library can take a lot of time. Nor are all requests for assistance equal. Directional questions are quickly answered, whereas some questions can be quite complicated and require multiple sources to answer. Some library activities never show up in library statistics at all. Of course, all the costs do appear, but they are spread over other activities.

Counting the Same Items Twice Inflates and Misleads

The Association of Research Libraries (ARL), in its annual rankings reports, gives an unrealistic picture of many elements. For example, these reports include (see Figure 4.5):

- Volumes held per student
- Volumes held per faculty
- Expenditures per student
- Expenditures per faculty
- Serials per student
- Serials per faculty

All are based on the total. Using expenditures as an example of distorted statistics, let us consider a library that spends $4,550,000. The service population includes 21,889 students and 1,222 faculty. To report that the library spends $208 per student and $3,723 per faculty member overstates reality. In truth, the library spends about $197 per capita on its likely customer population ($4,550,000 divided by 23,111—the combined total of students and faculty).

Are All These Really Apples?

To make comparisons meaningful and fair, it is necessary to agree on definitions about what is being compared and on a standard procedure for comparison. In most instances, that is not done. Take a simple thing like volumes in a library. There is no consensus in the profession about uniformity in reporting volumes. Here are some of the issues/questions about volume counting:

- Should volumes be counted as bibliographic or physical items?
- Is an encyclopedia one volume, or is each part a volume?
- Should CD-ROMs be included in the volume count, and if so, as bibliographic or physical items?

Further complicating matters, some libraries collect and report volume counts, whereas others either maintain title counts or both volume and title counts.

Comparability issues can be found in every area of library activity. Unfortunately, too many comparisons are made without taking into account that not every library is counting the same way. These counting practices are not, however, usually stated or questioned when comparing libraries.

New Options and Technologies Must Be Included

The most compelling reason to rethink the data in current reports of library activity is that the nature of information access and provision has been, and still is, changing radically. Libraries now offer more options for customers than ever, but these new options—perhaps dealing with information in electronic formats—have not been incorporated into current reports about service. On the other hand, continuing to concentrate on statistics about physical items grossly understates the actual access provided.

Summary

Library managers must be certain about what they want and need to know: what use they will make of the data collected, how they will interpret the data, what decisions the data will impact, and how the data will be used to improve library service. As Richard L. Lynch and Kelvin F. Cross explain,

performance measures must help managers and workers:

- Measure what is important to . . . customers;
- Motivate operations to continually improve against customer expectations;
- Identify and eliminate waste—of both time and resources;
- Shift the focus of their organizations from bureaucratic, vertical empires to more responsive, horizontal business systems;
- Accelerate organizational learning and build a consensus for the change when customer expectations shift or strategies call for the organization to behave differently.[4]

As a result, meaningful assessment should focus on nine overlapping dimensions:

Reliability—the delivery of the promised library service dependably and accurately, and collections containing information appropriate to customer needs

Responsiveness—readiness of the staff to provide service, quick resolution of problems, and timeliness of information

Assurance—knowledge and courtesy of the staff and their ability to convey confidence, be polite and friendly, and possess the knowledge necessary to provide information about collections and services

Access—sufficient numbers of staff and equipment, adequate hours of operation, access to remote collections and resources, and access to senior management team when necessary

Communications—keeping the customers informed in language understandable to them, and listening to them

Credibility—reputation of the service

Tangibles—maintenance of the physical facilities and serviceability of the equipment, as well as the environment

Security—safety

Understanding the customer—recognition of regular customers and understanding the individual needs of customers[5]

Using these nine dimensions, Figure 5.1 offers examples of questions meaningful to customers, for whom the library could develop performance indicators and, in reports and elsewhere, relate the findings to a customer service plan and to organizational goals and objectives (see Chapter 3). After all, a library, like other organizations, operates in a political context and may have to collect and report input and output measures. Nonetheless, it should also "stay close to . . . [its] customers."[6]

FIGURE 5.1
Service Dimensions That Can Be Converted to Performance Indicators and Reported

Reliability
- Are telephone calls returned when promised?
- Does equipment work when it has been repaired?
- Are errors made in overdue and fine notices?
- Are reference questions answered correctly?
- Is the OPAC and other equipment functional?

Responsiveness
- Are new periodicals and newspapers checked in promptly?
- Are books reshelved promptly?
- Is turnaround time for interlibrary loan requests minimized?
- Are customer complaints quickly resolved?

(Continued)

Assurance

- Are staff members courteous to customers?
- Are staff members familiar with the equipment and the technology?

Access

- Are senior managers accessible when customers need them?
- How long is the waiting time at the circulation and reference desks, as well as at computers?
- How long does it take staff members to answer the telephone?

Communications

- Do staff members avoid the use of unnecessary jargon?
- Are staff members good listeners?
- Are customers who complain assured that their problem or concern will be addressed?

Credibility

- What is the reputation of the library, individual units in the library, and specific services?

- How much faith can customers place in the information provided by the library?

Tangibles

- Is the library an attractive place to visit?
- Is the building too hot or too cold? Is the lighting adequate?
- What is the condition of the equipment?
- Are handouts attractive and clear?
- Are WWW sites and links "to" and "from" them clear?

Security

- How safe is it to be in and nearby the library?

Understanding the Customer

- To what extent are regular customers recognized and treated accordingly?
- To what extent do staff members understand customer expectations and try to satisfy them?

Adapted from "Measuring and Improving the Quality of Public Services: A Hybrid Approach," by Thomas Seay, Sheila Seaman, and David Cohen, *Library Trends* 44, no. 3, p. 476. © 1996 The Board of Trustees of the University of Illinois at Urbana-Champaign. See also Peter Brophy and Kate Coulling, *Quality Management for Information and Library Managers* (Hampshire, England: Gower Publishing Limited, 1996), 49–50.

NOTES

1. Allan D. Pratt and Ellen Altman, "Live by the Numbers, Die by the Numbers," *Library Journal*, 122, no. 7 (April 15, 1997): 48.
2. Peter Hernon and Charles R. McClure, *Evaluation and Library Decision Making* (Norwood, N.J.: Ablex, 1990), 214.
3. Pratt and Altman, "Live by the Numbers," 48–49.
4. Richard L. Lynch and Kelvin F. Cross, *Measure Up! Yardsticks for Continuous Improvement* (Cambridge, Mass.: Blackwell, 1991), 8.
5. See Valerie A. Zeithaml, A. Parasuraman, and Leonard L. Berry, *Delivering Quality Service: Balancing Customer Perceptions and Expectations* (New York: The Free Press, 1990).
6. Lynch and Cross, *Measure Up*, 98.

6

Compliment and Complaint Management

[Complaining customers] are, in essence, asking firms to listen to their concerns and foster their loyalty.

—Michael D. Johnson[1]

If a complaint is handled well, it sustains and strengthens customer loyalty and the . . . [organization's] image as a leader. It also tells the customer that the . . . [organization] cares and can improve because of their contact.

—National Performance Review[2]

Customer complaints . . . represent valuable information about recurrent problems.

—National Performance Review[3]

"If ever you are dissatisfied with one of our tires, please feel free to bring it back" intones the announcer as a little old lady hurls a tire through the showroom window. Over the sound of shattering glass, the announcer says, "Thank you." This long-running television commercial is a prime example of one organization's commitment to customer satisfaction. The commitment must be genuine because the stores' windows remain intact despite the invitation to express dissatisfaction by destroying them. Clearly, the management of this multicity chain of tire stores has developed policies and instructed store personnel about how to solve the problems of customers who complain. Even more important, however, is that top management views complaints as opportunities both to fix the customer's problem and to learn about defects in the products. Library managers might ponder their own attitude toward dealing with dissatisfied or disappointed customers.

A number of articles and books have appeared in the past few years on the topic of dealing with "problem patrons." Usually the situations presented describe behaviors that violate library policies or the law. Some of these writings, however, present persons who are upset, frustrated, or annoyed as problem patrons, a characterization that, in some instances, is unfair.[4] Customers have a right to express their opinions about mistakes and about perceived quality of the service, good or bad, and to make specific complaints (e.g., about the length of time that material is at the bindery, the length of time it takes to receive material through interlibrary loan, and borrowed material that has been returned but is still shown in the OPAC records as checked out). Smart managers recognize, accept, encourage, and profit from customer complaints: One recent book on customer service is titled *A Complaint Is a Gift*.[5]

Even the federal government recognizes that customer service and resolving customer problems with its agencies is increasingly important. The Clinton administration's National Performance Review (NPR), which aims to make the government function more effectively and efficiently and to be more responsive to customers, produced a most interesting report. Titled *Serving the American Public: Best Practices in Resolving Customer Complaints*, it links customer service to the president's 1993 Executive Order on "Setting Customer Service Standards."

What Is a Complaint?

Serving the American Public defines a customer complaint "as any indication that the service or product does not meet the customer's expectations."[6] That definition is rather broad, so let us examine it more closely in the context of libraries.

The most frequent customer disappointments in libraries center around the unavailability of materials (e.g., cannot find, do not own, or missing). Having people serve themselves as they do in most libraries has obvious advantages, but also certain disadvantages, the most serious of which is loss of information about unmet needs, wants, or demands. Customers not finding what they want, unless the need is urgent, may simply leave the building or terminate an online session; some never return.

In other instances, customers unable to locate the desired item or information are likely to approach the first person who seems to be an employee and ask for help. In the stack area of a large library, that employee is probably a part-time shelver whose knowledge may be insufficient to be helpful. More persistent customers, perhaps driven by the importance of the search, might go to the reference or circulation departments for assistance. If the request concerns a missing item, the staff will likely check the OPAC record. Should the record indicate that the item is in, the customer will be told to search again—looking on tables and book carts—and be sent back to the stack area where the item is supposed to be. If the item is still not found, the customer either leaves without the desired item or information, or must accept alternatives. In the case of such departing customers, the library may be missing an opportunity to learn how it might better meet their expectations, assuming that they will return.

Complaints are not all the same. They can range from minor annoyances to major problems. Items being unavailable may seem minor. Yet, unavailability represents a "situation where customers are deprived of the specific satisfaction [the library's] service was supposed to give them."[7] Unless library managers establish some mechanism to capture and record data about items or information desired but unavailable, they have no way of knowing if availability is a minor or major problem, nor do they have any information about how to improve availability.

In some libraries a complaint has to be specifically labeled as such to make it "official." The dissatisfaction or disappointments of people who just grumble to the staff are seldom brought to management's attention. Thus, problems that might have been corrected remain unnoticed except by the customers. The people who complain or just grumble about the service should be thanked and appreciated because they may be reporting flaws in the system and because they represent only a fraction of the disappointed customers.

Why People Do Not Complain

Customers believe that the way your . . . [library] treats them is the way you intend to treat them.

—Clay Carr[8]

The consensus in the business literature is that 96 percent of all dissatisfied customers will never complain, but 90 percent of them will not return either. In addition, each one of that 90 percent will tell at least nine other people about their unsatisfactory experience with the organization. Another 13 percent will tell 20 or more people about the poor service they received. One writer estimated that if an organization had just 10 unhappy customers a month, that as many as 101 people would become aware of poor service quality in that organization.[9] In other words, one person complained; nine other people were just as unhappy, and now as many as 101 people could have a poor opinion of the service. The reasons why people do not complain have been repeatedly verified:

- You do not care about me.
- You make it hard for me to tell you that I am dissatisfied (which proves you do not care about me).
- Why should I do your work for you, such as finding mistakes. You do not even deserve my comments.[10]
- You will not do anything about my problem anyway.

You Do Not Care about Me

The viewpoint that "you do not care about me" is reflected in three ways:

1. The system itself is not customer friendly.
2. A policy regarding dissatisfied customers is not known or understood by frontline staff.
3. Staff seem disinterested or unhelpful in solving the customer's problems.

A lot of customer frustration arises from an inability to understand the "system" or because the system itself is not working properly. How to use the library and how to find desired items may be unclear to many customers, especially new ones. Some people even claim that the system is deliberately confusing in order to ensure continued employment for the staff.[11]

Many libraries have no policies for dealing with complaints. Rather, each complaint is treated on an ad hoc basis. As a result, managers have not thought about such basic elements as what is a complaint, how customers are informed about the complaint policy, the mechanisms by which complaints can be made, who is responsible for responding, and how responsive the library wants to be.

Customers who feel annoyed or frustrated tend to vent their feelings to the first library employee they encounter. The reaction from the staff greatly influences the customer's perception of the service. The worst, and most common, enemies of responsive customer service are indifference and defensiveness. When people have trouble finding materials in the stacks, they may go to the main floor and report the item as missing. Staff, especially part-time staff and students in academic libraries, usually have not been trained how to respond, so they simply shrug off the customer with the attitude, "It is not my job" or "It is probably stolen." Staff in some libraries are not permitted to leave the service area to help customers in the stacks. Or, customers might be instructed to go to a particular service area for assistance. If they do so, they might find the area unstaffed, understaffed, or congested, or the staff unhelpful.

One major problem is that all too often employees receiving a complaint or negative comment about the service react defensively. This is shown by body language that bristles although no verbal response is made. "When a frontline person reacts negatively to a customer, . . . [that person] communicates not that the customer has a problem, but that he [or she] is the problem."[12] Others try to make the customer feel guilty for complaining by responding with the cliché that "we are doing the best we can!" Such a comment is an admission that the library's service is less than excellent—and likely to stay that way.

Both customers and library staff members, as Ann Curry explains, have rights. She analyzes 11 rights, which, by the way, would make an excellent discussion document for library staff. For instance, she notes that customers have "the right to be treated equally" and "to dislike libraries," while the staff have "the right to dislike a customer. . . . [That right] is acceptable as long as the rights of those customers are not infringed."[13]

You Make It Hard for Me to Tell You That I Am Dissatisfied

To Whom Can Customers Complain?

Many large department stores, such as Kmart and Wal-Mart, have telephones at various places so that customers can ask where certain merchandise is located and whether the store carries a particular item. Telephones in unstaffed stack areas connected to a central point might be an effective way to assist customers in their searches and also serve as a mechanism for receiving queries about missing items.

If customers grumble or complain at the library's public service desk, will a staff member try to solve the problem, or at least promise that the complaint will be passed on to the person responsible for resolution? Or, do customers have to go to another desk or office to file a complaint formally? How many times do customers have to explain the problem? If they want to see a manager or supervisor, is one available?

How Can Customers Complain?

Organizations that actively discourage complaints require that the complaint be submitted in writing—sometimes with extra copies. Ideally, every complaint should be recorded in order to track it to resolution or stalemate, but should the customer actually have to write out a statement? Responsive organizations make complaining easy. Complaint forms are available at every public service point, but using the form is not required (Figure 6.1 shows two copies of a sample form). Complaints can be made online through the library's Web homepage. Complaints can be phoned in and the specifics taken either through audio equipment or by an employee filling out a form. Staff are encouraged to pass along customer grumbles even though a customer may have declined to make a formal complaint. Figure 6.2, the Problem Report Form, is an example of how staff can report problems and complaints. The form can also be put on a template for the library's internal computer network.

Why Should I Do Your Work for You?

Just as the staff consider that supervisors get paid to deal with certain situations, customers think that library personnel should be responsible for library service performance and that they should look for and correct problems. A factor inhibiting customers from mentioning mistakes, such as misshelved items, is that they are unsure of the staff's reaction to the report. Staff who welcome being told about problems encourage reporting, but other staff may react stiffly, causing customers to vow never to mention another mistake.

You Will Not Do Anything about My Problem

Believing that nothing will be done about the problem is one of the most common reasons that customers do not complain. They believe that the library does not operate for them. They feel like outsiders, having to cope with rigid rules and procedures, and staff who are not there to serve them.

FIGURE 6.1
Complaint Form (two copies)

Something Wrong? Missing? Out of Place?
Let us know so we can fix it.

Today's date: _____

Nature of the problem (Please be as specific as you can. Tell us when, where, and how you encountered the difficulty.):

```
┌─────────────────────────────────────────────────────────┐
│                                                         │
│                                                         │
│                                                         │
│                                                         │
│                                                         │
│                                                         │
│                                                         │
└─────────────────────────────────────────────────────────┘
```

If you'd like a response, let us know how to reach you. (Optional)

Name: _____

Address: _____

Phone: _____

E-mail address: _____

- -

Something Wrong? Missing? Out of Place?
Let us know so we can fix it.

Today's date: _____

Nature of the problem (Please be as specific as you can. Tell us when, where, and how you encountered the difficulty.):

```
┌─────────────────────────────────────────────────────────┐
│                                                         │
│                                                         │
│                                                         │
│                                                         │
│                                                         │
│                                                         │
│                                                         │
└─────────────────────────────────────────────────────────┘
```

If you'd like a response, let us know how to reach you. (Optional)

Name: _____

Address: _____

Phone: _____

E-mail address: _____

FIGURE 6.2
Problem Report Form (for staff use)

Problem Report Form

Date of Incident: _____

Location in Library: _____

Reported by:
☐ Patron
☐ Library Staff
☐ Other

Problem Report # _____

Description of Problem:

Action Taken:

User Satisfied?   ☐ Yes   ☐ No

If no, why not? Is further action required? If so, describe it.

Comments?

Optional: Complete if user wishes to be notified of actions taken.

Name _____

Address _____

Phone _____   E-mail _____

Today's Date: _____   Recorded by: _____

Attitude and Actions

Simply announcing that the library wants to satisfy customers is insufficient. The real task is to turn satisfied customers into loyal ones, customers who will return often to use library service. Creating loyal and delighted customers requires both an attitude and action. The attitude is recognition that keeping customers is important and that the entire organization has a commitment to customer service. The actions are steps for developing and maintaining a system for handling complaints. Such a system should also deal with compliments. Compliments reinforce good service performance and make staff feel that they make a difference and that they are appreciated. Thus, the library should have a compliment form (see Figure 6.3) as well as a complaint form (see Figure 6.1).

Some lessons from the NPR can serve as guides to action:

Make it easy for customers to complain, and they will make it easy for the organization to improve.

Respond to complaints quickly and courteously with common sense. The purpose is to improve customer loyalty.

Resolve complaints on the first contact and: (1) save money by eliminating unnecessary, additional contacts that escalate costs, and (2) build customer confidence.

Develop an automated compliment and complaint handling system.

Recruit and hire the best staff members to fill customer service jobs.[15]

Establishing a Compliment and Complaint Tracking System

As discussed in a business guide developed by the Department of Commerce, the key ingredients for a compliment and complaint tracking system are:

- Management commitment
- Publicity for the system
- Accessibility of complaint management staff
- Promptness and courtesy of response
- Personalized response, whenever possible
- Simple, clear communication with customers
- Objectivity and flexibility in determining the proper resolution
- Uniform, consistent and computerized record keeping[17]

Computerization provides a mechanism for "enabling management to monitor the efficiency and effectiveness of the complaint management system" and for "providing market research through complaint trends."[18]

FIGURE 6.3
Compliment Form (two copies)

Something Right? Well Done?
Let us know so we can thank the people who did it.

Today's date: _____

Describe what we did that you thought we did well:

```



```

If you'd like a response, let us know how to reach you. (Optional)

Name: _____

Address: _____

Phone: _____

E-mail address: _____

- -

Something Right? Well Done?
Let us know so we can thank the people who did it.

Today's date: _____

Describe what we did that you thought we did well:

```



```

If you'd like a response, let us know how to reach you. (Optional)

Name: _____

Address: _____

Phone: _____

E-mail address: _____

A library that wants a first-rate compliment/complaint tracking system should follow these steps:

1. Establish an implementation team with diverse representation—both managers and nonmanagers—to oversee the development of the system.

2. Develop a policy statement that says that the organization embraces complaints and views them as opportunities for improvement. For example,

   > The library embraces complaints and thrives on compliments. Let us know what you like and dislike. We view complaints as opportunities to improve. We may not always be able to resolve your complaints, but we can sure try. Compliments tell us that we are going in the right direction.

3. Identify each step necessary for creating a useful tracking system and then establish the system. The staff should record and classify both compliments and complaints so that the data can be analyzed and reported to top management.

4. Develop recommendations to improve core processes and empower frontline employees to resolve complaints on first contact.

5. Develop an action plan for implementing approved customer recommendations and for publicizing the value of customer input.[19]

The implementation team must consider ways to draw attention to the tracking system. To this end, it should interact with various stakeholders to determine the most effective ways of encouraging customers to express their compliments and complaints.

Many businesses reward employees for good service by maintaining employee of the week or month awards. Some of the rewards are as simple as being able to use a parking spot with a sign reading "Reserved for the Employee of the Month." The library need not adopt the same reward system, but the implementation team should consider various options, as it works with library administration and other staff members to shift the focus from collections to customer services.

Issues to Consider

The questions listed in Figure 6.4 serve as a basis for developing the building blocks of the compliment and complaint tracking system. The implementation team should invite library staff, library managers, and library customers to express their views and perspectives. It is important that the managers and library staff do not become defensive, no matter what customers have to say. Discussions might consider these questions:

- What types of complaints and problems should be addressed?

- What changes in the library—its services and operations—have resulted from financial and resource stringencies?

- Are certain problems caused by problem or disorderly patrons, or by problem staff?

- Does the library act on complaint data?
- How does it act on such data?
- To what extent are customers' complaints heeded?

These questions should guide the implementation team as it interacts with internal and external customers, and develops the compliment and complaint tracking system. The team might meet with customers in groups and listen to their discussion of certain questions (see Chapter 8 on focus group interviews).

The questions in Figure 6.4 can be answered by all the regular staff as an indication of the organizational climate for handling complaints and as a means of enlightening managers about staff knowledge and attitudes in helping customers solve problems. The discussion of these questions serves a dual purpose. First, it indicates the extent to which library staff members are prepared to deal with the community they serve as valued customers. If they are not prepared, steps should be taken to remedy the situation. Second, the discussion helps staff to understand

FIGURE 6.4
Discussion Questions for Library Staff

1. What has the department [or library] done to make sure it listens to the voice of the customer?

2. How does the organization listen to the voice of the employee who directly serves the customer?

3. How do the leaders in the organization view complaints?

4. How does the organization make it easy for customers to complain?

5. What does the organization do to make it easy for employees to solve customers' problems?

6. How does the organization support frontline employees so that they can serve customers with complaints?

7. Will staff receive incentives for participation and not be put "on the spot"—each episode or encounter becoming public or known throughout the organization?

8. How does the organization currently track and analyze complaints?

9. How does the organization use information about complaints to identify and address underlying problems?

10. How well are resource decisions aligned with the desire to meet customer expectations and to ensure customer satisfaction?

11. How does the organization train frontline employees to handle complaints and to produce satisfied customers?

12. How do you delight customers who have problems?

13. What access do customers have to the organization so that it is easy for them to complain?

14. How do you make sure that you understand what customers want?

15. How do you manage customer expectations?

16. How does the organization design its complaint-handling processes?

17. Does the organization invest in the infrastructure needed to make the complaint-handling process effective both in customer recovery and minimizing costs?

18. How does the organization use complaint information to make operational improvements?

Adapted from National Performance Review, *Serving the American Public: Best Practices in Resolving Customer Complaints* (Washington, D.C.: Government Printing Office, 1996).

Compliment and Complaint Management

the benefits of monitoring customer responses voiced as complaints or compliments.

It merits repeating that the assumption is not that customers are always right and must be given whatever they ask. Rather, the purpose is to review those customer expectations that the library wants to meet and the extent to which it does so. In cases where the library cannot act on complaints, it might be important to explain why. Of course, special attention must be given to the forum in which the explanation is provided. How effective is it? How well was the message explained and received? These discussions will reveal the extent to which managers are willing to act on the results—to build them into goals and objectives.

The next step (and it may not be an immediate one) is for the implementation team to develop a policy statement. Again, the statement should be widely discussed and everyone should realize the benefits of having it. The next step (and again, it may not be immediate) is to review the procedures involved in tracking complaints and compliments. Customers, through selected individual and group interviews, should provide feedback into the process; the purpose is to "develop a culture that supports teamwork with the customer as a part of the team."[20]

Considering Process and Procedure

The library must adopt a systematic strategy for complaint and compliment management. In developing the procedures for the system, the implementation team needs to consider the following questions:

- Will it be easy for customers to complain or make a compliment?
- Will the system be decentralized, with each employee responsible for resolving complaints; centralized in one location; or a "combination of both, with larger or more serious complaints resolved in a central office?"[21]
- What training will complaint management staff receive? Will that training be adequate?
- How will the library periodically survey customers to ensure that they are satisfied with the complaint management system? Will the library encourage feedback?
- Will the system be regularly reviewed to make necessary improvements? Will the computer program be flexible enough to accept any revisions?
- Will the system be used (and how will it be used) "for more than settling individual complaints? For example, for quality control and problem prevention?"[22]
- Does the system "swiftly generate systematic information about causes of complaints and complaint trends?" Do the data meet the needs of managers?[23]
- Will regular reports be generated from the system, and what will be the nature of those reports?

Using the Tracking System

It is important to analyze complaints and compliments to see what patterns emerge. Just as Federal Express tracks all shipments, identifies bottlenecks, and provides customers with feedback on the delivery status of their packages, so libraries can monitor complaints and how the staff dealt with them. The purpose is to identify problems and, when necessary, develop an effective mechanism to explain why something cannot be done. Furthermore, complaints should not be treated as isolated instances; rather, the library should analyze the reasons, look for patterns, and ensure that the organization learns from both complaints and compliments.

Data from complaints can be "scattered, biased, and fragmentary and [are] as apt to be misleading as to be helpful. Not everyone likes or dislikes the same things."[24] To help sort out patterns and minimize the impact of isolated minor instances, the compliment and complaint tracking system should be automated. Any database or spreadsheet package can be used. The important thing is to enter all compliments and complaints, and assess the patterns for improving the system and service.

Figure 6.5 outlines sample categories for inclusion in a compliment and complaint system that covers both internal and external customers. The system recognizes that both stakeholder groups must be listened to and respected, and their concerns addressed. Categories should be coded by number for ease of data processing.

Using the information provided in the Problem Report Form (Figure 6.2), the following data must be entered into the spreadsheet: the date the complaint was made, status of complainer, type of problem, action taken, the extent to which the customer professes satisfaction, and length of time taken to resolve the problem (speed to resolution is an issue, especially if fines are accruing). Figure 6.6 is an example of the "Problem Resolution Tracking Database" form. Regarding compliments, the system should monitor the reasons and extent to which the same items gain repeated praise. Library managers can also gauge the extent of *mixed signals*—complaints and compliments for the same service.

Making the Automated System Available

Library staff must be apprised of progress in developing the system, participate in the field test, and be informed of system procedures. Once the system is installed, all staff in the library should be able to access it. The reasons are quite simple. Looking at how similar problems were handled may be a guide for new staff or for staff dealing with a problem for the first time. Other reasons are accountability and encouraging staff to participate in maintaining a compliment and complaint tracking system. According to David Osborne and Ted Gaebler, "What gets measured gets done."[25] They recount how the number and kinds of errors decreased in welfare offices in Massachusetts after the data gathered were made available statewide to all employees.

FIGURE 6.5

Sample Categories for a Compliment and Complaint Tracking System

	Compliments	
	Internal Customers	**External Customers**
System		
Appreciated instruction in use		
Policies consistently applied		
Service delivery: meet or exceed expectations		
Environment		
Good ambiance		
Attractive building		
Spacious		
Staff		
Helpful		
Knowledgeable		

	Complaints (Suggestions for Improvement)	
	Internal Customers	**External Customers**
Resources		
Item		
Not owned/purchased		
Owned but missing		
Mutilated		
Delays in making it available (e.g., still in process)		
On order; not received		
In poor physical condition		
Inappropriate for library or age group		
Inaccurate or missing OPAC information about it		
Insufficient number of copies held		
Prefer its availability in electronic form (e.g., CD-ROM)		
Why no longer held in library?		
Delays in its receipt from storage		
Dated holdings		
Reserve material		
Long wait for their return		
Insufficient copies		

	Complaints (Suggestions for Improvement)	
	Internal Customers	External Customers
Mutilated		
Lost		
Too slow in placing material on reserve		
Need more videos and recordings		
Intralibrary loan delays		
Fines erroneously charged		
Charges too high for		
Fines		
Interlibrary loans		
Reserves		
Photocopies		
Rental items		
Videos		
Policies		
Information required for registration too personal (e.g., age or social security number)		
Policy not to give children's record of current borrowing to parent(s)		
Policy not to restrict children's borrowing to children's materials		
Other customers using inappropriate Internet materials		
Internet access not filtered or restricted for children's use		
Have to wait in line too long		
Problems with phones (e.g., getting through, cut off, placed on hold, or getting a recording instead of a person)		
Need for Internet/OPAC/CD-ROM instruction		
Environment		
Parking problem		
Lighting		
Temperature		
Too hot		
Too cold		
Too noisy		
No seats available		
No seminar or conference rooms available		
Other customers who smell or stare, or are distasteful		

(Continued)

	Complaints (Suggestions for Improvement)	
	Internal Customers	External Customers
Concern about personal safety		
Theft of customer belongings		
Equipment		
Insufficient number		
Not in working order		
None available at moment (in use)		
Hard to use		
Screens hard to read		
Keyboards dirty		
Poor quality printing		
Unable to connect to dial-up service		
Modem too slow		
Water fountains/restroom facilities not working or dirty		
Reader area messy		
Too many unshelved items		
Garbage from people eating and drinking		
Elevators not working		
Hours library open		
Staff		
None present in service area		
Long queue for service		
Circulation desk		
Information desk		
Do not seem to know collection or sources		
Not helpful		
Discourteous/rude		
Aloof/uninterested		
Unresponsive (e.g., using OPAC without saying a word)		
Too busy talking with each other		
Answer telephone before helping customers awaiting service		

FIGURE 6.6

Problem Resolution Tracking Database

Problem Number	Date	Problem Type	Location	Reported by	Responsible Person	Action Required?	Action Taken	Date Taken	Reply Required?	Date Sent

Problem Number: Assigned by staff
Date: Date incident was reported
Problem Type: Mechanical (copier, computer, etc.), shelving error, etc.
Location: Where in building(s) the problem occurred
Reported by: Staff member who filled out problem report
Responsible Person: Name of person responsible for fixing this kind of problem.
Action Required?:   Is any further action needed to fix this problem?
Action Taken: If action is required, what was done?
Date Taken: If action was taken, when?
Reply Required?:   Did patron request a response?
Date Sent: If so, when was it sent?

FIGURE 6.7
Framework for Maximizing Customer Satisfaction and Loyalty

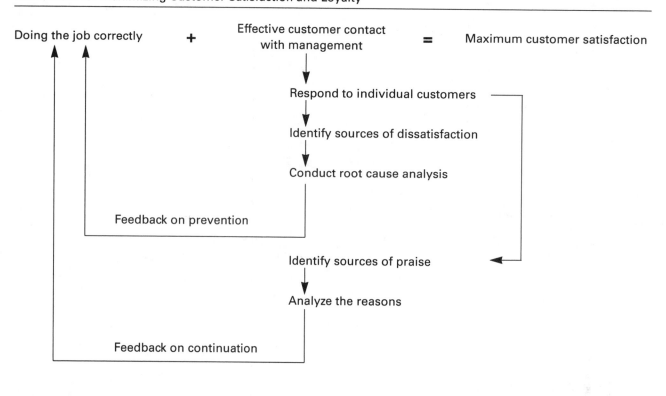

Adapted from National Performance Review, *Serving the American Public: Best Practices in Resolving Customer Complaints* (Washington, D.C.: Government Printing Office, 1996), 29.

Continuous Improvement

Figure 6.7 provides a framework for maximizing customer satisfaction and loyalty. The focus here is on continuous improvement within the context of stated goals and objectives, in which the library sets benchmarks and seeks to improve service delivery and staff interactions with customers. "The key to continuous improvement is to refine, redesign, and improve . . . [the] process while putting the customer first."[26] Thus, the compliment and complaint process is

> viewed as a loop with the customer at the beginning and at the end and with the core operating processes in the middle. Constant feedback from both customers and employees and constant reevaluation based on satisfaction measurement assure constant improvement.[27]

As Figure 6.8 indicates, organizations can compute and include in regular reports various measures that reflect customer satisfaction with the complaint resolution process, and the timeliness and efficiency of the resolution. As well, complaint managers should monitor employee

FIGURE 6.8
How Does the Library Measure Up?

1. The percentage of complaints handled on first contact
2. The amount of time required to resolve complaints
3. The percentage of instances in which the customer was kept informed through the resolution process
4. The percentage of instances in which complaints were resolved within a specified deadline
5. The extent to which that deadline is acceptable to the customer and the organization
6. The size of the backlog of unresolved complaints
7. The satisfaction level of customers as a result of complaining
8. The amount of repeat business from customers who have complained

Adapted from: National Performance Review, *Serving the American Public: Best Practices in Resolving Customer Complaints* (Washington, D.C.: Government Printing Office, 1996), 31–33.

satisfaction with the results of the measures and the effectiveness of staff training in customer service. They should determine the number of hours spent in customer service training per employee and per department or organizational unit (e.g., team), and monitor attrition rates among the staff and the reasons for leaving.

"As complaint data and other customer feedback are used to eliminate underlying problems, the number of complaints should decline."[28] It is hoped that the library can stimulate the number of compliments given and that the number of complaints will decline. The measures depicted in Figure 6.8 can reflect a marked improvement in the quality of service performance and in repeat business.

Summary

By making it "easy for customers to complain" and handling "complaints quickly and courteously with common sense," organizations not only "save money by eliminating unnecessary additional contacts that escalate costs [but also] build customer confidence."[29] That confidence produces or improves customer satisfaction and loyalty. Effective complaint handling, therefore, "sustains and strengthens" customer loyalty to a service or organization.[30] Loyalty is interrelated with satisfaction, and the correlation can be either positive or negative; if the latter, the number of complaints increases—or at least does not decrease—and the organization may become more resistant to customer grievances.[31] A concept known as "vicious circle complaints" may emerge: The more complaints that an organization receives, the less responsive it becomes. Instead of making use of customer complaints, the organization behaves dysfunctionally.[32] Furthermore, more customers may be "lost" as they desert the library and go elsewhere for the resolution of their information needs, and as they convey their negative experience(s) to friends and colleagues.

In summary, two objectives of complaint handling are to: (1) turn a dissatisfied customer into a loyal customer, and (2) reduce barriers or problems that might have a negative impact on other customers. After all, if complaints indicate, for instance, that a service fails to meet customers' expectations or that customers feel they have not been heard or treated fairly, it might be appropriate to approach complaints more as opportunities for improved service delivery and to accept the challenges of creating a more customer-focused, service organization.[33]

Paul Hawken, author and specialist in garden and horticultural mail-order businesses, has specified how to be a good customer:

- Complain
- Praise
- Be articulate in expressing needs/wants
- Demand quick service
- Be quick yourself (complain immediately)
- Be kind
- Be persistent[34]

To this list, we add *be knowledgeable* (know what you are talking about and where to go to make your voice heard). Library staff, therefore, should avoid saying "if only customers knew about . . ." and perpetuating the status quo. The library should constantly strive to improve its services and should let customers participate in shaping those services of highest priority to them.

Complaints should gain more attention from the library than is provided through notices on a bulletin board or in a centrally located notebook. "Complaint data are only part of customer feedback,"[35] but should not be ignored as library staff deal with the evaluation options presented in Chapters 7, 8, and 10.

NOTES

1. Michael D. Johnson, *Customer Orientation and Market Action* (Upper Saddle River, N.J.: Prentice Hall, 1998), 66.
2. National Performance Review, *Serving the American Public: Best Practices in Resolving Customer Complaints*, Federal Benchmarking Consortium Study Report (Washington, D.C.: Government Printing Office, 1996), 6.
3. Ibid.
4. See Ann Curry, "Managing the Problem Patron," *Public Libraries* 35, no. 3 (May/June 1996): 181–88; Nathan Smith, "Active Listening: Alleviating Patron Problems through Communication," in *Patron Behavior in Libraries: A Handbook of Positive Approaches to Negative Situations*, edited by Beth McNeil and Denise J. Johnson (Chicago: American Library Association, 1996), 127–34.

5. Janelle Barlow and Claus Moller, *A Complaint Is a Gift: Using Customer Feedback as a Strategic Tool* (San Francisco: Berrett Koehler, 1996).

6. National Performance Review, *Serving the American Public*, 6.

7. Clay Carr, *Front-line Customer Service: 15 Keys to Customer Satisfaction* (New York: Wiley, 1990), 26.

8. Ibid., 23.

9. Ibid., 20–21.

10. Ibid., 21.

11. Curry, "Managing the Problem Patron," 183.

12. Carr, *Front-line Customer Service*, 79.

13. Curry, "Managing the Problem Patron," 183.

14. Catharine G. Johnston, *Beyond Customer Satisfaction to Loyalty* (Ottawa: Conference Board of Canada, 1996), 35.

15. National Performance Review, *Serving the American Public*, 1–2.

16. Benjamin Schneider and David E. Bowen, *Winning the Service Game* (Boston: Harvard Business School Press, 1995), 67.

17. Department of Commerce, Office of Consumer Affairs, *Managing Consumer Complaints: Responsive Business Approaches to Consumer Needs* (Washington, D.C.: Government Printing Office, 1992), 5.

18. Ibid.

19. National Performance Review, *Serving the American Public*, 2.

20. Ibid., 28.

21. Ibid., 29.

22. Department of Commerce, *Managing Consumer Complaints*, 13.

23. Ibid.

24. Carr, *Front-line Customer Service*, 135.

25. David Osborne and Ted Gaebler, *Reinventing Government* (Reading, Mass.: Addison-Wesley, 1992), 146.

26. National Performance Review, *Serving the American Public*, 8.

27. Department of Commerce, *Managing Consumer Complaints*, 13.

28. National Performance Review, *Serving the American Public*, 6.

29. Ibid., 1, 2.

30. Ibid., 6.

31. See Claes Fornell, "A National Customer Satisfaction Barometer: The Swedish Experience," in *Performance Measurement and Evaluation*, edited by Jacky Holloway, Jenny Lewis, and Geoff Mallory (London: Sage, 1995), 95–123.

32. Ibid., 113.

33. National Performance Review, *Serving the American Public*, 6.

34. Paul Hawken, *Growing a Business* (New York: Simon & Schuster, 1987).

35. National Performance Review, *Serving the American Public*, 17.

7 Listening to Customers through Surveys

The "best-in-class" organizations use aggressive and varied ways to locate and listen to the "Voice of the Customer."

—National Performance Review[1]

Sometimes users can be very clear and helpful in stating expectations. Clear enough to help us find our service bearings.

—John L. Lubans[2]

Information about service quality can be garnered from customers in many ways; some take little effort, others take considerably more, and all require thought about what to ask and how the information solicited might be used to improve services. Figure 7.1 identifies various ways in which libraries can listen to customers, identify their expectations, and compare their expectations to perceptions of service delivery or to the actual service provided. Library staff members or outside evaluators might collect data *actively* (from customers directly), perhaps through a survey or focus group interview (see Chapter 8). In so doing, they request a *favor* of or make an *imposition* on respondents. As an alternative, they might collect data *passively*—"meaning (a) any solicitation of feedback . . . done without direct customer interaction, and (b) the customer initiates any response given."[3]

According to Scott E. Sampson, examples of passively solicited customer feedback "include customer comment cards (left on a table, a wall display, etc.), toll-free telephone numbers, and comment links on World Wide Web pages."[4] He notes that "passive methods generally have lower response rates and are inherently biased, but have cost and sample frame advantages when used to monitor quality on a continuing basis."[5] Passive methods are less time consuming, do not require a major campaign to invite response, and can more easily be assumed as part of regular staff duties and responsibilities. The findings, however, require great caution in interpretation and application, in part because customers must be motivated to respond. Because those customers who are the most satisfied or dissatisfied are the most likely to respond, there is a risk of response bias.

Sampson, who surveyed customers staying at a hotel, concludes that "customers who spontaneously register complaints generally record higher ratings of the service provider than customers who complain in response to a complaint solicitation."[6] This important finding, if transferable to library settings, is a reminder to encourage customers to complain or to compliment, in such a way that libraries ensure spontaneity and prompt resolution of problems, when feasible.

Another way to collect information about customers is to train library staff members to make objective observations and consult records that provide insights into potential problem areas. For instance, they might monitor the number of busy signals received on a telephone line, connectivity problems to the library's homepage, and the working condition of equipment. The focus of such methods is less on the identification of customer expectations and more on the condition or state of the actual service delivered. Thus, by comparing active methods to other methods, library staff members can monitor discrepancies between expectations and the service provided. They can then seek to reduce the gap between the two. Whatever methods the library uses for characterizing the service actually delivered must be objective and must produce valid comparisons to customer expectations.

Librarians can engage in data collection that produces *quantitative* results (in which numbers are reduced to measurement) or *qualitative* results (which lack that reduction). Whenever possible, they should collect both types of data about operations, services, and customers. Each one provides a portion of the picture; together, they provide rich insights useful for better serving customers and attracting new or lost ones. This chapter fills in a portion of the picture—that part requiring quantitative data collection. Together, Chapters 6 through 8 and Chapter 10 offer strategies for assessing service quality and satisfaction. A library needs to select those strategies most relevant to its particular situation (see Figure 7.1).

Measuring Customer Expectations

A key question is: How can librarians measure customer expectations and perceptions about the service actually provided, or determine the width of the gap between perceptions of library performance and customer expectations? Standard techniques developed in other fields or disciplines, such as SERVQUAL or SERPERF, might be applied as is or

FIGURE 7.1

Some Ways to Listen to Customers

Suggestion Boxes, Forms, and Comment Cards. These are customer initiated and tend to focus on problems. The survey might take the form of comment cards similar to those found in hotels and restaurants. Such methods, however, lack the tracking and management features of complaint tracking systems (see Chapter 6).

Advantages	Information can be collected with little effort and low cost. Data come in continuously.
Disadvantages	Data are subject to extreme bias. There may be no linkage to a tracking and management system.

Customer Surveys. The intent is to identify customers' expectations and perceptions—presumably those that the library is willing to meet. Such surveys might be repeated as part of customer follow-up over a predetermined time frame. Methods might include rating cards placed in a service area or near the exit. Customers can then rate the quality of service they received and comment on the extent to which their expectations were met. Library WWW homepages might also contain brief surveys that rate services and the extent to which expectations were met; any questions eliciting background information should not infringe on customers' privacy.

Questionnaires. These must be constructed carefully and distributed according to a sophisticated sampling plan.

Advantages	Can explore many aspects of service. Usually obtain some demographic information about respondents. Sampling is controlled by the researcher. High rates of response are possible. Data may well reflect the characteristics and opinions of the customer population. Costs less than interviewing. Can be self-administered. May survey large numbers of people.
Disadvantages	Produces a snapshot of the situation at a particular point in time. May be time consuming to analyze and interpret results.

Produces self-reported data. Data lack the depth resulting from interviewing.

Focus Group Interviews. Common in marketing and in political campaigns, focus groups bring customers together to discuss a product, a service, or an issue. Libraries can use them to gather insights into customer expectations, the willingness of library staff members to meet those expectations and embrace customer service plans, and the ability to regain lost customers or to attract first-time customers.

Advantages	Unstructured nature can allow for deeper exploration of customers' views. Sampling is controlled by the researcher. Groups can represent one type of customer or customers in general, depending on what the library wants to know. See Chapter 8 for other advantages.
Disadvantages	Requires a skilled moderator able to be objective in data collection; such an individual may be difficult to find. See Chapter 8 for other disadvantages.

In-person or Telephone Interviews. Interviews gather opinions on a service, a product, or an issue from customers on a one-to-one basis. In one type of telephone survey, customers calling the library are asked to participate in a short interview while on the line. An alternative is the telephone recontact, in which the staff member asks if the customer would agree to being called later and, if so, obtains the person's name and phone number. Or, instead of getting the phone number for telephone recontact, the customer might be asked to provide an address for a mail survey or comment card.

Advantages	Sampling is controlled by the researcher. Data may be representative of the population. More topics can be explored than by passive data collection (not surveying customers directly).

In-person interviews permit in-depth probing of opinions and elaboration of issues; telephone surveys may not.

Permits interaction with respondents.

Disadvantages   Cost is high to medium.

Chance for error in transcription is medium to high.

Time-consuming to set up and administer.

Interviewers must be well trained.

Data collected may be self-reports.

May produce low response rate.

May be hard to find interviewers who have the voices and verbal skills to gain compliance and high-quality data.[1]

Not all households may have telephones.

Toll-free or Special Telephone Number(s). As a companion to other methods for registering complaints, offering compliments, or identifying special expectations, library staff might provide a toll-free or local telephone number. Such numbers might be listed on brochures (e.g., service pledges) and on signs scattered throughout the library.

Advantages   Data collection is quick and continuous.

Disadvantages   May produce response bias if most customers are angry.

Cost of maintaining phone line may be high.

Electronic Mail. Through the library's homepage, or independent of it, customers can communicate directly with library staff and convey problems, expectations, and degree of satisfaction.

Advantages   Information can be collected with little effort and low cost.

———————
1. See Lois Oksenberg, Lerita Coleman, and Charles F. Cannell, "Interviewers' Voices and Refusal Rates in Telephone Surveys," *Public Opinion Quarterly* 50, no. 1 (1996): 97–111.

Data can be collected continuously.

Method is self-administered.

May provide an opportunity for interaction and follow-up with subjects.

Disadvantages   Population may be unknown.

Responses are all self-reported.

Risks self-selected sample.

Electronic mail can also be used as a means of conducting customer surveys.

Advantages   The survey reaches a geographically dispersed group of customers

The method is faster and cheaper than mailed, telephone, and in-person surveys.

The likelihood of a prompt response is high.

The survey can target a specific group of customers.

Disadvantages   Respondents may not be representative of the population.

Respondents are likely to be better-educated, urban, white-collar, and technologically literate.

Problems may occur in telecommunications transmissions.

Response rate, if it can be determined, may be low.

It is more difficult to show legitimacy of the study (e.g., demonstrate authority of those doing the investigation).

Customers may resent receiving surveys among their e-mail communication.

Complaint Tracking Systems. As discussed in Chapter 6, these systems track responses to inquiries and complaints, for the purpose of improving response time, resolving problems, and creating and maintaining customer loyalty. Data received from suggestion boxes, e-mail, and special phone lines can be incorporated into the compliment and complaint tracking system.

Advantages   Data are useful for tracking quality on a continuous basis.

Disadvantages   Some costs are incurred to establish and maintain the system.

with modification. SERVQUAL, for instance, which was developed originally through marketing research in the profit sector, has been used in academic, public, and special libraries in the United States, Canada, Australia, and the United Kingdom.[7] It measures what customers value as important across five dimensions:

Assurance—knowledge and courtesy of employees and their ability to inspire trust and confidence

Empathy—caring and individualized attention

Reliability—ability to perform the promised service dependably and accurately

Responsiveness—willingness to help customers and provide prompt service

Tangibles—physical facilities, equipment, and appearance of personnel

As the designers of SERVQUAL note, "Quality evaluations are not made solely on the outcome of a service; they also involve evaluations of the process of service delivery."[8]

Vicki Coleman et al. surveyed faculty, students, and some community users on service quality using a modified version of SERVQUAL. They administered it in two parts:

Part 1 (see . . . [Figure 7.2] for a partial sample survey) contains three sets of twenty-two questions each, where a customer indicates his or her minimum, perceived, and desired service acceptable levels on a scale ranging from a low of 1 to a high of 9. The twenty-two questions can be divided into five sets, each of which represents one of the five dimensions of quality (reliability, responsiveness, assurance, empathy, and tangibles). Part 2 (see . . . [Figure 7.3] for a partial sample survey) allows the customer to give an overall rating of library service quality and to weigh five different dimensions of quality pertaining to services offered in academic libraries.[9]

Coleman et al. note that "quality is measured by determining where perceived performance falls with respect to the zone of tolerance, . . . the area between the minimum and desired acceptance levels. . . . Scores . . . can be weighted to measure quality with respect to the dimension(s) most important to the customer."[10]

An examination of Figures 7.2 and 7.3 indicates that customers must take great care in the completion of the surveys and the allocation of the points. More importantly, the statements deal only with certain aspects of service quality. Why are those chosen more important than others? On what basis do customers assign points? How can library evaluators produce an acceptable response rate?[11] This last question will be discussed later in this chapter.

In her dissertation, Danuta A. Nitecki adapted the SERVQUAL instrument to measure the quality of interlibrary loan, reserve room services, and reference services.[12] She also applied that instrument to

FIGURE 7.2
Customer Satisfaction Survey (SERVQUAL), Part 1

We would like your impressions about Evans' [Library, Texas A&M University] service performance relative to your expectations. Please think about the two different levels of expectations as defined below:

Minimum Service Level: **the minimum service performance you consider adequate**
Desired Service Level: **the level of service performance you desire**

For each of the following statements, please indicate: (a) your minimum service level by circling one of the numbers in the first column; (b) your desired service level by circling one of the numbers in the second column; and (c) your perception of Evans' service by circling one of the numbers in the third column.

When it comes to ...	*My Minimum Service Level Is:*		*My Desired Service Level Is:*		*My Perception of Evans' Service Performance Is:*		
	Low	High	Low	High	Low	High	No Opinion
	1 2 3 4 5 6 7 8 9		1 2 3 4 5 6 7 8 9		1 2 3 4 5 6 7 8 9		N

Q.1 Prompt service to customers

Q.2 Employees who are consistently courteous

Q.3 Employees who deal with customers in a caring fashion

Q.4 Providing service at the promised time

Q.5 Employees who understand the needs of their customers

Q.6 Visually appealing materials associated with the service (e.g., clear and concise forms)

Q.7 Having the customer's best interest at heart

Q.8 Willingness to help customers

Q.9 Maintaining error-free customer and catalog records

Q.10 Keeping customers informed about when services will be performed

Q.11 Providing services as promised

Q.12 Employees who instill confidence in customers

Q.13 Employees who have the knowledge to answer customers' questions

Q.14 Readiness to respond to customers' questions

Q.15 Dependability in handling customers' service problems

Q.16 Performing services right the first time

Q.17 Visually appealing facilities

Q.18 Giving customers individual attention

Q.19 Employees who have a neat, professional appearance

Q.20 Convenient business hours

Q.21 Modern equipment

Q.22 Assuring customers of the accuracy and confidentiality of their transactions

Source: Vicki Coleman, Yi (Daniel) Xiao, Linda Blair, and Bill Chollett, "Toward a TQM Paradigm: Using SERVQUAL to Measure Library Service Quality," *College & Research Libraries* 58, no. 3 (May 1997): 239.

reference services at Sterling Memorial Library at Yale University, and Joan Stein adapted Nitecki's instrument to examine interlibrary loan services at Carnegie Mellon University. Nitecki's SERVQUAL instrument for reference services, is reprinted at the end of this chapter. The *Proceedings of the 2nd Northumbria International Conference on Performance Measurement in Libraries and Information Services* reproduces both the Nitecki and Stein instruments.[13]

In an important discussion of service quality and the use of SERVQUAL, Danuta A. Nitecki reminds us that the survey measures customer expectations and perceptions of service performance, thus enabling librarians to determine the extent of the gap between the two.[14]

FIGURE 7.3
Customer Satisfaction Survey (SERVQUAL), Part 2

1. How would you rate the overall quality of service provided by Evans Library?
   (Circle one number below.)

Extremely Poor   **Extremely Good**

1   2   3   4   5   6   7   8   9

2. Listed below are five general features pertaining to academic libraries and the services they offer. We would like to know how important each of these features is to you when you evaluate an academic library's quality of service.

   Please allocate a total of 100 points among the five features according to how important each feature is to you—the more important a feature is to you, the more points you should give it. Please be sure the points you give add up to 100.

   1. The appearance of the library's physical facilities, equipment, personnel, and communications materials. ____ points

   2. The library's ability to perform the promised services dependably and accurately. ____ points

   3. The library's willingness to help customers and provide prompt service. ____ points

   4. The knowledge and courtesy of the library's employees and their ability to convey trust and confidence. ____ points

   5. The caring, individualized attention the library provides its customers. ____ points

   Total Points Allocated   **100 points**

Source: Vicki Coleman, Yi (Daniel) Xiao, Linda Blair, and Bill Chollett, "Toward a TQM Paradigm: Using SERVQUAL to Measure Library Service Quality," *College & Research Libraries* 58, no. 3 (May 1997): 241.

Thus, SERVQUAL, despite its limitations, is one way to view the gap between perceptions of expectations and perceptions of service performance. Furthermore, it can be applied to discrete services, such as reference, interlibrary loan, and reserve.

As this book reflects, library staff members have choices about the types of comparisons they make. First, using, as Nitecki did, a modified version of SERVQUAL, they might compare customer expectations and perceptions of service performance. Second, they might compare customer expectations to objective indicators of service quality. Or, third, they might compare customer expectations to library staff members' or management's perceptions of service performance.

Although this book does not emphasize the first approach, it is still a viable choice. (Readers wanting to use this approach can adapt the ideas discussed in this chapter.) This book focuses on the second choice and shows that libraries can pursue various choices and develop customer-related indicators. The third choice is the most risky if library staff members assume that they already fully understand service performance and become defensive in responding to customer expectations. Any use of the third choice must seek ways to minimize rationalization of the status quo and the attitude that the customer is never or seldom right.

Whatever the choice, librarians should remember that customers are not merely recipients of the services offered; they are "partners in the development and implementation of services" to make library experiences more successful from the perspective of customers.[15]

A Form and Process Tailored to Library Needs

Figure 7.4 includes more than 100 statements about customer expectations, developed by Peter Hernon and Ellen Altman,[16] Hernon and Philip J. Calvert,[17] and Calvert and Hernon.[18] The set of statements, although far-reaching, does not cover every conceivable aspect for which customers from any stakeholder group might have expectations.[19] Library staff may still want to develop statements pertaining, for instance, to: bibliographic instruction and information literacy, multicultural customers, physically challenged customers, and other special groups (e.g., the elderly, children, and members of the business community).

Figure 7.5 identifies the various aspects of service quality and suggests numerous options and choices for examining them; the statements in Figure 7.4 can be modified with these in mind. Most importantly, the pool of statements adequately covers the five dimensions of SERVQUAL (assurance, empathy, reliability, responsiveness, and tangibles),[20] and the reconceptualization of these dimensions by Chris Manolis and Scott W. Kelley.[21]

Discussions with internal and external customers, however, may reveal additional choices for possible statements to include in a survey. For example, staff might probe the extent to which customers:

- Expect term loans (for faculty and graduate students) for books.
- Dislike the placement of items on two-hour reserve.
- Have to bring their own disks for downloading bibliographic citations from CD-ROM and other database searching. The library might no longer provide printers in public service areas. How do the general public and others using an academic library feel about this policy?
- Expect library computers providing access to the WWW to have sound and multimedia capability.
- Expect the machinery that opens, closes, and locks compact shelving to be in good working order.

With a number of libraries concerned about the expense of supplying customers with computer paper, questions about disk provision become more important, as do issues related to willingness to pay for paper and the ability of customers to download files. Issues like these could easily form the basis of a survey or focus group interview (see Chapter 8).

FIGURE 7.4
Sample Statements on Service Quality Expectations

Guidance

Online Catalog

1. The online catalog is an accurate source of information about all material held by the library.

2. The online catalog computer is in good working order (it is not "down" when I want to use it).

3. The information displayed on the online library catalog computers is clear and easy to follow.

4. Instructions on remote access to the online library catalog are easy to follow.

5. The online library catalog displays information about material "on order" and "in process."

6. Using the online library catalog, I can request materials.

7. The online library catalog shows me materials I have:
   a. Requested.
   b. Borrowed.

8. Using the online library catalog, I can renew materials.

9. The online library catalog has a "Help" option that I can easily understand.

10. Online library catalog computers are conveniently distributed throughout the library.

11. I can gain easy access to the online library catalog and other electronic resources from outside the library buildings.

12. When I connect remotely to the online library catalog, I do not get a busy signal or get disconnected.

13. The online library catalog supplies the holdings of branch libraries.

14. I can print a list of titles from the online library catalog.

15. I can download to disk titles of works from the online library catalog.

16. The online library catalog indicates the number of prior reserves and copies available.

17. The online library catalog enables me to request loans from other libraries.

Other

18. Directional signs in the library are clear, understandable, and helpful.

19. When I enter the library I can see where to go for help.

20. It is easy to find out, in advance, when the library is open.

21. The library provides timely, accurate, and clear information when equipment is not in good working order.

22. The information displayed on the screen for electronic sources other than the online library catalog (e.g., CD-ROMs) is clear and easy to follow.

23. Electronic periodical indexes note library holdings beside each citation.

Waiting Times

24. I do not have to wait more than *three* minutes when I:
    a. Ask for assistance at a reference or information desk.
    b. Phone the library for assistance or information.
    c. Borrow material.
    d. Use the closed reserve collection.
    e. Use microfilm and microfiche readers.
    f. Use photocopiers.
    g. Use self-issue machines.
    h. Use the online library catalog.
    i. Use electronic resources (e.g., CD-ROMs and electronic databases).
    j. Need to print from a computer.

Library Staff

25. Library staff are:
    a. Approachable and welcoming.
    b. Willing to leave the desk area to help me.
    c. Available when I need them.
    d. Courteous and polite.
    e. Friendly and easy to talk to.

26. All public service desks throughout the library are served by knowledgeable staff.

27. Knowledgeable staff are available to assist whenever the library is open.
28. Library staff:
    a. Give accurate answers to my questions.
    b. Communicate with me using terms I understand.
    c. Encourage me to come back to ask for more assistance if I need it.
    d. Understand what information I am looking for.
    e. Do not overwhelm me with too much information and detail.
29. Library staff:
    a. Offer suggestions on where to look for information in other parts of the library.
    b. Offer suggestions on where to look for information outside the library.
    c. Take me to where the material is shelved instead of just pointing or telling me where to go.
    d. Direct me to library brochures and helpsheets.
    e. Mention interlibrary loan as a means to obtain materials that the library does not have.
30. Library staff:
    a. Help me select appropriate electronic resources.
    b. Personally help me use electronic resources.
    c. Show me how to use the online library catalog.
    d. Demonstrate and teach the use of electronic sources (e.g., CD-ROMs and electronic databases).
    e. Help me in using the World Wide Web.
    f. Demonstrate and teach the use of the World Wide Web.
31. Library staff demonstrate:
    a. Cultural sensitivity.
    b. Sensitivity toward those who are physically challenged.

Finding Materials

32. The materials I want are in their proper places on the shelves.
33. Materials are reshelved promptly.
34. It is easy to find where materials (books, journals, videos, maps, etc.) are located in the building.

Equipment

35. Equipment is in good working order:
    a. Audiovisual (e.g., video players and slide projectors).
    b. CD-ROM and database computers.
    c. Computer printers.
    d. Microfilm and microfiche readers.
    e. Multimedia/interactive computers.
    f. Photocopiers.
    g. Self-issue machines.

Requesting Materials

36. When I request material, I am told how long it will take to arrive by interlibrary loan.
37. Material I have requested comes within the time frame quoted by interlibrary loan.
38. When I request material, I am told how long it will take to arrive from storage.
39. Material I have requested comes within the time frame quoted from storage.
40. When I request material, I am told how long it will take to arrive if it is currently on loan.
41. Material I have requested comes within the time frame quoted if it is currently on loan.
42. If I make a recommendation for the purchase of new material, staff provide me with feedback on whether it is ordered and when it is received.

The Building and the Library Environment

Comfort

43. I find the:
    a. Humidity in the building is comfortable.
    b. Temperature in the building is comfortable.
    c. Ventilation in the building is comfortable.

Lighting

44. The lighting in the building is adequate to my needs.

Furniture

45. Library furniture is:
    a. Available (e.g., I can find a seat or study desk).
    b. Comfortable.
    c. Functional.

Other Utilities

46. Online library catalog keys are clean.
47. Online library screens are clean.
48. The drinking fountains are clean.

(Continued)

FIGURE 7.4

Sample Statements on Service Quality Expectations (Continued)

49. The number of drinking fountains in the building is sufficient.

50. The toilets are clean.

51. The number of toilets in the building is sufficient.

52. Talking is permitted in some study areas.

53. A sufficient number of group study rooms is available.

54. The library has an attractive interior.

Materials for Course Needs

55. The range of materials held by the library meets my course needs.

56. The library purchases new materials that are relevant to my course needs.

57. The information I get from library materials is accurate.

58. The material I need from the reserve collection is usually available when I want it.

Popular Material

59. Popular items are available in sufficient copies.

60. Popular items are available for rental.

61. Videos are available.

62. CDs are available.

Miscellaneous

Condition of Materials

63. The material I need has not been mutilated (e.g., torn pages or highlighted text).

64. The library material I need is in good condition (e.g., not brittle or falling apart).

Noise Level

65. Study areas in the library are kept quiet.

Complaint Resolution

66. It is easy to make a compliment, complaint, or suggestion about library services or conditions.

67. The library acts promptly when I make a complaint.

Supplying Equipment

68. The library provides personal computers for me to use within the building.

69. The library provides services such as staplers, hole-punchers, pencil sharpeners, and change machines.

Other

70. Librarians provide teaching programs that enable me to make more effective use of library materials and services.

71. The information displayed on the screen for electronic sources other than the online library catalog (e.g., CD-ROMs) is clear and easy to follow.

72. The library's World Wide Web page contains correct and useful information about library services and materials.

73. When faculty request that material be placed on reserve, it is done promptly.

74. I feel safe in the library.

75. I feel the library is located in a safe area.

76. I am able to find a parking place when I visit the library.

Adapted and expanded from Philip J. Calvert and Peter Hernon, "Surveying Service Quality within University Libraries," *Journal of Academic Librarianship* 23, no. 5 (September 1997): 408–15.

FIGURE 7.5
Aspects of Service Quality

Resources: Information Content

1. Appropriateness of fit (match) between content and customer
2. Accuracy/trustworthiness
   a. Degree of correctness (misinformation)
   b. Inaccuracy: Subject to misconduct, e.g., fraud (disinformation)
3. Currentness or timeliness
4. Degree of comprehensiveness (e.g., thoroughness and extent to which an electronic product duplicates a print source)
5. Medium
6. Packaging: Aesthetics
7. Relevance[1]

The Organization: Its Service Environment and Resource Delivery

1. Availability/accessibility
   a. Choices
      * Medium
      * Means of delivery (e.g., fax)
      * Source of service (e.g., a particular library or CARL UnCover)
      * Packaging: Aesthetics (e.g., screen display)
   b. Convenience
      * Assistance for electronic services (e.g., help screens, online tutorials, and publicized phone numbers for assistance)
      * Hours of operation
      * Location (e.g., of library or collection)
      * Staffing (service time and availability)— queuing
   c. Equipment
      * In operating condition
      * Lines of users waiting their turn
      * More needed
      * Out of order—needing repair
      * Written/visual instructions correct/not misleading
   d. Information itself (ease of its use)
2. Responsiveness, including complaint and compliment procedures
   a. Ease of making complaint or compliment

b. Response for receiving *good* service
c. Response/redress for receiving *poor* service

3. Maintenance
   a. Items in collection: On shelf, in proper location, no sizable backlog needing reshelving, and length of time item is part of backlog (speed of reshelving)
4. Physical condition of material in collection (e.g., brittle materials, restricted use, or quality of photocopied material on reserve)
5. Physical surroundings
   a. Ambient conditions
   b. Noise level
   c. Perceived level of personal safety
   d. Point of public service contact (e.g., branch libraries might have circulation, not reference, desks)
   e. Signage
   f. Spatial layout
   g. Temperature: Too hot or too cold
6. Service costs
7. Service reputation (e.g., service-oriented)
8. Creates customer loyalty

Service Delivery Staff[2]

Public Service Staff

1. Ability to train/educate customers (e.g., in use of CD-ROM products)
2. Accuracy in answering questions
3. Behavior
   a. Approachable
   b. Appropriate body language and a smile
   c. Courteous
   d. Empathetic
   e. Friendly/pleasant
   f. Include, user in search process (i.e., not ignoring his or her presence)
   g. Maintain eye contact
   h. Not too busy to help; receptive to questions
   i. Willing to leave the desk

---

1. Patrick Wilson, "Unused Relevant Information in Research and Development," *Journal of the American Society for Information Science* 46, no. 1 (1995): 45–51.

2. In some libraries, staff perform both public and technical service functions.

FIGURE 7.5
Aspects of Service Quality (Continued)

4. Communication skills
   a. Ability to communicate with staff in other units of the library
   b. Ability to determine what customers need/want
   c. Ability to negotiate library system and records (e.g., the library's and other libraries' catalogs, and MARC records) to assist customers
   d. Conduct reference interview going beyond the initial question asked
   e. Use follow-up question inviting user to return (willingness to return)
5. Knowledge
   a. Issues (e.g., intellectual property rights)
   b. Referral
   c. Subject
   d. Technical expertise (e.g., formats, accessing electronic information, and Internet access)
6. Speed of delivery (mechanical and human)

7. Sufficient amount of assistance provided, including the amount of time needed to respond to a request
8. Appearance of personnel

Systems/Technical Service Staff

1. Ability to communicate with staff in other units of the library
2. Accuracy
3. Knowledge of (and ability to anticipate) user needs and information-seeking behavior
4. Knowledge of standards
5. Service orientation
6. Speed of delivery (e.g., in order processing)
7. Technical knowledge of systems (e.g., technology-based)

Adapted from Peter Hernon and Ellen Altman, *Service Quality in Academic Libraries* (Norwood, N.J.: Ablex, 1996), 66–67.

As reflected in Figure 7.5, service quality encompasses three general areas: resources, the organization, and service delivery. Figure 7.6 places the expectations for these three areas within the context of expectations and, more broadly, service quality and satisfaction. More importantly, it shows that satisfaction and service quality are interrelated but are not the same. Chapter 10 clarifies this point.

How to Proceed

As the first step—before conducting any survey—library staff, meeting in departments or teams and across departments/teams, should review: (1) the organization's mission for its coverage of customer-based services, and (2) any strategic planning documents. Everyone should understand that customers comprise "one of the key drivers in planning for the future."[22] As explained by the National Performance Review, any customer-driven organization "maintains a focus on the needs and expectations, both spoken and unspoken, of customers, both present and future, in the creation and/or improvement of the product or service provided. . . . Spoken and unspoken means that not only must the ex-

FIGURE 7.6
Satisfaction and Service Quality

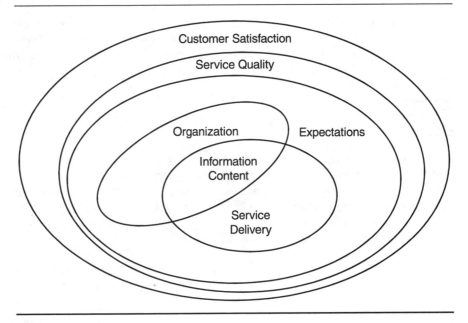

pressed needs and expectations of the customers be listened to, but also that information developed independently 'about' customers and their preferences . . . will be used as input to the organizational planning."[23] The U.S. General Accounting Office has referred to such planning and the resulting information or learning that managers and others obtain as "an investment in success."[24]

Asking customers to rate more than 100 statements is excessive, and not all the statements reflect priorities that a library has the resources to meet. Thus, this section describes how to query customers so that the results will be meaningful to library planning and decision making. As a first step, it is important to determine the extent of the staff's customer orientation. If they do not understand the importance of customer service, that lacuna must be addressed first. Do the library's mission statement and strategic planning documents contain statements about service? If so, the library has a starting point for emphasizing the need to learn how well a service meets customer expectations.

Library staff members should review the customer service plans in Figures 3.1 and 3.2 and those of Wright State University (WSU) Libraries (pp. 37–38). They should discuss WSU Libraries' "Commitment to Excellence" and determine whether they can develop a similar pledge. If they cannot develop a customer service plan or pledge, they should determine why not and how they should proceed. At a later date, they could revisit their attempt and see whether opinions have changed.

Staff should also review the statements in Figure 7.4 and identify those they regard to be the highest, second-highest, and third-highest priority. Such a list of priorities serves as a reminder that the intent is to identify those expectations that staff believe are most essential to meet and to lay the foundation both for expanding the list over time and for deciding where to set benchmarks. Perhaps together with selected customers, they might select an initial pool of, say, 30 statements and rewrite them or make substitutions as they desire. Then, using a nominal group technique, each staff member might vote for his or her three *most important* priorities.[25] The statements that receive the most votes become the basis for conducting a customer survey such as Figure 7.7.

FIGURE 7.7
Library Customer Survey

We ask you to spare about ___ minutes of your time to identify what you think are the *most important* indicators of high-quality service that you expect a library to provide. Some items are probably more important to you than others. The information that you provide will enable us to understand your service needs and priorities.

Please circle the number that indicates how important each of the following points is for the high-quality service that you expect a library to provide. *(The range is from 1 = of no importance to 7 = of highest importance.)*

If you don't use a particular service, please DO NOT
circle a number for that statement

	No Importance						Highest Importance
1. The online catalog is an accurate source of information about all material held by the library.	1	2	3	4	5	6	7
2. When I connect remotely to the online library catalog I do not get a busy signal or get disconnected.	1	2	3	4	5	6	7
3. I do not have to wait in line more than three minutes when I ask for assistance at a reference or information desk.	1	2	3	4	5	6	7
4. I do not have to wait in line more than three minutes when I borrow material.	1	2	3	4	5	6	7
5. Library staff are:							
a. Approachable and welcoming.	1	2	3	4	5	6	7
b. Willing to leave the desk area to help me.	1	2	3	4	5	6	7
c. Available when I need them.	1	2	3	4	5	6	7
d. Courteous and polite.	1	2	3	4	5	6	7
e. Friendly and easy to talk to.	1	2	3	4	5	6	7
6. Library staff:							
a. Communicate with me using terms I understand.	1	2	3	4	5	6	7
b. Give accurate answers to my questions.	1	2	3	4	5	6	7
c. Encourage me to come back to ask for more assistance if I need it.	1	2	3	4	5	6	7
d. Demonstrate cultural sensitivity.	1	2	3	4	5	6	7
7. Materials are reshelved promptly.	1	2	3	4	5	6	7
8. Equipment is in good working order:							
a. Computer printers	1	2	3	4	5	6	7
b. Microfilm and microfiche readers	1	2	3	4	5	6	7
c. Photocopiers	1	2	3	4	5	6	7

Thank you for your participation.

The review discussed above will take time and may require administrative leadership to support the development of a customer-service commitment and to supply the necessary resources to maintain that commitment. The intended outcome is achievement of the managerial perspective depicted in Figure 7.8. The review should encourage staff to:

- Become more customer-focused
- Finalize the set of expectations they want to meet
- Feel a sense of empowerment
- Pursue strategies for seeking a relationship with customers and for gaining their loyalty
- Identify the data-collection strategies to be pursued, such as a survey
- Ensure that customers can easily provide feedback
- Relate findings to actions, policies, and processes that the library can follow to make improvements

The initial stage will probably require: (1) customer service training and sensitivity to issues that are important to customers, and (2) the selective involvement of some *valued* customers in the discussions.

FIGURE 7.8
Customer-Driven Service

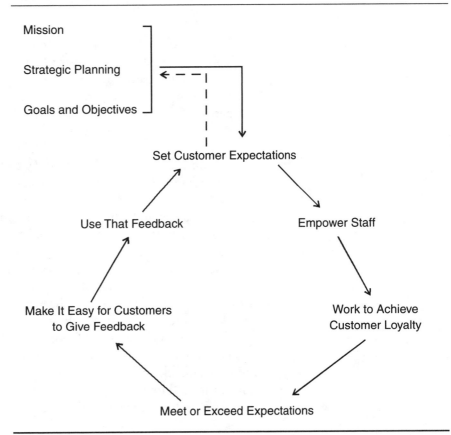

To recap, this procedure enables the organization to involve the staff in deciding on priorities for service quality. The staff discuss potential priorities among themselves, sharing what they consider important as internal customers and what they are prepared to do for external customers. They do not, however, want to develop expectations that are unimportant to customers or are unrealistic to attain. Data collection becomes a means to test the importance of specific expectations to customers, as the library determines which expectations have the highest priority and which ones the organization will consistently provide the resources to meet.

Once these decisions have been made, the staff can move to the next phase—surveying customers about selected expectations and measuring the gap between those expectations and the actual service provided. They can then work on reducing that gap. To begin, however, they need to frame relevant customer-related indicators, decide on how to interpret the results (benchmarking), and set the time frame for retesting and for interpreting later benchmark results. As the next step, they need to decide on the survey method and develop guidelines for ensuring an acceptable return rate.

Customer-Related Measures

As David Osborne and Ted Gaebler discuss in their widely acclaimed *Reinventing Government,*

> When public organizations set out to measure performance, their managers usually draw up lists that measure how well they carry out some administrative process: how many people they serve; how fast they serve them; what percentage of requests are fulfilled within a set period of time. In essence, they measure their volume of output. But *outputs* do not guarantee *outcomes*.[26]

As they further explain, "the tendency to focus on process is natural. . . . If . . . [individuals] follow those processes faithfully and produce the expected volume of output, they are doing their jobs."[27] One way to view outcomes is through the voice of customers and issues of satisfaction, expectations met, materials obtained, and willingness to return, as an organization sets long-term targets and strives to achieve them.

Osborne and Gaebler issue a reminder: "If an organization sets too few measures, they may not reflect all of its goals. Hence, its service providers may be driven to emphasize some goals at the expense of others. If it sets too many, it will dilute the power of all measures."[28]

As shown in Figure 4.7, "Countables and Assessables," libraries have choices about what data they collect. Customers cannot provide meaningful feedback in every instance; however, when libraries focus on questions of "How well?," "How valuable?," and "How satisfied?," they can. Also, as previously discussed, the answers to these questions can be analyzed through the use of customer-related indicators. Thus, as the staff develop the questionnaire, they can determine the types of indicators to develop. For example, if they are concerned about customers having to queue at service desks, they might decide customers should not have to stand unacknowledged at a desk for more than three minutes. Before reassigning staff to accommodate the three-minute limit, they might want to verify its importance to customers. (As a note of caution, library staff should avoid raising false expectation and should be willing to act on any survey statements they include.) Let us assume that the survey discovers that the time limit is very important to customers; then the staff could develop a customer-related measure. Thus, a survey becomes the basis for determining what is important to customers and what would be meaningful to develop into performance indicators.

Using the preceding example, a measure might be:

$$\frac{\text{Number served within three minutes}}{\text{Number of people waiting in line}} = \underline{\hspace{1cm}} \times 100 = \underline{\hspace{1cm}}\%$$

Given the focus of the ratio, the percentage should be large and, over time, should increase even more.

The survey tests the importance of certain expectations to customers. Library staff must then translate the findings into something measurable. Again using the example of waiting in line, the staff can periodically monitor service areas, count the number of people in line, and use a stopwatch to monitor the three-minute limit. Thus, data collection is not an imposition on customers, and the results, if properly gathered, comprise a "reality check."

Figure 7.9 provides some examples of measures that have direct implications for customers and for which customers can provide insights. Survey statements pertaining to the amount of time in line or to material awaiting reshelving produce yardsticks that are quantifiably measured, whereas statements about the staff have a more subjective focus. Having a subjective base does not mean that the data should not be collected, but, rather, that greater caution should be used in the interpretation.

Within the survey itself, specific time frames, such as three minutes, should not be set arbitrarily. Such numbers must come from extensive discussion among the staff and managers as they develop a time frame that is realistic for them to achieve. Further, as the figure illustrates, there are different types of customer-related measures; Chapters 9 and 12 offer more choices.

Developing the Survey Instrument

Target Audience

Customers are either internal or external. Internal customers are fellow staff members—it is they who must feel empowered and appreciated by

FIGURE 7.9
Customer-Related Measures

$$\frac{\text{Number of customers served within three minutes}}{\text{Number of customers seeking reference desk service}} = \underline{\quad} \times 100 = \underline{\quad} \%$$

$$\frac{\text{Number of customers served within three minutes}}{\text{Number of customers waiting to check out items}} = \underline{\quad} \times 100 = \underline{\quad} \%$$

$$\frac{\text{Number of staff approachable/welcoming}}{\text{Number of staff approached (per service area)}} = \underline{\quad} \times 100 = \underline{\quad} \%$$

$$\frac{\text{Number of staff courteous/polite}}{\text{Number of staff approached (per service area)}} = \underline{\quad} \times 100 = \underline{\quad} \%$$

$$\frac{\text{Number of books reshelved within 24 hours after being removed from the shelves}}{\text{Number of books needing reshelving}} = \underline{\quad} \times 100 = \underline{\quad} \%$$

$$\frac{\text{Number of current periodicals reshelved after being removed from the shelves}}{\text{Number of current periodicals needing reshelving}} = \underline{\quad} \times 100 = \underline{\quad} \%$$

$$\frac{\text{Number of bound periodicals reshelved after being removed from the shelves}}{\text{Number of bound periodicals needing reshelving}} = \underline{\quad} \times 100 = \underline{\quad} \%$$

$$\frac{\text{Number of microfiche filed after being removed from the cabinets}}{\text{Number of microfiche needing refiling}} = \underline{\quad} \times 100 = \underline{\quad} \%$$

$$\frac{\text{Number of computer printers in working order}}{\text{Number of computer printers in public service areas}} = \underline{\quad} \times 100 = \underline{\quad} \%$$

the organization if they are to go out of their way to meet the needs and preferences of customers, and, thus, maintain satisfied and loyal customers. All staff members must agree on a minimal set of expectations they will meet; individual members may go beyond this, but they will require a supportive organization.

Although internal staff might be the first surveyed, they need not be. Chapter 8 offers another method for seeking information from internal customers. In either case, a draft of the survey should be shared with staff as a discussion document; paraprofessional staff, student workers, and volunteers should also be brought into the process.

External customers can include a wide assortment of stakeholder groups, especially for public libraries that serve a community of broad interests, educational and income levels, lifestyle preferences, and age groups. Academic libraries traditionally have served faculty, staff, administrators, students, and, sometimes, community residents, especially those who use the government documents collections of libraries participating in the federal depository library program. In addition, as the student population becomes increasingly diverse, not only ethnically, but also in terms of age, work history, and life experiences, and as the World Wide Web becomes a common delivery system for credit courses to students far beyond the campus, library services may have to change to accommodate an expanded external customer base.

It is difficult to tell whether the people who place notes in the suggestion box, fill out forms on WWW pages, or make complaints reflect the views of the general customer population. To ascertain the expectations and perceptions of the customer base overall, it is necessary to take a formal survey. In some states and municipalities, government entities are required to conduct an annual customer opinion survey. Usually, these are short and the questions are general. For example, in 1997, the Phoenix Public Library annual survey asked about satisfaction with types of library materials, the overall appearance of the facility, and staff-delivered service. Respondents were entirely self-selected in that the forms were placed near the checkout desk, with no signs soliciting participation. Thus, the library risked skewed representation in survey findings and interpretation.

For various reasons, a library might prefer to survey a subpopulation (e.g., students, users of a particular library facility, or users of a particular collection). In such cases, the statements selected for customer response must be tailored to the interests and knowledge of the subpopulation surveyed. It is important to understand that the survey statements presented in this book can be answered only by customers. Do not assume that the staff know what a broad range of respondents would say. Such an assumption might forestall customer input and simply continue the status quo.

A key question becomes: Does the library need to generalize the findings to the population, or can it study the perceptions of selected customers without having to make generalizations? Sometimes, government bodies are required to generalize survey results to a specified population—recipients of an agency's service. Thus, critical questions for library staff and evaluators to consider include:

- Should we focus on a particular population or subpopulation? Why?
- Do we need to produce generalizable data?
- If so, is this for a certain time period?

Representativeness

Questions about where, when, and how to distribute surveys can influence the representativeness of the responses. Representativeness is the degree to which the characteristics of the respondents match the characteristics of the population under consideration. The population for purposes of the survey can be any group under study. For example, an academic library at a university offering night classes for working adults wants to sample its student customers. To obtain a cross section of student opinion, survey forms will have to be available at times when those adult students come to campus—nights and weekends. Certain times during the school year can also influence the results. For example, surveys distributed right before final examination week or during any period of campus upheaval are likely to result in low responses and high levels of customer angst.

Distribution of surveys in public libraries having multiple branches with different hours of operation is more complicated. The distribution plan needs to take into account the customers who come at various times throughout the day and week.

The two basic types of sampling method are *probability sampling* (representativeness) and *nonprobability sampling* (lacking in representativeness). With nonprobability sampling, it is not possible to generalize from the sample to the population because the sample may not be representative of the population. Such sampling may, however, be easier and cheaper to conduct, while still producing useful insights. Probability sampling might involve *random sampling*—the selection of cases or subjects so that each one has an equal and known chance of inclusion and the selection of one case or subject does not influence the selection of another—or *systematic sampling*, in which each member of the population is not chosen independently. With systematic sampling, once the first member of the population has been chosen, other members of the sample are automatically determined. For example, staff members might decide to select for participation every tenth person leaving the library.

Sampling extends to who will be surveyed and when (e.g., day, week, month, or school term). You might consult *Measuring Academic Library Performance* or *Output Measures for Public Libraries* and follow the suggestions for data collection.[29] In a general survey of customers, evaluators might distribute the questionnaire to anyone entering the library. With this method, one needs to consider how the forms will be collected, and how many will never be completed. (They may be found all over the building.) A variant of the door distribution method is to ask persons leaving the library to fill out a form. This method makes collection easier, but some people will claim the press of time as an excuse not to participate. As an alternative, evaluators might walk throughout the library and ask customers to complete the form. This method requires a decision about remaining with the person until the form has been completed, returning later to pick up the completed form and to answer any questions, or providing a centralized collection location. Of course, the person may leave, may only partially complete the form, or may decide against participation. If there is interest in a particular branch, service area, or location within the building, then only customers using that site should receive forms.

When library staff collect data for a so-called *typical* day or week, they are really using a type of nonprobability sample. How is *typical* defined, and how is that time period identified without the use of a probability sample to select from among various choices?

Number of Customers to Survey

Because customer participation is voluntary, the gap between the number of forms distributed and the number completed must be considered. Another major factor is the confidence that evaluators can place in the results; confidence is influenced by the size of the population to be surveyed and the number of forms completed.

In *Measuring Academic Library Performance*, Van House et al. recommend that "in most cases you will need at least 100 completed forms; closer to 400 is preferable."[30] One hundred forms corresponds to a sample size for a population of less than 140 at a 95 percent confidence level with a standard deviation of ±5, whereas 400 pertains to a population of well over 100,000 (with a similar confidence level and standard deviation). Librarians wanting a more precisely determined sample size should consult Figure 7.10, which is a general guide to determining sample size for a random sample.

Given the widespread use and acceptance of *Measuring Academic Library Performance* and similar manuals, we believe it legitimate to follow their advice. If the population served by the library is very small (does

FIGURE 7.10

Survey Sample Size[1]

Number	Sample Size	Number	Sample Size
50	44	850	264
75	62	900	269
100	79	950	273
150	107	1,000	277
200	131	1,500	305
250	151	2,000	322
300	168	2,500	332
350	183	3,000	340
400	195	3,500	346
450	207	4,000	350
500	217	4,500	353
550	226	5,000	356
600	234	6,000	361
650	241	7,000	364
700	248	9,000	368
750	254	10,000	369
800	259		

1. Reflects 95 percent confidence level and ±5 standard deviation.

not exceed 100), all the customers might be surveyed. For small populations, a sample size of 100 is viable; the larger the population, the more likely the sample should be between 300 and 400.

A note of caution should be inserted, however. If the larger organization expects the library to produce insights that accurately reflect a population's perceptions, it is best to consult with a statistician and draw a representative sample.

Formulating Survey Questions

The statements labeled as highest priority—no more than 20 of them—become the basis for exploring customer expectations (see Figure 7.7). The questionnaire should neither exceed two pages nor impose much of a burden on respondents for completion. The questionnaire might conclude with a few questions about respondent demographics. For college or university students, the survey designers might select questions regarding:

- Class level (e.g., graduate or undergraduate; freshman, sophomore, junior, or senior; lower division [freshman and sophomore] or upper division [junior and senior] undergraduate; master's or doctoral student)
- Major
- Gender
- Residence (on campus or commuter student)
- Status (full- or part-time student)

In the case of faculty members, variables might include rank, department, areas of specialization, and status (full-time or adjunct).

In the case of public libraries, respondents might be asked about:

- Gender
- Level of schooling completed (e.g., some or all of elementary school, some or all of junior high school, some or all of high school, vocational school, some or all of college, master's or doctoral degree)
- Occupation (e.g., homemaker; manager or proprietor; operator, fabricator, laborer [machine operator, inspector, assembler; transportation and material moving; handlers, equipment cleaners, helpers, and laborers]; precision, production, craft, and repair; professional [teacher, doctor, accountant, etc.]; technical sales and administrative support [including technicians and related support, sales, and administrative support—clerical]; retired; student; unemployed; other [specify]).[31] As an alternative, staff might complete this category if respondents are unsure where their job falls in a list or if they have more than one occupation.

It is possible to add variables related to age, race and ethnicity, language spoken at home, or income, but these types of data may be technically complex and publicly controversial.[32] Any list of variables, however, should be short and essential to know. Does the library want to distinguish among customers? If yes, the questions become "Why?" and "In what regard?"

Because Figure 7.7 contains 17 items, a couple of variables relating to demographics might be added at the end. Again, the form should not exceed two printed pages and should be well presented, using good quality paper and attractive layout of the statements on the pages (assuming the survey is not conveyed via e-mail).

Evaluators should pretest the instrument on library staff (both professional and nonprofessional), and on a few well-known customers. The pretest might involve a group discussion, a one-on-one discussion, or written responses to the wording and interpretation of questions, and to ways of enticing the survey population to respond.

Distributing the Survey

Figure 7.1 assesses different methods of survey distribution and shows that each has strengths and limitations. Library staff members should review the options and make the choice that best meets their needs. Clearly, it is essential that customers understand why the library needs their comments and why they should accept the imposition. For this reason, the survey approach is probably best used for preexisting customers, rather than those labeled as lost or never-gained. (Chapter 8 will address these other groups.) If the library does not want to target never-gained or lost customers specifically, it might survey a population of faculty, staff, students, or community residents and gain responses from some present, some lost, and some never-gained customers. The findings, however, might, be skewed in favor of actual customers because the other two groups might have little incentive to participate.

Response Rate

The response rate is the percentage of people who return completed and usable surveys:

$$\text{Response rate} = \frac{\text{Number completed and usable}}{\text{Number distributed}} = \underline{\quad} \times 100 = \underline{\quad} \%$$

The number distributed includes the number of refusals.

Thus, if library staff members distribute 500 questionnaires and 410 are completed and usable, the response rate is 82 percent. If 100 are returned, the response rate is 20 percent. In the latter instance, if the staff distribute another 300 questionnaires and receive 250 in return, they might mistakenly define the response rate as 70 percent [(100 + 250) ÷ 500]; in fact, the response rate is 43.8 percent [(100 + 250) ÷ (500 + 300)].

P. L. Erdos, among others, indicates that "no mail survey can be considered reliable unless it has a minimum of 50 percent response . . . (or verifies a lack of nonresponse bias)."[33] The same advice applies to surveys distributed to customers within libraries. According to Nancy Van House, Beth Weil, and Charles R. McClure, "Response rates in academic libraries run about 50 to 90 percent."[34] For a satisfaction survey, they estimate a response rate of approximately 80 percent.[35]

The lower the return rate, the greater the risk that the answers of respondents and nonrespondents differ, thereby inhibiting generalization to a population. For this reason, library evaluators should take great care to explain the value of participation and do all that they can to achieve response rates no lower than 70 to 80 percent. In the case of mailed questionnaires, library staff should consider a follow-up procedure(s), whereby they approach nonrespondents and invite their participation; again, they should offer compelling reasons for why they are asking a favor and why the individual should accept the imposition.[36]

Errors

Every survey has the possibility of error, which can invalidate the results. Examples include: noncoverage (not surveying the right customers); nonresponse bias (customers' failure to participate); measurement bias (misinterpreting questions); response bias (failing to answer truthfully); and technical errors in recording, coding, tabulating, or analyzing data.[37] Using the procedures discussed in this chapter and consulting sources such as those in the list beginning on page 128 can minimize nonsampling errors.

Continuous Evaluation

Evaluation within the context of customer-driven strategic planning should be an ongoing or continuous process. The staff should set internal benchmarks, meet those delivery expectations over time, and set more lofty benchmarks as the organization becomes more effective and efficient and as customers become completely satisfied. As any customer-focused pledge becomes more meaningful, staff aspire to meet or exceed it.

Summary

In preparation for conducting a survey of external customers or a population such as faculty or students (consisting of present [infrequent to high-volume] customers, lost customers, and never-gained customers), the library should review its customer service plan and the staff should engage in self-assessment. Self-assessment reveals the extent to which the library is oriented toward satisfying and delighting customers. Figures 7.11, "Customer Service Inventory," and 7.12, "Reasons and Remedies for Customer Dissatisfaction," offer sample questions that libraries can adapt as the staff engage in an internal dialogue about their service role.[38] Such a discussion, especially if customers are brought into the dialogue, may delay the necessity of surveying external customers.

FIGURE 7.11

Customer Service Inventory (to be completed by staff)

I am interested in providing the best customer service that I and the library can.

Using the scale of 1 to 5, with 5 being the best, please rate how well you and other staff members provide each of the following services.

	Myself	Other Staff
1. Courteous answering of telephone	_____	_____
2. Accurate responses to telephone queries	_____	_____
3. Courteous and friendly service to in-person customers	_____	_____

Place a mark in the box that most clearly corresponds to your level of agreement with the statement. Do not attach your name or department to the form. Thank you for your participation.

	Strongly Agree	Agree	Neutral	Disagree	Strongly Disagree
4. Only rarely do customers have to wait in line longer than a few minutes for service.	_____	_____	_____	_____	_____
5. The telephone is answered by the fourth ring.	_____	_____	_____	_____	_____
6. Customers are placed on hold for no more than one minute.	_____	_____	_____	_____	_____
7. The atmosphere of the library is warm and inviting.	_____	_____	_____	_____	_____
8. Customer complaints are resolved quickly and satisfactorily.	_____	_____	_____	_____	_____
9. I like my job.	_____	_____	_____	_____	_____
10. The staff demonstrate a caring attitude toward each other.	_____	_____	_____	_____	_____
11. Other staff demonstrate a caring attitude toward customers.	_____	_____	_____	_____	_____
12. The library has a good reputation in the community.	_____	_____	_____	_____	_____
13. The customer pays my salary.	_____	_____	_____	_____	_____
14. Top management puts the customer first.	_____	_____	_____	_____	_____
15. Middle management puts the customer first.	_____	_____	_____	_____	_____
16. The rest of the staff puts the customer first.	_____	_____	_____	_____	_____

(Continued)

FIGURE 7.11
Customer Service Inventory (Continued)

	Strongly Agree	Agree	Neutral	Disagree	Strongly Disagree
17. Management asks, "What is best for the customer?" and makes decisions based on hard data relating to customer expectations and satisfaction.	_____	_____	_____	_____	_____
18. Customers are not the victim of telephone tag.	_____	_____	_____	_____	_____
19. Staff know how to transfer calls without cutting off the caller.	_____	_____	_____	_____	_____
20. The customer is the ultimate judge of quality and, ultimately, determines quality collections and services.	_____	_____	_____	_____	_____
21. There is a strong commitment to product/service quality in the library.	_____	_____	_____	_____	_____
22. The morale among staff in the department is excellent.	_____	_____	_____	_____	_____
23. The morale among staff in the library is excellent.	_____	_____	_____	_____	_____

	Yes, most definitely	Somewhat	Not sure	Definitely no
24. Do you think your job has an impact on how satisfied customers are about using the library?	_____	_____	_____	_____

	Much Better	Better	About the Same	Worse	Much Worse
25. Over the past year, do you think the library has done better or worse in providing high-quality customer service?	_____	_____	_____	_____	_____

26. The three things I like MOST about working here are:

    1. _____

    2. _____

    3. _____

27. The three things I like LEAST about working here are:

    1. _____

    2. _____

    3. _____

28. If I could change ONE thing about how the library helps customers, it would be: _____

    _____

    _____

FIGURE 7.12

Reasons and Remedies for Customer Dissatisfaction (to be completed by staff)

Customers become dissatisfied for various reasons. Please identify the three *most important* reasons why you think customers become dissatisfied with library services. Also, please suggest ways to overcome those points of dissatisfaction.

Internal Customers

Reasons	Possible Remedy
One:	
Two:	
Three:	

External Customers

Reasons	Possible Remedy
One:	
Two:	
Three:	

Figure 7.13 highlights key steps discussed in this chapter. Within the context of Figures 7.4, 7.5, and 7.7, a library can determine which expectations are important for it to meet. Customers should play a key role in the decision. As a first step, library staff should discuss service quality among themselves and with a few valued customers, using a self-assessment process such as the one discussed earlier. The staff should not presume to know what customers expect, nor should they downplay the importance of letting customers voice their expectations and of customers seeing policies shaped around those expectations. Development of a survey provides a rich opportunity for library staff to refine the list of priority expectations to meet now and in the near future—for the majority of customers. Once these have been met on a regular basis, library staff can move to meeting new (additional) expectations. Equally important, the staff enter a dialogue with customers, and both parties begin to know each other better.

Clear choices must be made regarding who is surveyed, when, and by what means. Whatever the decision, the staff should seek to obtain a respectable return rate—no lower than 70 percent. With the data obtained, the staff can continue the planning of customer-driven service (see Figure 7.8), become empowered, and achieve customer loyalty. These are worthy goals, but they require dedication and hard work to achieve and maintain on a broad scale.

FIGURE 7.13
Key Steps to Conducting a Survey

Plan

1. Conduct surveys for purposes that are clearly stated and designed to improve services to customers.

2. Assign responsible staff to conduct the survey.

3. Follow standard research methods, such as those explained in this chapter and the sources cited, to minimize errors and other potential problems.

4. Involve the staff in the process and in developing a commitment to customer service and the outcome of the survey.

Identify Customers

5. Decide if the survey will focus on a particular population or subpopulation, and for what time period.

6. Determine when, where, and how the forms will be distributed.

7. Try to obtain responses from the greatest possible percentage of those selected and, if relevant, check to ensure that those who respond are representative of customers receiving the services being studied.

Construct and Ask Questions

8. Review the more than 100 statements given in Figure 7.4, selecting, rewriting, and adding as

necessary; or consider the use of SERVQUAL or another instrument.

9. Decide on any variables relating to individual customers (e.g., occupation).

10. Treat respondents respectfully and remember that you are imposing on them.

11. Be careful about the appearance of the survey form.

12. Conduct a pretest on some library staff and valued customers—bring eight to 10 individuals together and review each statement and variable with them, ensuring that the wording is clear and deals with what the library really wants to know.

Edit and Archive Data

13. Make every attempt to ensure that the data are technically error-free.

14. Make it possible for others to confirm the results later.

Analyze Data and Results

15. Objectively analyze all data.

16. Interpret results with the appropriate level of precision and express the proper degree of caution about conclusions that can be drawn from the results.

17. Use the data as input in outcome measures, where feasible.

Adapted from Minnesota Office of the Legislative Auditor, *State Agency Use of Customer Satisfaction Surveys: A Program Evaluation Report* (St. Paul, Minn.: The Office, 1995), 5.

SELECTED SOURCES ON RESEARCH METHODS

Ary, Donald, Lucy C. Jacobs, and Asghar Razavieh. *Introduction to Research in Education*. New York: Holt, Rinehart and Winston, 1985, 1990; Harcourt Brace, 1995.

Greenbaum, Thomas L. *The Handbook of Focus Group Research*. Thousand Oaks, Calif.: Sage, 1997.*

*Sage also offers "The Focus Group Kit," a series of books edited by David L. Morgan and Richard A. Krueger.

Hernon, Peter. *Statistics: A Component of the Research Process.* Norwood, N.J.: Ablex, 1994.

Isaac, Stephen, and William B. Michael. *Handbook in Research and Evaluation.* San Diego: EdITS, 1995.

Miller, Delbert C. *Handbook of Research Design and Social Measurement.* Newbury Park, Calif.: Sage, 1991.

Powell, Ronald R. *Basic Research Methods for Librarians.* Greenwich, Conn.: Ablex, 1997.

Rossi, Peter H., and Howard E. Freeman. *Evaluation: A Systematic Approach.* Thousand Oaks, Calif.: Sage, 1993.

Salant, Priscella, and Donald Dillman. *How to Conduct Your Own Survey.* New York: Wiley, 1994.

Swisher, Robert, and Charles R. McClure. *Research for Decision Making.* Chicago: ALA, 1984.

NOTES

1. National Performance Review, *Serving the American Public: Best Practices in Customer-Driven Strategic Planning* (Washington, D.C.: Government Printing Office, 1997), 1.

2. John L. Lubans, "Sherlock's Dog, or Managers and Mess Findings," *Library Administration & Management* 8, no. 3 (summer 1994): 144.

3. Scott E. Sampson, "Ramifications of Monitoring Service Quality through Passively Solicited Customer Feedback," *Decision Sciences* 27, no. 4 (fall 1996): 601.

4. Ibid.

5. Ibid.

6. Ibid.

7. See Peter Hernon and Ellen Altman, *Service Quality in Academic Libraries* (Norwood, N.J.: Ablex, 1996).

8. A. Parasuraman, Valarie A. Zeithaml, and Leonard L. Berry, "A Conceptual Model of Service Quality and Its Implications for Future Research," *Journal of Marketing* 49, no. 4 (fall 1985): 42.

9. Vicki Coleman, Yi (Daniel) Xiao, Linda Blair, and Bill Chollett, "Toward a TQM Paradigm: Using SERVQUAL to Measure Library Service Quality," *College & Research Libraries* 58, no. 3 (May 1997), 240.

10. Ibid.

11. When Coleman et al. reported on a survey to measure service quality, they based their findings on a 38 percent return rate and generalized their findings to the population. Clearly, they fall well short of Erdos' recommendation (page 124). A key question becomes, Why do library journals accept for publication papers that have low survey return rates and do not verify a lack of nonresponse bias? The answer may well be that the reviewers (and perhaps a number of editors) do not have a background in research methodology and design.

12. For copies of all three instruments, see Danuta A. Nitecki, "An Assessment of the Applicability of SERVQUAL Dimensions as Customer-based Criteria for Evaluating Quality of Services in an Academic Library," Ph.D. dissertation, University of Maryland, 1995.

13. See Danuta A. Nitecki, "Assessment of Service Quality in Academic Libraries: Focus on the Applicability of the SERVQUAL," in *Proceedings of the 2nd Northumbria International Conference on Performance Measurement in Libraries and Information Services* (Newcastle upon Tyne, England: Department of Information and Library Management, University of Northumbria at Newcastle, 1998), pp. 193–96; Joan Stein, "Feedback from a Captive Audience: Reflections on the Results of a SERVQUAL Survey of Interlibrary Loan Services at Carnegie Mellon University Libraries," in *Proceedings of the 2nd Northumbria International Conference on Performance Measurement in Libraries and Information Services*, pp. 217–22.

14. Danuta A. Nitecki, "Changing the Concept and Measure of Service Quality in Academic Libraries," *Journal of Academic Librarianship* 22, no. 3 (May 1996): 181–90.

15. Ibid., 188.

16. Hernon and Altman, *Service Quality in Academic Libraries*.

17. Peter Hernon and Philip J. Calvert, "Methods for Measuring Service Quality in University Libraries in New Zealand," *Journal of Academic Librarianship* 22, no. 5 (September 1996): 387–391.

18. Philip J. Calvert and Peter Hernon, "Surveying Service Quality within University Libraries," *Journal of Academic Librarianship* 23, no. 5 (September 1997): 408–415.

19. See Rowena J. Cullen and Philip J. Calvert, "Stakeholder Perceptions of University Library Effectiveness," *Journal of Academic Librarianship* 21, no. 6 (November 1995): 438–448; Thomas Childers and Nancy Van House, "Dimensions of Public Library Effectiveness," *Library & Information Science Research* 11, no. 3 (1989): 273–301; Nancy A. Van House and Thomas Childers, "Dimensions of Public Library Effectiveness II: Library Performance," *Library & Information Science Research* 12, no. 2 (1990): 131–152.

20. See Hernon and Altman, *Service Quality in Academic Libraries*, 106–107.

21. Chris Manolis and Scott W. Kelley, "Assessing Service Quality via the Contributions of Service Employees and Customers," *Journal of Customer Service in Marketing and Management* 2, no. 4 (1996): 31–48.

22. National Performance Review, *Serving the American Public*, 6.

23. Ibid., 7.

24. General Accounting Office, *The Government Performance and Results Act: 1997 Governmentwide Implementation Will Be Uneven*, GAO/GGD-97-109 (Washington, D.C.: The Office, 1997), 79.

25. The nominal group technique is a method for producing group consensus. See William P. Anthony, *Practical Strategic Planning* (Westport, Conn.: Quorum Books, 1985), 47.

26. David Osborne and Ted Gaebler, *Reinventing Government: How the Entrepreneurial Spirit Is Transforming the Public Sector* (Reading, Mass.: Addison-Wesley, 1992), 350.

27. Ibid.

28. Ibid., 358.

29. Nancy A. Van House, Beth Weil, and Charles R. McClure, *Measuring Academic Library Performance: A Practical Approach* (Chicago: ALA, 1990); Nancy A. Van House, Mary Jo Lynch, Charles R. McClure, Douglas L. Zweizig, and Eleanor Jo Rodger, *Output Measures for Public Libraries*, 2d ed. (Chicago: ALA, 1987).

30. Van House, Weil, and McClure, *Measuring Academic Library Performance*, 44.

31. Charles R. McClure and Peter Hernon, *Users of Academic and Public GPO Depository Libraries* (Washington, D.C.: Government Printing Office, 1989), 63.

32. See, for instance, General Accounting Office, "Statistical Agencies: Collection and Reporting of Race and Ethnicity Data," statement of Bernard L. Ungar, Associate Director, Federal Management and Workforce Issues, General Government Division, GAO/T-GGD-97-92 (Washington, D.C.: The Office, 1997).

33. P. L. Erdos, *Professional Mail Surveys* (New York: McGraw-Hill, 1970): 144.

34. Van House, Weil, and McClure, *Measuring Academic Library Performance*, 28.

35. Ibid.

36. Why should the customer be motivated to respond? This question becomes even more important when library staff try to survey lost or never-gained customers.

37. Peter Hernon, *Statistics: A Component of the Research Process* (Norwood, N.J.: Ablex, 1994), 64–65.

38. For examples of other self-assessment forms, see Rebecca L. Morgan, *Calming Upset Customers: Staying Effective during Unpleasant Situations*, rev. ed. (Menlo Park, Calif.: Crisp Publications, 1996).

SECTION A *Directions:* Based on your experiences as a user of reference services, please think about the kind of library that would deliver excellent quality of reference services. Think about the kind of library which you would be pleased to use. Please show the extent to which you think such a library should possess the feature described by each statement. If you feel a feature is "not at all essential" for excellent libraries such as the one you have in mind, circle the number "1". If you feel a feature is "absolutely essential" for excellent libraries, circle "7". If your feelings are less strong, circle one of the numbers in the middle. There are no right or wrong answers—all we are interested in is a number that truly reflects your feelings regarding libraries that would deliver excellent quality of reference service.

	Not at all Essential						Absolutely Essential
1. Excellent libraries' reference units will have modern-looking equipment.	1	2	3	4	5	6	7
2. The physical facilities at excellent libraries' reference units will be visually appealing.	1	2	3	4	5	6	7
3. Employees at excellent libraries' reference units will be neat-appearing.	1	2	3	4	5	6	7
4. Materials associated with the reference services (such as pamphlets or statements) will be visually appealing in an excellent library.	1	2	3	4	5	6	7
5. When excellent libraries' reference units promise to do something by a certain time, they will do so.	1	2	3	4	5	6	7
6. When a user has a problem, excellent libraries' reference units will show a sincere interest in solving it.	1	2	3	4	5	6	7
7. Excellent libraries will perform reference services right the first time.	1	2	3	4	5	6	7
8. Excellent libraries will provide reference services at the time they promise to do so.	1	2	3	4	5	6	7
9. Excellent libraries' reference units will insist on error-free records.	1	2	3	4	5	6	7
10. Employees in excellent libraries will tell users exactly when reference services will be performed.	1	2	3	4	5	6	7
11. Employees in excellent libraries will give prompt reference services to users.	1	2	3	4	5	6	7
12. Employees in excellent libraries' reference units will always be willing to help users.	1	2	3	4	5	6	7
13. Employees in excellent libraries' reference units will never be too busy to respond to users' requests.	1	2	3	4	5	6	7
14. The behavior of employees in excellent libraries' reference units will instill confidence in users.	1	2	3	4	5	6	7
15. Users of excellent libraries will feel safe in their reference transactions.	1	2	3	4	5	6	7
16. Employees in excellent libraries' reference units will be consistently courteous with users.	1	2	3	4	5	6	7
17. Employees in excellent libraries' reference units will have the knowledge to answer users' questions.	1	2	3	4	5	6	7
18. Excellent libraries' reference units will give users individual attention.	1	2	3	4	5	6	7
19. Excellent libraries' reference units will have operating hours convenient to all their users.	1	2	3	4	5	6	7

		Not at all Essential				Absolutely Essential		

20. Excellent libraries' reference units will have employees who give users personal attention.

    1 2 3 4 5 6 7

21. Excellent libraries' reference units will have the user's best interests at heart.

    1 2 3 4 5 6 7

22. The employees of excellent libraries' reference units will understand the specific needs of their users.

    1 2 3 4 5 6 7

23. Do you have any other expectations for excellent reference services not mentioned thus far on this questionnaire?
    _____ Yes _____ No [If no, proceed to section B].

24. *Identify additional expectations you have of excellent reference services and rank how important you feel each expectation is in evaluating the quality of reference services.*

Expectations of excellent reference services

	Not at all Essential					Absolutely Essential	

a. _____   1 2 3 4 5 6 7

b. _____   1 2 3 4 5 6 7

c. _____   1 2 3 4 5 6 7

SECTION B *Directions:* Listed below are five features pertaining to libraries and the reference service they offer. We would like to know how important each of these features is to you when you evaluate a library's quality of reference service. Please allocate a total of 100 points among the five features according to how important each feature is to you—the more important a feature is to you, the more points you should allocate to it. Please ensure that the points you allocate to the five features add up to 100.

1. The appearance of the library reference unit's physical facilities, equipment, personnel, and communication materials. _____ points

2. The library's ability to perform the promised reference service dependably and accurately. _____ points

3. The library's willingness to help reference users and provide prompt reference service. _____ points

4. The knowledge and courtesy of the library's reference unit employees and their ability to convey trust and confidence. _____ points

5. The caring, individualized attention the library provides its reference users. _____ points

                                                       TOTAL points allocated   **100** points

6. Which one feature among the above five is most important to you? (please enter the feature's number) _____

7. Which feature is least important to you? _____

8. Is there anything else not included in these five factors which you find important in evaluating the quality of reference services?
    _____ Yes, please specify: _____
    _____ No

(Continued)

SECTION C *Directions:* The following set of statements relate to your feelings about the Yale University Sterling Memorial Library's reference services. For each statement, please show the extent to which you believe Sterling Memorial Library (SML) has the feature described by the statement. Circling a "1" means that you strongly disagree that Sterling Memorial Library has that feature, and circling a "7" means that you strongly agree. You may circle any of the numbers in the middle that show how strong your feelings are. There are no right or wrong answers—all we are interested in is a number that best shows your perceptions about Sterling Memorial Library's reference services.

	Strongly Disagree					Strongly Agree		No basis to judge
1. SML Reference unit has modern looking equipment.	1	2	3	4	5	6	7	0
2. SML Reference unit's physical facilities are visually appealing.	1	2	3	4	5	6	7	0
3. SML Reference unit employees are neat-appearing.	1	2	3	4	5	6	7	0
4. Materials associated with the reference services (such as pamphlets or statements) are visually appealing at SML.	1	2	3	4	5	6	7	0
5. When SML Reference unit promises to do something by a certain time, it does so.	1	2	3	4	5	6	7	0
6. When a reference user has a problem, SML shows a sincere interest in solving it.	1	2	3	4	5	6	7	0
7. SML performs reference services right the first time.	1	2	3	4	5	6	7	0
8. SML provides its reference services at the time it promises to do so.	1	2	3	4	5	6	7	0
9. SML Reference unit insists on error-free records.	1	2	3	4	5	6	7	0
10. Employees of SML tell you exactly when reference services will be performed.	1	2	3	4	5	6	7	0
11. Employees of SML give you prompt reference services.	1	2	3	4	5	6	7	0
12. Employees of SML Reference unit are always willing to help you.	1	2	3	4	5	6	7	0
13. Employees of SML Reference unit are never too busy to respond to your requests.	1	2	3	4	5	6	7	0
14. The behavior of employees of SML Reference unit instills confidence in users.	1	2	3	4	5	6	7	0
15. You feel safe in your reference transactions with SML.	1	2	3	4	5	6	7	0
16. Employees of SML Reference unit are consistently courteous with you.	1	2	3	4	5	6	7	0
17. Employees of SML Reference unit have the knowledge to answer your questions.	1	2	3	4	5	6	7	0
18. SML Reference unit gives you individual attention.	1	2	3	4	5	6	7	0
19. SML Reference unit has operating hours convenient to you.	1	2	3	4	5	6	7	0
20. SML Reference unit has employees who give you personal attention.	1	2	3	4	5	6	7	0
21. SML Reference unit has your best interests at heart.	1	2	3	4	5	6	7	0
22. Employees of SML Reference unit understand your specific needs.	1	2	3	4	5	6	7	0

SECTION D *Directions:* Please answer just a few more questions about your experiences with library services in Sterling Memorial Library.

1. Overall, how would you rate the quality of the Sterling Memorial Library's reference services?

   Extremely   **Extremely**
   Poor   **Good**
   1   2   3   4   5   6   7   8   9   10

2. Have you experienced a problem with reference services at the Sterling Memorial Library within the past year?

   _____ Yes _____ No (if no, skip to question 5)

3. Please briefly describe the problem:

4. Were you satisfied with the resolution of the problem?

   _____ Yes _____ No

5. Was the information you obtained through your most recent experience with reference services at the Sterling Memorial Library valuable to you?

   _____ Yes _____ No

6. Would you recommend the reference services to a friend?

   _____ Yes _____ No

SECTION E *Directions:* Your help will be appreciated in this final section to understand better the characteristics of the Sterling Memorial Library's reference users. Please check the categories in each question which best apply.

1. How many times have you used the reference services in SML during the past three months? _____ times

2. At how many libraries, other than Sterling Memorial Library, have you used reference services during the past two years?

   _____ none   _____ 1   _____ 2   _____ 3   _____ 4 or more

3. Your most recent use of the reference services in the Sterling Memorial Library was primarily in support of (check one);

   _____ course work   _____ teaching   _____ mix of several purposes

   _____ research   _____ current   _____ other: _____
                                  awareness

4. Which best describes your activities on the Yale campus?:

   _____ undergraduate   _____ graduate   _____ faculty
          student   student

   _____ staff   _____ other: _____

(Continued)

5. Your study or research falls within which of the following academic areas?:

Humanities and Area Studies

_____ African-American Studies	_____ History	_____ Near Eastern Lang & Civilizations
_____ American Studies	_____ History of Art	_____ Religious Studies
_____ Classics	_____ History of Med & Science	_____ Renaissance Studies
_____ Comparative Literature	_____ Italian	_____ Russian & East European Studies
_____ East Asian Languages & Lit	_____ Judaic Studies	_____ Slavic Languages & Literatures
_____ East Asian Studies	_____ Latin American Studies	_____ Spanish and Portuguese
_____ English	_____ Film Studies	_____ Linguistics
_____ Studies in the Environment	_____ French	_____ Medieval Studies
_____ Theater Studies	_____ German Studies	_____ Middle East Studies
_____ Philosophy	_____ Germanic Lang & Lit	_____ Music

Social Sciences · **Sciences** · **Professional School**

Social Sciences	Sciences	Professional School
_____ Anthropology	_____ Astronomy	_____ Art
_____ Economics	_____ Biology	_____ Architecture
_____ Ethics, Politics & Economics	_____ Chemistry	_____ Divinity
_____ International Studies	_____ Computer Science	_____ Drama
_____ Political Science	_____ Engineering (all areas)	_____ EPH
_____ Psychology	_____ Geology & Geophysics	_____ Forestry
_____ Sociology	_____ Mathematics	_____ Law
_____ Statistics	_____ Molecular Biology	_____ Medicine
_____ Women's Studies	_____ Operations Research	_____ Music
	_____ Organismal Biology	_____ Nursing
		_____ School of Management

_____ **Undeclared Undergraduate**

_____ Other: _____

6. You are: _____ Male _____ Female

7. How old are you? _____

Thank you very much for participating in this study.

Adapted from the work of A. Parasuraman, Valarie A. Zeithaml, and Leonard L. Berry by Danuta A. Nitecki. For application of the SERVQUAL instrument in libraries, readers may want to contact Danuta A. Nitecki, Associate University Librarian, Sterling Memorial Library, Yale University, P.O. Box 208240, New Haven, CT 06520-8240.

8

Listening to Customers through Focus Group Interviews

He who listens well learns well. . . . Listening should be an opportunity to learn.

—J. W. Marriott, Jr., and Kathi A. Brown[1]

Chapter 7 discussed listening to customers through surveys administered within the library or having customers visit the library, or externally by surface or electronic mail, telephone, or making visits to library customers. Surveys might even be administered in residence halls or the student union, shopping malls, or other high-traffic locations. The more the library reaches out, the less likely that customers participating in the survey will be regular or the most frequent users of the library. What incentive do noncustomers or infrequent customers have to participate? As previously noted, survey participation involves an imposition; why should the noncustomer or infrequent customer be willing to accept an imposition? Traditionally, survey cover letters have stressed the value of participation to the organization and offered respondents a summary of the findings. Such a summary is a delayed reward for participation but still will not appeal to some individuals.[2]

Key questions become: (1) Does the study need to produce findings generalizable to a population and, if so, how are those doing the research most likely to achieve an acceptable response rate—one much higher than

50 percent? and (2) From which customers do librarians want to compile findings leading to improved service performance? Options include:

Internal customers

External customers—regular users of library services (present customers)

External customers—infrequent users (present customers)

External customers—nonusers: former users (lost customers)

External customers—nonusers (*never-gained* customers)

The purpose of this chapter is to present focus group interviews as a means of studying each group and for overcoming some of the inherent weaknesses of other types of surveys. Focus group interviewing is a powerful and significant way to gather data on specific issues and problems; Figure 8.1 assesses the strengths and weaknesses of this data-collection technique.

Case Studies

Case studies are useful both for exploratory research and for descriptive and explanatory purposes. According to the congressional General Accounting Office, there are three general bases for selecting instances applicable to case studies: convenience, purpose, and probability. "Each has its function and can be used to answer certain questions. . . . [A] good case study will use a basis for instance selection that is appropriate for the question to be answered. Using the wrong basis for selecting an

FIGURE 8.1
Strengths and Weaknesses of Focus Group Interviews

Strengths	Weaknesses
Address a wide variety of issues, and anyone can participate	Limited generalizability to a large population
Provide data more quickly and cheaply than in-person interviewing	Dominating moderators inhibit discussion and may bias the discussion; they might fail to be objective
Encourage interaction among participants; therefore, the findings reflect more than the cumulated responses of individuals	Some participants may be quiet and not feel comfortable about revealing their opinions in a group setting
The comment of one individual may produce responses from others	Summarization and interpretation of open-ended responses may be difficult
Provide opportunity to clarify and probe responses, and to ask follow-up questions	
Produce data in respondents' own words	

FIGURE 8.2
Instance Selection in Case Studies

Selection Basis	When to Use and What Questions It Can Answer
Convenience	In this site selected because it was expedient for data-collection purposes, what is happening, and why?
Purpose	
Bracketing	What is happening at extremes? What explains such differences?
Best Cases	What accounts for an effective program?
Worst Cases	Why is the program not working?
Cluster	How do different types of programs compare with each other?
Representative	In instances chosen to represent important variations, what is the program like, and why?
Typical	In a typical site, what is happening and why?
Special Interest	In this particular circumstance, what is happening, and why?
Probability	What is happening in the program as a whole, and why?

Source: General Accounting Office, Program Evaluation and Methodology Division, *Case Study Evaluations,* Transfer Paper 9 (Washington, D.C.: The Office, 1990), 23.

instance is a fatal error in case study designs, as in all designs."[3] These instances suggest choices for the selection of actual participants, and focus groups may consist of individuals selected by convenience, purpose, or probability sampling.

Figure 8.2 summarizes the three instances, when to use them, and what questions they address. Purposive selection requires a justification about how the site or participants fit one of the seven categories. For example, focusing on *typical* customers raises the question: What does "typical" mean and encompass? Expediency or convenience is an option, but evaluators likely will be unable to generalize responses to a population. Probability sampling is possible in academic institutions for faculty, students, and administrators, where the population and its characteristics are known. Public libraries may lack sufficient insights into the population, except one based on customers who visit during a particular time frame, or on a group such as public school teachers. Probability sampling, in comparison to convenience selection, may be too time consuming to conduct. Clearly, libraries have choices depending on what question or questions are important to the development and maintenance of a customer service plan.

Focus Group Interviews

Case Study Selection

In focus group interviews—a type of case study application—between six and 10 people participate in an interactive group discussion on highly focused issues or problems; "the open-ended approach of focus groups allows subjects to comment, to explain, and to suggest notions quite different from any they would offer in answers to highly structured questions."[4] It is possible to base selection of participants—ones willing to donate approximately 45 to 90 minutes of their time—on either a probability or nonprobability (convenience or purposive) sample. If the library is required to produce findings generalizable to a population (e.g., present customers who are students; faculty; children under the age of 12), then the staff must select a probability sample, as noted in the preceding chapter. If the library managers do not need to make broad generalizations, they should pursue a nonprobability sample, especially if the intent is to ascertain the views of *lost* or *never-gained* customers—groups for which a population is not easily identified (or always possible to identify). Lost and never-gained customers, especially a sufficient portion, are unlikely to respond to a written or telephone survey, especially if they, a friend, or a colleague experienced unsatisfactory service.

As more libraries want to expand their customer base and penetrate the noncustomer segment of the population, convenience selection becomes more attractive. It affords an opportunity to listen to some individuals who share a certain characteristic—lost or never-gained status—without having to mount a large, time-consuming data-collection effort.

An area to probe with present customers, especially students, relates to the extent to which they expect (and the library can provide) technology and software (e.g., Internet use) that is on a par with what they have at home or can find elsewhere. This is a topic of concern to a number of librarians. The students might be selected by a nonprobability sample.

Purpose of the Interview

Library staff might use a focus group interview as a pretest for reviewing and refining the list of statements to include on a survey, such as the one highlighted in the preceding chapter. A focus group interview, however, might be the primary (perhaps only) means or a secondary means (used in conjunction with another method to reinforce or enrich the findings) of data collection. In the latter instance, participants might even be asked to complete a brief questionnaire after the session or to review a subsequent transcript of the session; researchers would thus elicit additional and quantifiable data, or receive further validation of the findings. As this example illustrates, different methods of data collection can be combined to produce a more in-depth picture. Such research is known as *triangulation* or *multimethod* research.

In another instance, customers might complete the SERVQUAL instrument (see Figures 7.2 and 7.3) or a survey of selected statements (see Figure 7.7). From among the respondents—those willing to supply their names and participate in a follow-up study—the library staff could select a subset for participation in one or more focus group interviews. The findings from a survey might shape the questions asked in focus group interviews and enable participants to clarify and expand on general findings.

When using focus group interviews as either a primary or secondary means of data collection, researchers must validate that the research presented is a balanced, realistic, and authentic reflection of participants' views and beliefs. After all, the criteria for good case study research of a qualitative nature are: trustworthiness, credibility, transferability, confirmability of the data, and consistency or dependability of the data.[5]

The Group

The mixture of participants for a focus group interview should be carefully considered so that they complement one another and can provide the library with the desired feedback. The staff should ask: Why do we want this individual in a focus group? If the library anticipates holding more than one group interview, then a second question is: Why do we want that person in this particular session? Behind the second question is the need to determine how many focus group interviews are convenient, realistic, and necessary to conduct. Will there be one? Two? More? The answer to this question depends on the amount of time that the staff have to engage in data collection, what they want to know, what they intend to do with the findings, and how far they want to generalize the findings.

Even one focus group in which the participants were selected by convenience represents a type of generalizability of findings: generalizable to the one group. The inclusion of additional groups expands the generalizability of the findings, but it merits noting that the purpose is not to show consensus within, between, and among groups; rather, it is to obtain varied and in-depth perceptions on a defined area of interest in a permissive, nonthreatening environment. Even when the moderator, near the conclusion of a focus group session, shares the findings of previous sessions, conclusions about the extent of similarity and dissimilarity across groups are tenuous. Nevertheless, they can provide additional insights as a group has more information to consider.

Another potentially difficult issue revolves around getting customers, potential or actual, to participate. Why should they accept the invitation and agree to participate? In brainstorming sessions, the staff can review rationales for attracting people and letting them know the value of their contribution and how the information obtained will be related to improving service performance. This does not mean that the library will accept all the suggestions offered.

The meeting area should be inviting, some refreshments provided, and participants given an opportunity to visit briefly and get acquainted, if they do not know one another. An informal setting may help the participants relax. Arranging the furniture so that participants face one another reinforces a positive, friendly atmosphere.

The Moderator

The moderator conducts the session, explains the purpose of the session, helps participants to feel at ease and willing to contribute, asks the questions, and maintains the constant flow of the conversation. A good moderator, however, blends into the background and lets the dialogue develop among the participants. For many libraries, it may be difficult to find an impartial moderator who can elicit the desired information and ensure that participants leave the session feeling positive about the experience and believing that they benefited personally from the discussion. In several well-conducted focus group interviews that we have witnessed, many participants thanked the moderator for being invited; they enjoyed the experience and did not regret the imposition on their time!

The moderator does not become defensive if customers criticize library policies or services. A key question is: Can someone on the staff perform this function impartially? If the answer is no, the library might draw on staff from another library, on the community, or, in the case of academic institutions where such an office exists, on institutional researchers. These individuals often know how to conduct focus group interviews, but they would need training to ensure that they understand the library's needs and the intent behind each question being asked.

Lost and Never-Gained Customers

In addition to gathering the opinions of present customers, a library may want to explore the attitudes of lost or never-gained customers, ascertaining their needs and expectations and seeing what role to play in converting them to actual customers. Given the complexity of and, more than likely, the limited time available for data collection, the groups should be limited to *either* lost customers *or* never-gained ones.

In a brainstorming session, library staff members—both professional and nonprofessional—should be able to identify a sufficient number of lost or never-gained customers to ensure enough participants for at least one focus group interview. Of course, those individuals asked to participate will be selected based on convenience. Some people will refuse to participate and others might require some persuasion.

Careful consideration must be given to the five to seven open-ended questions to be discussed (see Figure 8.3), the welcome, and the beginning of the session. The moderator (or someone else) might demonstrate or explain a document delivery or other service and then question the participants about its potential value to them. The moderator must be careful that the session does not exceed 90 minutes. (We have had participants tell us that they can only give us 30 minutes. Sixty minutes into the session they are still enjoying the interaction! Still, their time should not be abused. Remember that one purpose, albeit a secondary one, is to gain and retain their goodwill. Part of that goodwill might be to let others know about the experience and to encourage them to participate in another session at some future date.)

Other than for a brief demonstration, no library staff (except the moderator and perhaps a note-taker) should be present. The session might be taped, if the participants agree and if the library wants to pay for transcription. The moderator might take brief notes, but cannot be

FIGURE 8.3
Sample Questions for Lost and Never-Gained Customers

Lost Customers

1. What types of information do you need? Where do you turn to meet these needs?

2. What was your experience with the library?

3. Did you tell friends and colleagues about that experience? What did you say?

4. What might this library do to regain your business?

5. How can you tell whether service employees are truly interested in providing you with outstanding service? Do you think they know what customers expect?

Never-Gained Customers

1. What types of information do you need? Where do you turn to meet these needs?

2. Do you use a library? Which one? Why? When did you last use a library? For what purpose(s)?

3. What might this library do to gain your business?

---

expected to pace discussion while simultaneously recording responses. The moderator can, however, periodically recap the key points mentioned by participants to ensure that their views are represented correctly. (After the session, the moderator should develop a more complete written record of the interview.)

At the end of the session, the moderator might ask participants to identify peers who might be willing to participate in a subsequent focus group. This *snowball* technique represents an effort to go beyond the initial pool of people known to the library staff. Perhaps the original participants will be willing to let the library staff say that "'so and so' suggested your name. If you have any questions, please contact 'so and so.'"

For lost and never-gained customers, it may be important to conduct some type of follow-up (on a regular basis, at irregular intervals, or just once, say, six months later) to see if their information-seeking patterns changed, and why or why not. The typical focus group interview discussed in the literature of library and information science occurs once with no follow-up session; however, for monitoring perceptions of customer expectations about service, follow-up produces useful (comparative) insights.

Internal Customers

The literature on service quality agrees that the staff must be satisfied, trained and able to cope with customers, and empowered to resolve problems. Clearly, they must think like a customer and realize that they are customers themselves: Library staff members provide service to one another. Thus, focus group interviews should not be confined to external customers. Library staff should participate, and their participation

FIGURE 8.4
Sample Questions for Internal Customers

1. Do you see working here as a privilege? Are you proud to represent the library to its customers?

2. What image does the library project?

3. Overall, how satisfied are you with the service provided by the library?

4. How do you arrive at this sense of overall satisfaction? What aspects or dimensions of library services and operations are you basing your satisfaction on? (Examples might be staff helpfulness, convenient hours, and attractiveness of the environment.)

5. How can you tell whether or not library staff members are truly interested in providing outstanding service? Do you know what customers expect? Is there a gap between those expectations and the services actually provided? Do public service staff provide prompt answers to questions when asked, without making the customer feel like an intruder? Do you sense that the library is an impersonal organization? Do the staff treat customers with interest and respect?

6. Do you see competitors for the library? How does the library compare to them?

7. Would you recommend [name of the library or service] to others? Why or why not?

8. Do you feel comfortable telling those administratively higher than you about any problems? Is it easy to do so, or would you just not bother?

need not be confined to development of a customer pledge or survey. The questions depicted in Figure 8.4 would provide an excellent basis of discussion as the staff prepare to be more responsive to one another and to the expectations of external customers.

It may be that the library need not conduct many surveys of external customers, especially at first. Discussions among internal customers, such as new staff, provide a rich opportunity to put staff "in the shoes" of customers, anticipating expectations, and trying to resolve matters before they become problems.

Summary

Busy librarians who want to listen to customers but are unable to engage in a survey because of time and financial constraints, or who are questioning the application of a mail or telephone survey to lost or never-gained customers, might consider focus group interviewing (see Figure 8.5). Marketing researchers have used this technique most effectively to ascertain purchasing patterns of the public and subpopulations and to target products to teenagers and others. A cynical person might even suggest that many politicians decide their position on an issue based on what focus groups reveal. Clearly, the success of focus groups in other contexts suggests their usefulness to libraries wanting to listen to customers.

Surveys, focus groups, and complaint and compliment systems become ways to listen directly. Chapter 10 discusses other ways to gain insights into matters of importance to customers. Again, our intent is to identify choices from which individual libraries can select those most meaningful to them.

FIGURE 8.5
Focus Group Interviews: A Summary

Definition

Interactive group discussion on a specific topic. Not a freewheeling or unfocused discussion. Qualitative method of data collection. (Not lip-service consultation; rather, sincere listening and learning.)

Uses

1. Obtaining background for a survey; deciding on questions and response options

2. Exploring something not well understood

3. Confirming and testing a hypothesis

4. Engaging those not often asked for their opinions (e.g., lost or internal customers) to motivate them to become coproducers of service quality.

Participants

Six to 10 internal or external customers, such as students, administrators, faculty, or individuals from city government, local businesses, public schools, religious organizations, local heritage agencies, or friends of the library. They are selected through probability or nonprobability sampling, such as convenience and snowball.

Number of Groups

Depends on what staff want to know, funding, etc.

Persuading External Customers to Participate

Remember that an invitation is an imposition—you are asking a favor. Why should they accept it?

Length of Session

No longer than 90 minutes

Number of Questions

Maximum of seven

Single or Multiple Interviews

Depending on the needs of the staff, participants might or might not be invited back for follow-up group interviewing. Do not abuse the privilege of having them participate.

Atmosphere of the Session

Should be warm and inviting. Make participants feel comfortable.

Potential Problems

1. Getting enough people together who are willing to participate (donate their time)

2. Attracting a high-quality, neutral moderator

Moderator

Should be carefully selected. Not everyone can be neutral, maintain a conducive atmosphere, and be knowledgeable enough to facilitate meaningful discussion.

Transcription

Will the session be taped? Does taping affect the nature of comments? Does the moderator take selected notes, and is there a person present solely to take notes? Who is that person? Has that person been trained?

Reliability and Validity

For qualitative data collection, the issues are: confirmability, dependability, trustworthiness, and credibility. For instance, periodic summarization of the major points brought out in the discussion by the moderator; sharing of key findings among different focus groups; and later asking participants to verify copies of a written summary will help demonstrate confirmability, dependability, and trustworthiness. Also, participants might receive a demonstration of a technological application and respond to the value of what they observed; such an example seeks credibility in that participants have a common base of fact around which to respond.

Costs

Refreshments, moderator (perhaps), transcription, and any supplies or handouts

Complementary Data Collection

1. Asking participants to complete a written survey about key issues raised and to provide information about themselves

2. Sharing a written summary of the session for verification and additional comment.

NOTES

1. J. W. Marriott, Jr., and Kathi A. Brown, *The Spirit to Serve: Marriott's Way* (New York: HarperCollins, 1997), 50, 53.

2. Some researchers have used a variety of monetary and other gifts as enticements for survey completion. See, for instance, Anton J. Nederhof, "The Effects of Material Incentives in Mail Surveys: Two Studies," *Public Opinion Quarterly* 47, no. 1 (spring 1983): 103–11.

3. General Accounting Office, Program Evaluation and Methodology Division, *Case Study Evaluations*, Transfer Paper 9 (Washington, D.C.: The Office, 1990), 22.

4. Christopher K. McKenna, "Using Focus Groups to Understand Library Utilization: An Open Systems Perspective," *Journal of Management Science and Policy Analysis* 7 (summer 1990): 320.

5. General Accounting Office, *Case Study Evaluations*, 53, 76.

9

Customer-Related Indicators and Requirements

*The efficient collection of relevant statistics and their effective use
. . . [are] more important today than ever before.*

—Patricia M. Larsen[1]

Traditional library statistics and measures, whether for academic or public libraries, do not adequately describe the library's contributions or productivity. Nor do they reflect the significant changes that have occurred and continue to occur in library operations and services. Furthermore, a number of academic administrators and local government officials, under pressure to contain or reduce costs, now want proof, or at least reasonable indications, that each unit gives "value for money." The cost of higher education particularly is being scrutinized. Peter Drucker notes that "the cost of higher education has risen as fast as the cost of health care."[2] Because of the financial squeeze on middle-class families, Drucker predicts a bleak future for universities.

As resources shrink, statistical reports that emphasize budget, staff, and collection size reinforce the notion of the library as mainly a warehouse. Although rankings among peer institutions by specific types of resources might still exert some influence on academic administrators, they tend to carry little weight with local government officials. In a world of electronically delivered information, size no longer matters. A student using a computer in a dormitory room can access the same information as one sitting at a terminal in the library—and both can be using another library at the same time.

Figures showing staff workloads, such as the number of items cataloged, may raise disquieting (and enlightening) questions about productivity. The continuous improvement philosophy, now prevalent in many businesses, can easily be applied to various library processes. Shrewd administrators in academe and local government are likely to track workload statistics reported from year to year, looking for productivity increases equal to the increase in the annual budget. Alternatively, they may question why certain processes are still being done after the acquisition of new technology. Those individuals only casually acquainted with the World Wide Web may raise other questions about productivity and how people perform their work. They seem to believe that the WWW has (or is about to) become a prime source of information that will replace libraries.

Another reason that traditional statistics are no longer useful is that they do not reflect the new ways in which people gain access to information in libraries. The number and diversity of electronic resources will continue to multiply, and, as individuals become more adept at using them, that growth will have an impact on traditional measures, such as the number of reference questions posed to staff. The notion of maintaining a large number of annual journal subscriptions will become outmoded because, as more "articles" become available only online and are individually priced at reasonable cost, many people will prefer electronic delivery, even if a print article might be more appropriate for the topic. Librarians are already complaining that students prefer inferior material in electronic format to better material in the form of hard copy. As well, more libraries are subscribing to "virtual library collections" that provide access to periodical articles and other material. As these resources become available through online public access catalogs, usage statistics for the paper collection will decline while those for remote access will increase.

However, the most serious problem with traditional statistics is that they do not indicate either how well libraries serve customers or how libraries might change or improve their service. Also, except for its relationship to the operating budget, each measure is isolated from the others. Common sense indicates that not all measures are equally important, yet current statistical systems do not distinguish among measures, except to note the importance of the overall budget and its percentage increase or decrease.

We propose a more comprehensive system of indicators that fall into two different, but interrelated, areas: (1) customer-related indicators and (2) customer requirements, which focus on the internal workings and processes of the library. Customer-related indicators report on service. They are based on customer actions and expressed preferences, surely more reliable indicators than check marks on a survey purporting to measure customer satisfaction.

Libraries, like many other organizations, have surveyed customers about their satisfaction. Questions about overall satisfaction, or satisfaction with specific aspects of the service, might be "measured" on a five-point scale, ranging from "very dissatisfied" (1) through "satisfied" (3) to "very satisfied" (5). Common practice has been to interpret all responses of 3 or higher as "satisfied" and, thus, to arrive at rather elevated levels of customer satisfaction. Unrecognized bias is built in by summing responses to three categories as indicating *satisfaction* but summing responses to only two categories as indicating *dissatisfaction*. (A four-point scale that allots only one category to express dissatisfaction is even more biased.)

Research has shown that "satisfaction is an inadequate, incomplete, and maybe even inaccurate measure of customer loyalty."[3] A report from the Conference Board of Canada cites studies done for BancOne, Xerox, and AT&T Universal Card Services that indicate that scores of 3 and 4 on a five-point scale are relatively meaningless.[4] Some marketing experts have characterized these scores as a "zone of tolerance"—the difference "between customers' ideal or desired level of service and the level of service they would find minimally acceptable."[5] Figure 9.1, adapted from a chart created by Xerox, Inc., illustrates the tracking of customer responses. Customers rating satisfaction as 3 or 4 on a five-point scale are quite likely to take their business elsewhere, whereas customers who rate satisfaction as 5 tend to remain. Xerox's research characterized customers who are merely satisfied with a company or a service as being in a zone of indifference toward a continuing relationship with that company or service.[6]

FIGURE 9.1

Customer Satisfaction and Loyalty Zones

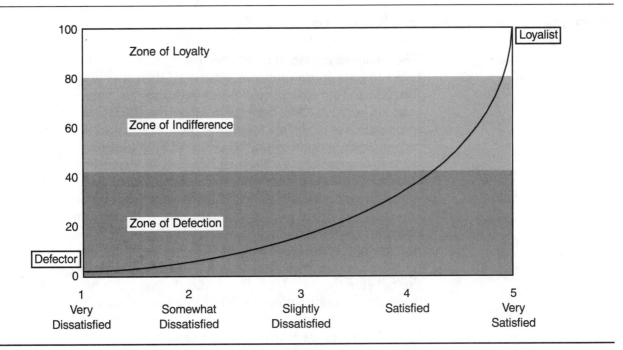

Adapted from Catharine G. Johnston, *Beyond Customer Satisfaction to Loyalty* (Ottawa, Canada: The Conference Board of Canada, 1996), 7. Reproduced with permission from The Conference Board of Canada.

Libraries might collect information about customer behaviors, thereby going beyond the collection of self-reported opinions. The customer-related indicators proposed here allow library managers to assess not only market penetration of the library among its community, but also such important things as the length and strength of customer relationships as measured by the frequency and intensity of library use. Such indicators are considered loyalty ratios.[7] They include the following:

Maintenance ratio—the number of current customers retained to the number who defect within a year

Retention ratio—the number of customers retained per dollar of investment

Amount/continuity ratio—comparison of the length and intensity of the relationship between core customers and all customers. Core customers are those who buy heavily, refer other customers, or have a long-standing relationship with a firm

Businesses rely on sales revenue to assess intensity. Libraries, on the other hand, can analyze borrowing, uses, and calls for service (e.g., reference queries, entries to the building, and access to electronic files) as surrogates for sales because they, in effect, represent sales to the library. Data reflecting customer behaviors can be obtained from those integrated automated systems that capture the information gathered. It may be possible to compare the borrower file to the circulation and use files.

Mining the Automated System

The computerization of library records gives staff a tremendous opportunity to learn more about customers and their uses in order to improve the service. Yet, as Stephen Atkins complains, "It is almost a crime how little this capacity has been utilized by the library community."[8] He places much of the blame for underutilization on vendors being "slow to recognize the potential marketability of this feature."[9] Some respondents in one survey said that their particular systems did not produce reports easily, or that those add-on packages that could produce such reports were "expensive."[10] Such attitudes are shortsighted, because the computer's abilities to count, manipulate, and perform mathematical functions can be exploited to generate an amazing amount of information useful for decision making.

Donna Mancini, director of the Nashville Public Library, describes the benefits that the DeKalb County Public Library gained from its management information system during her tenure as its director:

• Improves the management of resources

- Allows managers at all levels to monitor their particular operation
- Gives staff a holistic view of the library system and can reinforce the interrelatedness of the system despite expanding service points
- Supports the feeling that it is possible to solve problems through the study of everyday activities. Technology can be used to teach problem-solving skills.
- Improves the overall quality of data gathering. Staff understand they collect statistics for a reason—direct feedback through reports.[11]

The data provided in the computer records can be gathered easily, cheaply, and frequently. When designed to do so, the computer can monitor the pulse of many library activities. New releases of a number of automated systems have the ability to produce a variety of reports useful for managerial decision making.

Privacy Issues

Many organizations, including libraries, need certain information about individuals in order to conduct their business. Libraries, for instance, collect information about who owes fines, who has placed reserves, and how those with library cards can be contacted. Some libraries ask for social security numbers and dates of birth from people wanting cards; providing such information, however, is usually voluntary. Some libraries do not delete the identity of the two previous borrowers of an item so that, in case damage is detected, these individuals can be contacted for payment. When libraries turn over to collection agencies the names, addresses, telephone numbers, and fine amounts owed by borrowers with titles long overdue, they justify that action as necessary for the conduct of library business.

The data used for statistical reporting purposes in the customer-related indicators proposed here need not identify any individual borrower or any item borrowed. It is, however, not unusual for registration applications to state that data about cardholders may be used for administrative purposes, which would cover use in some of the indicators proposed in the following sections of this chapter.

Respecting privacy means that the people who work in the organization do not talk about customers to those not needing to know certain information for legitimate library purposes. The pharmacist does not discuss what medicines an individual takes. The bank teller who cashes a check is required to look at the person's account balance to see whether the amount can be recovered in case the check is bad; that teller does not, however, discuss the account balance with other customers (internal or external).

Tracking Trends

Most library surveys are snapshots of a situation at one particular point in time. They are seldom compared with earlier surveys, and the wording of questions may vary over time. Similarly, the current statistical reports of both academic and public libraries are essentially glimpses of the current reporting year. The data obtained from the customer-related indicators outlined here can be compared to a report card in that they give a picture of the current situation. These same data can also be tracked over a period of years to indicate whether the strength of the relationship between the library and its customers is increasing or diminishing.

Such information might give senior managers an indication that something is wrong in the system, but not specifically what has gone wrong. Gaining insight into problems that need to be addressed requires using *operational indicators*, which analyze where the system is malfunctioning. (Indicators relating to operations will be described later in this chapter.) Because of the differences in the operation of academic and public libraries, and in the needs of their customers, the sections on customer-related indicators are specific to each type.

The tables presented in this chapter are illustrative rather than prescriptive. The intent is to show how the data recommended could be categorized and presented. All data, whether daily, monthly, quarterly, or annual tallies, should be entered on whatever spreadsheet program is available. Many libraries already collect some of the data recommended in the indicators, such as number of new borrower registrations and number of visitors. If the current methods of collecting and tabulating these data are satisfactory, libraries should keep on using them. The summaries should, however, be entered into the spreadsheets for updating, tabulation, and analysis.

Capturing Virtual Visitors and Uses of Electronic Information

With the increasing use of electronic information and the existence of virtual customers, librarians need and want to collect information about electronic interactions between library resources and customers. Since 1994, representatives to the Steering Committee of Federal-State Cooperative System (FSCS) for Public Library Data have been pondering which measures related to electronic information to collect nationwide and how to collect them. Satisfactory answers, however, have been elusive. The technological challenges in gathering data are complex, as are the identification and definition of those measures to collect. Nevertheless, the concept of hits and the number of databases or gateways accessed seems to generate the most interest. Figure 9.2 offers a graphic illustration of the data-collection options presented to the FSCS Steering Committee in 1996.

FIGURE 9.2

Data Collection for Electronic Resources

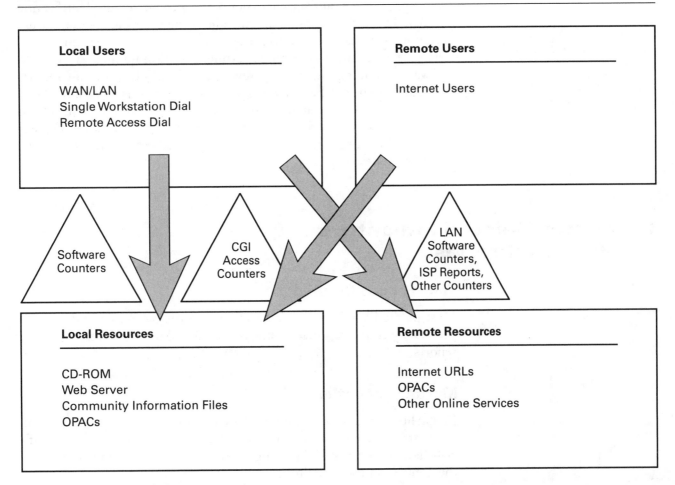

The top two boxes represent users, the bottom two boxes represent resouces. The arrows indicate user paths to resources and the triangles show the different types of data collection and where that data collection should be located.

Source: Mark Smith and Gerry Rowland, "To Boldly Go: Searching for Output Measures for Electronic Services," *Public Libraries* 36, no. 3 (May/June 1997): 171.

Mark Smith and Gerry Rowland, both former chairpersons of the Steering Committee, explain that local users—either in the library or via modem—can gain access to local or remote resources. Data about local use can be captured at either the workstation in the library or through the local area network (for customers whether inside or outside the library).[13] "Measuring local . . . use of remote resources via the Internet will require locating the data collection activity . . . either at the router level, or at the Internet Service Provider [ISP] level, if access is purchased through an ISP."[14] In essence, libraries should care only about what is used and the uses of library resources made by customers dialing in.

Because of licensing agreements with vendors, access to most newspaper and periodical indexes, and other text-based resources, via modem requires the would-be customer to key in a borrower identification number. Through that number, data about the customers and their use of resources are easy to capture. In some libraries, access to licensed materials is denied unless the borrower identification number is supplied. Software counters, common gateway interfaces (CGIs), and reports from ISPs can be used to tally hits. Because libraries use a variety of systems to support electronic resources, it is impossible to give instructions on how to obtain the information recommended in this chapter. Each library should consult its systems staff about the best way to capture the information desired.

Customer-Related Indicators for Public Libraries

Time Periods Covered

Most public libraries will want to tally records by month and then by year. Daily counts will need to be recorded and totaled for the monthly reports.

Market Penetration

Public libraries are supported on the basis of their being available to all residents of a community. Both the library management and local officials have an interest in knowing whether or not a large proportion of the population uses the library.

The indicators for market penetration presented here include registered borrowers and visitors to the library, both in-person and virtual through electronic transport. It is important for libraries to keep registration information current by annual reregistrations. Many libraries already have such a policy. Claims that registered borrowers exceed the service area's population, as can be found in the Public Library Data Service survey, invite distrust. Registration files that are years out of date need to be updated to make the following indicators useful.

The indicators proposed here need monitoring by day, month, year, or year-to-date. Many libraries already collect these data. To identify trends in market penetration, comparisons with the same point in time (e.g., the previous year, month by month, quarter by quarter, and year by year) are encouraged. Libraries with multiple outlets should keep data for each branch and then transfer branch information to a systemwide database for comparisons. (Again, many libraries already do this.)

Figures 9.3 through 9.7 illustrate some ways to format spreadsheets to record data about market penetration. Figures 9.3 and 9.4 cover daily and monthly tracking of new registrants, library visitors, and virtual visitors. Many libraries already record these data on their own forms, which negates their need for some of the tables.

FIGURE 9.3

Market Penetration Indicators:
Daily Tally of Real and Virtual Visitors and New Registrants

[Month/Year]	In-Person Visits	Virtual Visits	New Registrants
1			
2			
3			
4			
5			
...			
Totals			

FIGURE 9.4

Market Penetration Indicators:
Systemwide Report of Visitors and New Registrants

[Month/Year] Branch	In-Person Visits	Virtual Visits	New Registrants
Totals			

Registrants

New borrowers are those who have registered during the past 12 months. For them, measures might focus on the following:

- Number of new borrowers registered for the year-to-date for each outlet and for the whole system
- Number of new borrowers registered during the preceding year. If data are available by outlet for each month, so much the better for comparison. If not, the staff should use whatever data categories match those of the current year.
- Percentage of this year's new registrants to previous years. Are numbers of new registrations increasing or decreasing?

Figure 9.5 is an example of a format for making comparisons among new registrations month by month, year by year, and by each outlet as well as systemwide.

FIGURE 9.5

Market Penetration Indicator: New Registrants

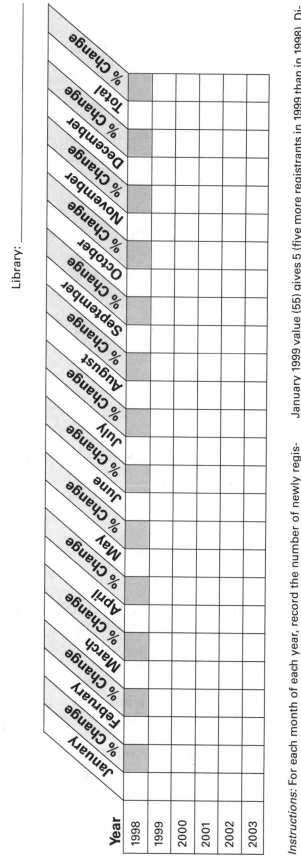

Library: _____

Instructions: For each month of each year, record the number of newly registered persons. After the first year, compute the percentage change for each month, and for the entire year. The calculation is as follows. Subtract the prior year's count from this year's count. Divide the result by the prior year's count. Multiply by 100. The result is the percentage change between the two months of the different years. Example: Suppose the January 1998 count is 50, and the January 1999 count is 55. Subtracting the January 1998 value (50) from the January 1999 value (55) gives 5 (five more registrants in 1999 than in 1998). Divide by the January 1998 count (50), giving 5/50, or 0.10. Multiply by 100, resulting in 10 percent. Even if the subtraction gives a negative number, the process is the same, but represents a decline. Suppose the January 1998 count was 55, and the January 1999 count was 50. The subtraction gives –5. Again divide by the earlier year's count (55): –5/55 = –.0909. Multiply by 100 to give 9.09 percent, a decline.

The changes in the registration rates over time will indicate how well the library is attracting new customers. If the "new customer" rate is falling off, steps should be taken to remedy this. However, though registration may be growing, the service area population may also be growing, so a further measure is needed to account for this. Population estimates can be gathered from several sources. Though the official census is taken only once every 10 years, annual estimates are usually available from state and local government agencies.

FIGURE 9.6

Proportion of Population Registered as Borrowers

Year	Population Estimate	Registered Borrowers	Percentage	Change from Prior Year
1998				
1999				
2000				
2001				
2002				
2003				

Instructions: Obtain the population and borrower registration figures for each year of interest. Divide the registration by the population and multiply by 100 to get the percentage of the population that is registered. After the first year, the extent of change from year to year will be a guide to the library's performance.

For all registrants, the staff might focus on the number and percentage of the population in the legal service area over X years of age registered as cardholders over the past five years.[15] Are the numbers increasing or decreasing out of proportion to the general change in the population? (Data about population are available from local government, the Chamber of Commerce, and other sources. Be sure to subtract the population too young to qualify as cardholders from the population total so that only those meeting borrower requirements are compared with actual cardholders.) Figure 9.6 illustrates how such data can be presented.

In-Person Visitors

The following measures apply only if the library has an automatic door counter:

- The number of visitors for the year to date. Data can be collected for each outlet and systemwide.
- The number of visitors for the previous four years and the percentage change by year for each outlet and systemwide.

A configuration similar to that of Figure 9.7 can be used for both the indicators.

Virtual Visitors

For customers who use library resources from off-site, it is possible to determine the following:

- Number of "visits" to the library's homepage for the year to date
- Number and percentage of homepage visits comparing current year with previous years

FIGURE 9.7
Library Visitors

Library: _____

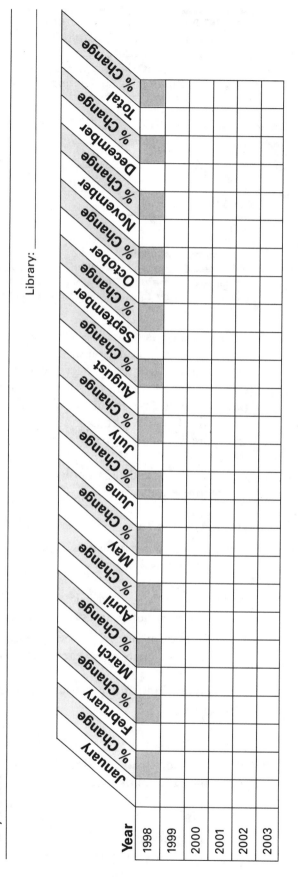

Year	January	% Change	February	% Change	March	% Change	April	% Change	May	% Change	June	% Change	July	% Change	August	% Change	September	% Change	October	% Change	November	% Change	December	% Change	Total	% Change
1998																										
1999																										
2000																										
2001																										
2002																										
2003																										

- Number of "visits" to OPAC via modem for the year to date
- Number and percentage of OPAC visits comparing current year with previous year

The data for homepage visits and the other types of visits specified here can be recorded in a format similar to that shown in Figure 9.7.

It is also possible to examine the number of hits by local and remote users to local databases by name of the database. Virtual visits via gateways to other information sources, such as the OPACs of other libraries, should also be recorded in the same manner as those described above.

Loyalty Indicators

Identifying and serving loyal customers—those who are very frequent users—is an important part of the success of any organization. It is far easier and cheaper to keep a current customer than it is to get a new one. Current customers who frequently use the library have already demonstrated their support.

Many businesses identify and reward customer loyalty. The frequent flyer programs of airlines are a conspicuous example. Libraries could adopt programs to encourage frequent use, but, at present, many of them cannot identify, much less encourage, the array of frequent use customers.

Analysis of circulation records and the use of electronic resources could produce useful information regarding those loyal customers; this is, however, infrequently done. Such data could indicate the library's holding power—both retention and the intensity of the relationship with its cardholders. Among the data that can be gathered from nearly any automated circulation system are the following:

- Number of customers who have been continuously registered as borrowers for three, five, ten, . . . n years
- Number of customers who have been continuously active borrowers for three, five, ten, . . . n years. In essence, how long has the most loyal customer used the library? With that person's consent, is the time sufficiently long to honor formally his or her years of loyalty? Figure 9.8 offers a format for recording both continuously registered and continuously active customers.
- Age and gender of cardholders in relation to the service area population. Figure 9.9 indicates the distribution of cardholders among the service area population.
- Demographic profile of loyal customers, using such data as gender, age, and ZIP code.[16] Which groups in the community are underrepresented? For example, what is the representation of teenaged boys among loyal customers? (Figure 9.10 is an example of how the data can be formatted for spreadsheet analysis. Data may be broken down to study customer patterns by library branch. As well, the figure can depict registered borrowers.)

FIGURE 9.8

Loyalty Indicators: Distribution of Customers
by Years of Continuous Registration and Activity

Years of Registration	Number of Registered Customers	Number of Active Borrowers
Less than 1		
1		
2		
3		
4		
5		
.		
.		
n		
Total		

- Demographic profile of virtual visitors, if they must supply a borrower number.[17] (System staff can offer helpful suggestions about compiling relevant data.) Figure 9.11 can be adapted to reflect such electronic customers.

- Distribution of circulation over borrowers (i.e., the number and percentage of cardholders who borrowed zero, one, two, three, . . . n items in the past year. This information, taken from the automated system, should reflect the frequency of use. Figure 9.11 is an example of the format.

Declining Loyalty?

People cease to be customers for predictable reasons, most notably moving out of the area or death. Thus, a certain percentage of customer loss (about 25 percent) is both expected and natural. This section, however, emphasizes cardholders who have not borrowed any materials during the past year. Relevant measures become the following:

- Number and percentage of cardholders to the total of registered customers who neither borrowed any items nor contacted the library electronically during the past year (see Figure 9.11).

- Number and percentage of cardholders to the total number of registered customers who have had no recorded contact with the library in each of the preceding four years. Such information, over time, can depict trends.

- Percentage of this year's number of customers with no recorded contact to that for the previous year. Is the number of persons increasing, decreasing, or remaining constant? (Figure 9.6 can be adapted for this type of data.)

FIGURE 9.9

Market Penetration by Age and Gender

| Age | Number of Registered Cardholders | | Service Area Population | | Percent Served by Library | |
	Male	Female	Male	Female	Male	Female
Under 10						
11–15						
16–21						
22–35						
36–50						
51–65						
66+						
Undetermined						
Total						

FIGURE 9.10

Profile of Active Customers by Age, Gender, and ZIP Code*

Age	ZIP: ___ Male	Female	ZIP: ___ Male	Female	ZIP: ___ Male	Female	ZIP: ___ Male	Female	ZIP: ___ Male	Female	Totals Male	Female
Under 10												
11–15												
16–21												
22–35												
36–50												
51–65												
66+												
Undetermined												
Total												

*Figure 9.10 can also be used to analyze registered borrowers and virtual borrowers when the card number is required for access.

FIGURE 9.11

Distribution of Circulation by Cardholders

Year	0 Items Number	Percent	1–5 Items Number	Percent	6–10 Items Number	Percent	11–25 Items Number	Percent	26–50 Items Number	Percent	51–100 Items Number	Percent	100+ Items Number	Percent
1998														
1999														
2000														
2001														
2002														
2003														

It is also possible to create a demographic profile of the cardholders who have no recorded contact with the library during the past year, using such data as gender, age, and ZIP code. Data might be subdivided to study use patterns by branch. (Figure 9.10 might be adapted for recording the profile.)

Comparisons of distributions and percentages, over a few years, will provide valuable insights into the library's customer base and the ability of the library to retain customers over time; retention is vital for organizational health and success. Emerging patterns regarding heavy-use, lost, and long-time customers can indicate areas for target marketing of library services. Such an identification of customers could allow the library to establish focus groups (see Chapter 8). With heavy-use customers, library staff can use focus groups to discuss what they like about the service and what improvements they would like. Groups of former customers might disclose their reasons for leaving the library and suggest changes that might result in regaining them as customers. The identification of long-time loyal customers is an opportunity to let them know that the library appreciates their patronage. Formal appreciation of long-time customers is also an excellent public relations opportunity for the library.

Information about Customer Preferences

Curiously, few libraries, with the notable exception of the Baltimore County Public Library, have made any serious analysis of customers' reading preferences by studying circulation patterns to see what circulates and what remains on the shelves. It is not our intent to enter the long-standing controversy over *meeting the demand* versus *trying to uplift preferences*. Nevertheless, two questions raised by Charlie Robinson, long-time director of the Baltimore County Public Library, seem pertinent:

- Should I buy what they don't want?
- Or, should I buy what they should want?[18]

The information recommended to be gathered about the collection is intended to make library managers more aware of customer preferences and how those preferences change over time. Data for the types of indicators listed here can be compiled monthly and cumulated annually. Data should be reported by branch for in-depth analysis.

Using data available from the OPAC, the staff might examine the following:

- Distribution of circulations by type of material; for example, video, adult fiction, adult nonfiction, picture books, juvenile nonfiction, and audio (including talking books). (Figure 9.12 is an example.) What is the ratio of circulations to holdings for these types of material? For example, assume that adult fiction represents 62 percent of circulations but only 50 percent of holdings.

FIGURE 9.12

Customer Preferences by Type of Material

Type of Material	Holdings	Circulation	Percent of Holdings	Percent of Circulation
Adult fiction				
Adult nonfiction				
Audio books				
Audio music				
Adult video				
Large print				
Young adult				
Maps				
Music scores				
Juvenile fiction				
Juvenile nonfiction				
Juvenile videos				
Periodicals				

Should the library consider acquiring more adult fiction or more talking books?

- Which areas of the collection are used most intensely? For example, what is the percentage of videos borrowed to videos owned? This is also called the *turnover rate*.
- Distribution of circulations for this year by call number groupings representing specific subjects or time periods. Generally, this means groupings by the tens for Dewey systems. The call number groupings can be expanded or contracted based on collection size (e.g., medicine titles by topic or U.S. history by time period).
- Distribution by the same call number groupings of items not circulating for two years. Data for the call number distributions can be formatted as shown in Figure 9.13.

Customer-Related Indicators for Academic Libraries

Market Penetration

One way to demonstrate that the library adds value to the educational program is to assess whether faculty require or encourage students to use the library for completing course assignments. Relating library use

FIGURE 9.13
Customer Preferences versus Holdings by Dewey Classification

Period covered: _____   Library: _____

Dewey Class	Holdings	Circulation	Percent of Holdings	Number Uncirculated
000–099				
100–199				
200–299				
300–319 Social Science				
320–329 Politics				
330–339 Economics				
340–349 Law				
350–359 Public Admin.				
360–369 Social Services				
370–379 Education				
380–389 Commerce				
390–399 Folklore				
400–499				
500–599				
600–699				
700–799				
800–899				
900–999				
Biography				
Totals				

The figure shows the 300s broken out as an example of a class that might be usefully subdivided to give more detailed information.

(and type of use) to courses gives the library an opportunity to discuss its contributions or value to the academic program. Although the indicators described here capture only a part of the usage stimulated by course work, such information and trend data about library involvement become more important for library managers as course packets and WWW pages replace libraries as the principal means of obtaining materials for many undergraduate courses.

Many of the indicators specify data collection for the year. The year's beginning should coincide with the start of classes in the fall and end at the conclusion of the last sessions before the start of a new academic year. Examples of indicators include the following:

- Number of courses offered by department (the course database from the Registrar can be imported for this compilation) compared with the number of courses utilizing the reserve service in each department. For example, how many courses from the economics department used the reserve service during the past year? Reserves can be paper or electronic, or local or remote. Summer courses should be included. (Figure 9.14 illustrates a spreadsheet format for these data.)
- Percentage of courses using reserve service to all courses taught by that department (see last column of Figure 9.14).
- Distribution of all presentations to classes made by library staff arranged by department in relation to all courses taught by each department. For example, how many presentations were made to classes in the history department, compared to all history courses taught during the academic year? Bibliographic instruction classes held in conjunction with courses should be counted here. Classes on library use and information literacy taught by library staff should not be counted in this section. (Figure 9.15 shows how these data can be presented.)
- What percentage of courses in each department used reserve collections and invited presentations by library staff over the past five years? If these data are not available, the staff should start from the point at which the data are available (see Figure 9.16). Which departments make heavy use of reserves and presentations? Which departments made little use of these services? The staff might rank departments by use of reserves and presentations in order to gain a clearer picture of how departments use the library for course work.

FIGURE 9.14

Market Penetration Indicator:
Use of Reserve Collection by Academic Department

Department	Number of Courses Offered	Number of Courses with Library Reserves	Percent of Courses with Library Reserves
English			
French			
Economics			
Math			
Physics			
Psychology			
Chemistry			
Totals			

Customer-Related Indicators and Requirements

FIGURE 9.15

Market Penetration Indicator: Course Presentations Given,
by Academic Department

Department	Number of Courses Offered	Number of Courses with Presentations	Percent of Courses with Presentations
English			
French			
Economics			
Math			
Physics			
Psychology			
Chemistry			
Totals			

FIGURE 9.16

Market Penetration Indicators: Percentage of Courses
Utilizing Reserves and Presentations, by Department

Departments	Percent Utilizing Reserves	Percent Utilizing Presentations
English		
French		
Economics		
Math		
Physics		
Psychology		
Chemistry		

For in-person library visitors, the staff might track, from the automatic door counter, the following:

- Number of visitors, for the year to date, for each departmental library as well as systemwide (see Figures 9.3 and 9.4)
- Number of visitors for the previous five years (see Figure 9.7)

Turning to virtual visitors, the staff might determine the following:

- Number of "visits" to the library's homepage for the year to date (see Figures 9.3 and 9.4)
- Number and percentage of homepage visits comparing the current year with previous years

- Number of "visits" to OPAC via modem for the year to date
- Number and percentage of OPAC visits comparing the current year with the previous year

The data for homepage visits and the other types of visits specified here can be recorded in a format similar to that shown in Figure 9.7.

The staff might also monitor:

- Database hits by local and remote users by name of the database
- Virtual visits via gateways to other information sources, such as the OPACs of other libraries

The data should be recorded in the same manner as those described above.

Loyalty Indicators

Because graduates leave and new students enroll at regular intervals, academic library managers may not have given much thought or attention to the retention of student customers. Most students are perceived as being in flux, as they move through the system, so to speak. This characterization overlooks, however, the importance of turning first-year students into customers for their remaining years on campus, and the value of building loyalty beyond graduation. Students tell one another about their experiences, both positive and negative, in selecting courses, dealing with faculty, using the library, eating in campus facilities, and so forth.

Faculty turnover is much lower than that of students, and faculty can be customers of high value in that the types of assignments they set strongly influence student use of the library. Examples of loyalty indicators include:

- The distribution of all recorded circulations by the type of borrower (i.e., the number and percentage of customers who borrowed 0, 1, 2, 3, . . . n items in the past academic year). As a base, staff might use the number of individuals from the campus community who are eligible to borrow. This may include support staff and other workers. Community borrowers can be excluded. (Figure 9.17 shows the format.)
- Comparison of data for the current year on these indicators with data for previous years (see Figure 9.18). Is the number of persons not using their cards increasing, decreasing, or remaining constant? Which groups in the campus community are consistently underrepresented as library borrowers? Is undergraduate borrowing increasing, or not?
- Demographic profile of faculty and graduate student borrowers by departments. What is the number of faculty departmental borrowers in relation to the number of faculty in each department?

FIGURE 9.17

Loyalty Measure: Number of Items Borrowed by Customer Status

Year: _____

Borrower Status	Number Eligible	0 Items		1–5 Items		6–10 Items		11–25 Items		26–50 Items		51–100 Items		101+ Items	
		Number	%	Number	%	Number	%	Number	%	Number	%	Number	%	Number	%
Lower Division															
Upper Division															
Graduate															
Faculty															
Staff															
Other															

Customer-Related Indicators and Requirements

FIGURE 9.18

Loyalty Measure: Overall Borrowing Trends by Type of Borrower

Type of Borrower	Number	Percent of Borrowing Each Year					
		1998	1999	2000	2001	2002	2003
Lower Division	0						
	1–5						
	6–10						
	11–25						
	26–50						
	51–100						
	101+						
Group Total							
Upper Division	0						
	1–5						
	6–10						
	11–25						
	26–50						
	51–100						
	101+						
Group Total							
Graduate Students	0						
	1–5						
	6–10						
	11–25						
	26–50						
	51–100						
	101+						
Group Total							
Faculty	0						
	1–5						
	6–10						
	11–25						
	26–50						
	51–100						
	101+						
Group Total							
Staff	0						
	1–5						
	6–10						
	11–25						
	26–50						
	51–100						
	101+						
Group Total							
Other	0						
	1–5						
	6–10						
	11–25						
	26–50						
	51–100						
	101+						
Group Total							

What is the ratio of graduate student borrowers to the number enrolled in each department? Figures 9.19 (current year) and 9.20 (comparisons over several years) show faculty distributions. These figures can be adapted for graduate student comparisons.

- Profile of virtual visitors, if they are required to supply a borrower number (see Figure 9.19).

Comparisons of distributions and percentages, over a few years, will provide valuable insights into the customer base. (Any such comparisons should not, however, assume that all departments and faculty have a similar level of need for library use.) Noncustomers will be identified, and, perhaps, their reasons for not using the library can be addressed. Knowing faculty usage by department allows library staff to discuss library–faculty cooperation more knowledgeably and to elicit suggestions for changes from faculty that might increase their usage and/or that of their students.

Information about Customer Preferences

The people who actually borrow from the library are the most useful source of information on borrower preferences. Although their preferences may shift over time, they are unlikely to change radically unless the academic program itself is radically transformed.

It is interesting to note that, of the 79 members of the Association of Research Libraries that responded to Dennis Carrigan's survey, only 34 used their automated system for any collection development decisions.[19] Amazingly, only three of these libraries used the data to adjust approval plans.

Libraries that have equated course numbers or departments with library classification numbers should analyze customer preferences for using material. Thus, they can show which courses or departments ostensibly use which areas of the collection. Libraries that have not connected courses and classification numbers might use one of the following methods:

- Track circulations in relation to holdings using the subjects specified in the major approval plan. This will produce gross information at the beginning, but the procedure can be refined with experience gained over time.
- Libraries that have implemented the Research Libraries Group (RLG) Conspectus might track circulations and holdings in relation to the levels desired when the Conspectus was implemented. For example, if the library specified a level four for particular subjects, it might examine how circulations for those subjects rated in comparison with subjects receiving other ratings.
- Compare circulation patterns, over time, to holdings. Figures 9.12 and 9.13 could be adapted for such an analysis.

FIGURE 9.19

Loyalty Measure: Number of Items Borrowed by Faculty, by Department

Department	Number of Faculty	0 Items		1–5 Items		6–10 Items		11–25 Items		26–50 Items		51–100 Items		101+ Items	
		Number	%	Number	%	Number	%	Number	%	Number	%	Number	%	Number	%
English															
French															
Economics															
Math															
Physics															
Psychology															
Chemistry															
Totals															

Year: _____

FIGURE 9.20

Loyalty Measure: Faculty Borrowing Trends, by Academic Department

Department	Number	Percent Borrowing by Year					
		1998	1999	2000	2001	2002	2003
English	0						
	1–5						
	6–10						
	11–25						
	26–50						
	51–100						
	101+						
Group Total							
French	0						
	1–5						
	6–10						
	11–25						
	26–50						
	51–100						
	101+						
Group Total							
Economics	0						
	1–5						
	6–10						
	11–25						
	26–50						
	51–100						
	101+						
Group Total							
Math	0						
	1–5						
	6–10						
	11–25						
	26–50						
	51–100						
	101+						
Group Total							
Physics	0						
	1–5						
	6–10						
	11–25						
	26–50						
	51–100						
	101+						
Group Total							

- Libraries can determine which databases receive the most use. If the databases tend to be full text, the libraries should investigate more access to such resources. If customers prefer periodical indexes, more of the titles indexed might be acquired, in print or electronic form.

Interpretation

Statistics, measures, and indicators are only as good as the use made of them. Two obvious uses are making comparisons and trend analysis. The most basic comparisons are over time, and they relate either this month's data with those of the previous month, or this month's data with those of the same month in the preceding year. If growth is important, the percentage of increase or decrease from the period being compared to the present is of interest, but it is not necessarily important if the time period analyzed is too short for meaningful interpretation. Public libraries often make comparisons among branches, despite the fact that the branches are not equivalent in resources, demographics, or size.

Comparisons of the types of materials circulating in each branch are of interest, but more interesting is a comparison among the demographics of the borrowers by gender, ZIP codes, intensity of borrowing, and so forth. Such comparisons produce new insights into the customer base and preferences, as do comparisons between classifications of materials borrowed and borrower demographics and intensity.

Academic libraries should look at their relationships to the various departments on campus in terms of the types of materials circulated, the proportion of faculty and graduate students actually borrowing materials, and the involvement of the library in the academic programs of departments. Of course, not every library use is included in these indicators. We have, however, tried to concentrate on the information about customers and how they use the library. Over time, and with better automated systems, more and better information about customers and their interactions with the library can be collected.

Customer Requirements for Both Academic and Public Libraries

Process measures, referred to by Catharine Johnston, relate to work units completed. For example, traditional statistics include the number of items purchased or cataloged, questions answered, and so forth. Productivity has long been a measure of performance, but productivity merely in terms of the number of units processed is not of much interest to customers. They have other standards by which to measure the quality of an organization's service.

In a book dealing with evaluating service quality, it is tempting to make a long list of items to be assessed and methods to assess them. Our earlier book, *Service Quality for Academic Libraries*, contains such lists for guidance about what service elements to assess and how to assess them.[23] A number of these relate to the list of statements presented in Figure 7.5. This section discusses service elements that customers of almost any service expect.

Most people have a lot of experience as customers and, as a result, hold some rather definite ideas about how service organizations should treat them. Some service elements cut across all types of service organizations, although the details differ from organization to organization. Regarding safety, for instance, expectations for an amusement park are rather different from those for a bank. Yet, customers expect both organizations to protect them.

Although most people might prioritize service elements differently depending on the service and organization used as well as on their particular needs, they would all agree about the importance of service quality and being satisfied with the service and its delivery. We refer to these attributes as *customer requirements*. Requirements important to customers, including internal ones, should replace process measures as indicators of performance. Library managers have some control and some power to change operations that affect the quality of the requirements proposed here. A variety of service organizations, ranging from appliance repair shops to zoos, recognize the importance of these requirements. Let us see how they might apply to libraries.

Acceptable Physical Facility

Just as there are different standards of housekeeping, any group has different levels of acceptability. *Acceptability*, as used here, means that, for most customers, satisfaction focuses on personal safety, the safety of their belongings, physical comfort in terms of temperature and noise, and the cleanliness of the facility. These are all factors over which the library has some control. Safety concerns will drive customers away faster than any other problem, as few people will place themselves or their possessions in jeopardy to use the library.

The library might establish a safety log to record incidents and reports from customers and staff. These can then be analyzed for ways to reduce problems.

Although noise tolerance varies among any group of customers, the degree of tolerance can be a significant factor in whether or not customers continue to use the facility. A survey taken at a university library in Wales found that noise problems were at the top of the list of customer complaints.[24] The level of background noise annoyed 34.1 percent of customers, while 33.7 percent were dissatisfied with the lack of control over noisy customers.

Concerns about cleanliness, or at least the appearance of cleanliness, are growing in importance as the media report more stories about bacteria and viruses identified as intractable to antibiotics. Even though janitorial services may be provided by another unit, the library has to monitor the acceptability of custodians' work, and also take responsibility for the cleanliness of its own equipment, such as OPAC keyboards and screens—items too often neglected.

Timeliness

Timeliness encompasses on-time delivery, short cycle times, and speedy handling of problems. Basically, timeliness means that what customers want is available when or soon after they request it. From retail establishments, customers expect fresh food, current news, and the latest fashions, just as they want the latest books, videos, and journal issues from the library. When customers make a request, pose a reference question, or file a complaint, they appreciate a quick response.

Timeliness is affected by:

- Process routines that are either streamlined or cumbersome
- Due dates, or the lack of them, for the completion of tasks
- Anticipating or ignoring customer requests based on past behaviors

Delays can be predicted when imbalances occur in a unit that produces work on which other units depend. Such imbalances can be caused by lack of staff, work overloads, or failure to smooth out predictable peaks and valleys in work flow.

Convenience

Convenience relates to hours, locations, and amenities, and to such questions as:

- Is the library open to accommodate people who work different shifts?
- Is the library open on weekends?
- Are service desks staffed so that people can obtain help?
- Are public restrooms, drinking fountains, and places to eat available, or must customers leave the building for these amenities?

Convenience also means saving customers' time. Saving readers' time is also one of Ranganathan's five principles of library science. Saving time means making the system so transparent that customers new to libraries can figure out what to do with minimal frustration.

Accuracy

Accuracy, or doing things right the first time, is much more important than most managers realize. Things done incorrectly make the organization look inept and cause customer frustration and anger. A study of *Fortune* 1000 executives indicated that accuracy was the most important factor in determining service quality; speed of response was a close second.[25]

Accuracy in the library means that:

- Items returned are discharged properly so that customers are not charged fines
- Fines paid are credited
- Materials are properly shelved the first time
- Shelves are regularly read for misplaced and hidden books
- Answers to reference questions are correct and complete, which means the library must ensure that information about current sit-

uations is kept up to date. Staff must remember that information contained in any source can become outdated.

Reliability and Dependability

Reliability and dependability mean that the organization provides what it purports to offer. Customers expect to be able to get a can of peaches in the supermarket, cough syrup in the drugstore, and bedrooms at the hotel. They also expect to get materials and answers to reference questions at the library. When an organization offers a new service, customers expect to be able to obtain it. These are not unreasonable expectations because they relate to the mission of the organization.

Federal Express has made reliability the cornerstone of its business. The company's 1997 advertising campaign featured an enlarged replica of a dictionary page containing the words from *reinforce* to *reliction*. The word *reliable* was boldly circled in red. Only by reading the tiny type at the lower left of the page does one learn that Federal Express is the advertiser. Federal Express tracks its reliability on a daily basis. That would be difficult for a library, but some efforts should be made to test reliability; otherwise, how can managers know if the mission is being fulfilled? Reliability is the basis for the reputation of many libraries.

Competent, Professional, and Knowledgeable Staff

Competent, professional, and *knowledgeable* are terms that apply to the ability of the staff to satisfy customers' information inquiries. Tests of reference accuracy from the early 1970s to the present have reaffirmed that customers are quite likely to be given incorrect answers or have their questions turned away as not answerable. Despite a rather low percentage of accuracy in answering questions, many libraries, both academic and public, on the grounds of economy, regularly staff reference desks, especially on evenings and weekends, with students and library assistants.

In an effort to establish standards for reference personnel, three librarians at Texas A&M University have developed lists of baseline competencies for the humanities, science, and the social sciences.[26] Anyone who cannot demonstrate knowledge of the sources in these lists is not considered qualified to work reference without supervision.

Courtesy

Customer interactions with staff in any service organization are crucial for producing repeat business. The professional literature is replete with articles describing both wonderful and woeful examples of such interactions, and indicating that many staff decide individually what levels of service or courtesy they will extend. By establishing standards of observable behaviors for staff, the library can make explicit what behaviors are expected. In January 1996, the Reference and Adult Services Division (now the Reference and User Services Association) Board of Directors approved a document titled, "Guidelines for Behavioral Performance of Reference and Information Services Professionals."[27] The guidelines offer excellent examples of desired behaviors designed to produce service of high quality. Any library seriously interested in achieving, maintaining, and monitoring the quality of public service should implement these guidelines.

Librarians are customers every day in various service organizations. They have clear ideas about what constitutes quality service and how they want to be treated. Customers in the library have the same ideas and want the same treatment.

Summary

The indicators and customer requirements presented here offer insights into and knowledge about the library's customer base and its reputation among the library's service community. Knowledge of who the customers are and the kinds of materials they prefer allows the staff to base service on evidence rather than on opinions, beliefs, or hopes. The evidence may or may not be pleasing, but, at the least, it provides a foundation on which to build, especially as it indicates segments of the population that could be targets of marketing.

These indicators allow us to think about service quality or library goodness in a different way. Resources no longer constitute the highest criterion of quality, nor is productivity of staff an independent standard. Instead, quality and goodness are understood as abstractions that exist in the minds of the people who interact with the library and react based on their experiences. We hope that data obtained from monitoring and analyzing these interactions will assist librarians to adjust service priorities to better meet customer expectations.

Some will resist these indicators for philosophical reasons or because of procedural difficulties in implementing them. We recognize that tradition is honored and that change is both difficult and usually slow. Yet, the information environment is experiencing rapid and unexpected changes—changes beyond the control of any library or the profession at large. If libraries fail to retain, maintain, and expand the customer base, they are likely to be in trouble. Getting and keeping customers is what it is all about, and all the platitudes about service, education, or imparting of knowledge will not change the need for customers.

NOTES

1. Patricia M. Larsen, "Mining Your Automated System for Better Management," *Library Administration & Management* 10, no. 1 (winter 1996): 10.
2. Robert Lenzer and Stephen S. Johnson, "Seeing Things as They Really Are: An Interview with Peter Drucker," *Forbes* 159 (March 10, 1997): 127.
3. Catharine G. Johnston, *Beyond Customer Satisfaction to Loyalty* (Ottawa: The Conference Board of Canada, 1996), 20.
4. Ibid., 20–21.

5. Benjamin Schneider and David E. Bowen, *Winning the Service Game* (Boston: Harvard Business School Press, 1995), 262.

6. Johnston, *Beyond Customer Satisfaction*, 6.

7. Ibid., 21–22.

8. Stephen Atkins, "Mining Automated Systems for Collection Management," *Library Administration & Management* 10, no. 1 (winter 1996): 16.

9. Ibid.

10. Dennis P. Carrigan, "Data-Guided Collection Development: A Promise Unfulfilled," *College & Research Libraries* 57, no. 5 (September 1996): 432.

11. Donna D. Mancini, "Mining Your Automated System for Systemwide Decision Making," *Library Administration & Management* 10, no. 1 (winter 1996): 14–15.

12. Ruth Alston, "Performance Indicators in Bromley—Purpose and Practice," *Library Management* 16, no. 1 (1995): 27.

13. Mark Smith and Gerry Rowland, "To Boldly Go: Searching for Output Measures for Electronic Services," *Public Libraries* 36, no. 3 (May/June 1997): 170.

14. Ibid.

15. The Public Library Data Service's statistical reports capture information on population and use age five and under as the cutoff.

16. Given the availability of geographic information systems (GISs) and numerous geo-coded datasets, it is possible to create demographic profiles of a community and to insert library data as additional components. Naturally, libraries would have to protect the privacy rights of individuals. For a background on GISs, see the special issues in the *Journal of Academic Librarianship* 21, no. 4 (July 1995) and 23, no. 6 (November 1997).

17. Ibid. See also John Carlo Bertot, Charles R. McClure, William E. Moen, and Jeffrey Rubin, "Web Usage Statistics: Measurement Issues and Analytical Techniques," *Government Information Quarterly* 14, no. 4 (1997): 373–95.

18. Baltimore County Public Library's Blue Ribbon Committee, *Give 'Em What They Want! Managing the Public's Library* (Chicago: American Library Association, 1992), 3.

19. Carrigan, "Data-Guided Collection Development," 432.

20. Alston, "Performance Indicators in Bromley," 28.

21. Johnston, *Beyond Customer Satisfaction*, 22.

22. Jack Dart, "Professional Service Quality: The Practice of the Professional?" *Journal of Customer Service in Marketing and Management* 2, no. 2 (1996): 22.

23. Peter Hernon and Ellen Altman, *Service Quality in Academic Libraries* (Norwood, N.J.: Ablex, 1996).

24. Annette Davies and Ian Kirkpatrick, "To Measure Service: Ask the Library User," *Library Association Record* 96, no. 2 (February 1994): 89.

25. Harry V. Roberts and Bernard E. Sergesketter, *Quality Is Personal: A Foundation for Total Quality Management* (New York: Free Press, 1992), 18.

26. Candace R. Benefiel, Jeannie P. Miller, and Diana Ramirez, "Baseline Subject Competencies for the Academic Reference Desk," *Reference Services Review* 25, no. 1 (spring 1997): 83–93.

27. Reference and Adult Services Division, Ad Hoc Committee on Behavioral Guidelines for Reference and Information Services, "Guidelines for Behavioral Performance of Reference and Information Services Professionals," *RQ* 36, no. 2 (winter 1996): 200–203.

10

Satisfaction and Service Quality: Separate but Intertwined

[C]ustomer satisfaction is not a passing fad.

—Michael D. Johnson[1]

Opinion polls, such as those conducted by telephone, according to Ann M. Turner, measure "library support with a tool that elected officials recognize. And [polls] also count the one thing they know best of all: votes."[2] Support, however, is a complex concept that includes satisfaction and the various questions raised in Chapter 4.

An academic institution or local government might distribute a questionnaire to ascertain the extent of satisfaction with a number of different services. One or two questions might be about the library and, as is often the case, respondents might give the library a high rating, especially in comparison to other services offered by the institution or local government. In the case of the public library in Wellington, New Zealand, the public has, over the years, rated the library more positively than other government agencies. Nevertheless, this did not stop the local government from believing that the Internet comprised a virtual library and, consequently, drastically reducing the level of public library services and the number of staff members.

Frequently, a satisfaction question is part of a customer survey that the local government requires the library to do periodically. High levels of overall satisfaction are usually considered good and a positive reflection on the library. Yet, the councilors in one city had a rather surprising reaction to a 95 percent satisfaction response. They decided that a lower percentage—perhaps something above 75 percent—would be quite acceptable, and cut the library's budget accordingly.

A college or university president, in an informal session, might ask students about their educational experience and be told that they are satisfied with library collections and services. That president would be concerned only if the students mentioned a problem. A problem might occur when parents or others question the accessibility of so-called pornography from the library's Internet terminals, and complain to central administration.

As the preceding examples indicate, the polling of satisfaction might be very general and not very revealing. Imagine, however, that a local television station, one night, runs one of its call-in surveys. The commentator asks, "Are you satisfied with the public library? If so, call this number. If not, call this other number." Either way, the phone company collects 65 cents per call, and the station reports to city officials the results of the survey. A negative response might be embarrassing for the library but it reveals little about specific problems or even who the respondents are. To what extent do they represent the taxpayers or others living in the community?

As an alternative to a general survey about city services, or those of an academic institution, the staff might want to probe customer satisfaction with library collections and services. The survey questions might ask about expectations, thereby equating expectations with satisfaction. In fact, determining expectations and comparing the perceptions about those expectations to any gap with the actual services delivered comprises service quality, not satisfaction. Complicating matters more, libraries might ascertain the percentage of satisfaction with various services (e.g., interlibrary loan service, reference desk service, and dial-in to the library's homepage) and compute various comparisons. Library A achieves a 57 percent rating on reference desk service, whereas Library B has a 72 percent rating and Library C has a 74 percent rating. What do these statistics, when compared, indicate?

Another library might produce a laundry list of services and ask customers to rate their level of satisfaction with each service, or that library might concentrate on a specific service and obtain a rating of satisfaction. The results might be translated into percentages that indicate, for instance, the number of respondents expressing any degree of satisfaction, or the ratio of satisfied to dissatisfied customers.

As these examples indicate, there is some confusion about the concept of satisfaction, and the results obtained may not be meaningful for library planning and decision making. All librarians can hope for is that the library comes out better—or at least no worse—than other city or academic institution services; and achieves, overall, a positive rating. The purpose of this chapter is to clarify the differences and interrelationships between service quality and satisfaction, and include ways that librarians can assess customer satisfaction for the purposes of planning and informed decision making.

Rachel Applegate offers an important reminder:

> Many studies that have used the term satisfaction did not attach it to a measurement of patron perception. Instead, it was often applied to a professional evaluation of the performance of an information system: a request, rather than a requestor, is "satisfied" with a match between a query and an answer.[3]

The focus of this chapter is on satisfaction as a reflection of the "customer's mind," but also as a driving force for "customer retention and future choice" about the use of a product, a service, or an organization.[4]

What Is Satisfaction?

The word *satisfaction* is derived from the Latin *satis* (enough) and *facere* (to do or make).[5] As Roland T. Rust and Richard L. Oliver explain, "satiation," a related word, "loosely means 'enough' or 'enough to excess.' These terms illustrate the point that satisfaction implies a filling or fulfillment. Thus, consumer satisfaction can be viewed as the consumer's fulfillment response."[6] Consumer researchers writing in the late 1980s and the 1990s "have moved away from the *literal* meaning of fulfillment or satisfaction and now pursue this concept as the consumer experiences and describes it."[7]

The general literature on customer services suggests that perceptions about service quality emerge in a fashion closely related to the same disconfirmation paradigm traditionally used in satisfaction research.[8] A consensus apparent in the literature, however, is that service quality and satisfaction are distinct constructs. The distinction centers on the view that service quality is a long-run overall evaluation, whereas satisfaction represents a more short-term, transaction-specific measure. Jagdip Singh, writing about patient care, defines satisfaction as a post-purchase phenomenon reflecting how much a patient likes or dislikes a service after experiencing it.[9] As noted in Chapter 1, Applegate defines "patron satisfaction . . . as a personal, emotional reaction to a library service or product."[10] Satisfaction with service delivery may have surprise, contentment, and pleasure dimensions.

Because satisfaction contains multiple facets and because there are many ways to judge it, Mary Jo Bitner and Amy R. Hubbert propose two perspectives for viewing satisfaction that are relevant to library services. The first is *service encounter satisfaction*—customer satisfaction or dissatisfaction with a specific service encounter—and the second is *overall service satisfaction*—customer satisfaction or dissatisfaction with an organization based on multiple encounters or experiences.[11] As discussed in the next section, perusal of various satisfaction surveys from the retail trade and hotel industries, and from libraries in the United States and elsewhere, reveals that *attribute satisfaction*, which examines views toward staff and the information provided, might be a subset of either service encounter or overall service satisfaction.

Figure 10.1, adapted from the work of Bitner and Hubbert, illustrates items indicative of service encounter satisfaction and overall service satisfaction. For service encounter satisfaction, customers reflect on a particular incident, and their satisfaction might be measured using a seven-point scale indicating that: (1) the service experience ranged from delightful to terrible, (2) they were satisfied with the service, (3) they were satisfied with the decision to use the service, (4) they would do the same thing again, (5) it was a wise decision to use the service, (6) they feel bad about the decision, and (7) they were dissatisfied or not happy about having used the service organization.

With overall service satisfaction, customers are asked to "step back" from the one encounter and to think about *all experiences* with that specific service provider.[12] Using a five-point scale this time, satisfaction might be gauged in terms of overall satisfaction (not limited to the one library or service provider), their level of dissatisfaction (with the one library), comparison satisfaction (compared with other libraries), and

---

FIGURE 10.1

Construct Indicators for Service Encounter Satisfaction and Overall Service Satisfaction

---

Service Encounter Satisfaction

1. How did you feel about the service you received today?[a]
2. I was satisfied with the service received.[b]
3. I was satisfied with my decision to obtain service from the library today.[b]
4. If I had it to do over again, I would *not* have gone to the library.[b]
5. My decision to use the library today was a wise one.[b]
6. I feel badly about my decision to go to the library.[b]
7. I was dissatisfied with my experience in using the library today.[b]
8. I think I did the right thing by going to the library today.[b]
9. I am *not* happy that I patronized the library today.[b*]

Overall Service Satisfaction

1. Based on *all of your experiences,* how satisfied overall are you with the library's service?[c]
2. Based on all of *my own experience* with the library, I am:[d*]
3. Compared to other libraries that you have used, how would you rate your satisfaction with this one?[c]
4. In general, I am satisfied with this library.[b]

---

[a] Fully anchored; end points: Delighted/Terrible
[b] Anchored at end points: Strongly agree/Strongly disagree
[c] Fully anchored; end points: Very satisfied/Very dissatisfied
[d] Anchored at end points: Very dissatisfied/Not at all dissatisfied
* Reverse scored

Adapted from Mary Jo Bitner and Amy R. Hubbert, "Encounter Satisfaction versus Overall Satisfaction versus Quality," in *Service Quality: New Directions in Theory and Practice,* edited by Roland T. Rust and Richard L. Oliver (Thousand Oaks, Calif.: Sage, 1994), 81. Copyright © 1994 (Sage Publications). Reprinted by Permission of Sage Publications, Inc.

general satisfaction. "Following the scaled items, an open-ended question . . . [might ask] respondents to describe what led them to rate their overall service satisfaction/dissatisfaction as they [did]."[13]

Ways to Measure Satisfaction

Any customer survey must limit the number of dimensions and questions on which customers comment. The more points probed through the survey, the fewer people will respond and do so with careful consideration. Thus, as with service quality, library staff must review the list of possible points and determine the subset of priority ones. In this case, however, they may include open-ended questions, giving customers an opportunity to elaborate with specific comments. (Service quality surveys avoid the use of open-ended questions because the intention is to probe only selected expectations, ones most relevant to service priorities.)

Figure 10.1 offers sample questions that examine satisfaction; Figure 10.2, which is a composite of questions from a number of library surveys and from surveys used in the retail industry that we have modified for possible application in libraries, suggests other potential survey items. The questions might be general and not probe specific services, or they might focus on specific services. A number of the questions tend to be open-ended, meaning that respondents must write something. Customers may not want to write much, however, and the more open-ended questions asked, the less likely that customers will respond and do so with care. As well, someone will have to review completed forms and develop categories representing the responses given. Data entry and analysis thus become labor-intensive activities, but, on the positive side, customers have the option of discussing whatever they want. The central question becomes: Which questions will provide the library with the most useful information for planning and decision making? Each library will have to answer this question for itself.

In reaching an answer, the staff might ascertain whether customers recommend library services to others (word of mouth) and whether they display loyalty to the library. Clearly, Figures 10.1 and 10.2 are suggestive rather than comprehensive.

Because a number of library and other satisfaction surveys that we have examined include items about the attributes of staff and the information provided or received, Figure 10.3 offers additional choices for libraries wanting to measure customer satisfaction. Such attributes might be dealt with through questions asking "How satisfied are you with. . . ." and the respondents might select from a five-point scale (very satisfied, somewhat satisfied, neither satisfied nor dissatisfied, somewhat dissatisfied, very dissatisfied).[14] Because attribute satisfaction is viewed within the context of service encounter satisfaction or overall service satisfaction, some examples are in order:

- In using the library today, I found the staff to be courteous (service encounter satisfaction).

FIGURE 10.2

Satisfaction: A Pool of Questions

Service Encounter Satisfaction

1. Overall, how satisfied are you with today's library visit? (Highly dissatisfied/Highly satisfied)

2. (Name specific services, facilities, and staff [by service points or location].) Ask respondents about which ones they used and how satisfied they are with the service provided. (Highly dissatisfied/Highly satisfied)

3. "How would you rate the *value* of your visit?" (Poor/Outstanding)

4. Did you find what you were looking for? Yes ___ No ___. If not, why?

5. If "yes," how satisfied were you with what you found? (four-point scale: very satisfied, satisfied, unsatisfied, very dissatisfied)

6. Did you experience any problems in the use of the library? If "yes," what was the problem or problems? How did the staff deal with the problem? Please assess the course of action they took to resolve the problem. Will you use the library again?

Overall Service Satisfaction

1. Based on all of your experiences in using the library, what are we doing that you particularly like?

2. Based on all of your experiences in using the library, what are we doing that you really don't like?

3. Based on all of your experiences in using the library, what are we doing that you really don't care about?

4. Based on all of your experiences in using the library, what aren't we doing that you would like us to do?

5. Based on all of your experiences in using the library, how and where could we most improve to provide high-quality service and guarantee 100 percent satisfaction?

6. Based on all of your experiences in using the library, what do you like *best* about us?

7. Based on all of your experiences in using the library, what do you like *least* about us?

8. If we could do ONE thing to improve, what should it be?

- In using the library today, I found the circulation desk staff to be courteous (service encounter satisfaction).
- Based on all of my experiences in using this library, I found the staff to be courteous (overall service satisfaction).
- Based on all of my experiences in using this library, I found the circulation desk staff to be courteous (overall service satisfaction).

In this instance, the five-point scale ranges from "strongly agree" to "strongly disagree." Clearly, the categories for any scale must match the question asked.

FIGURE 10.3

Attribute Satisfaction: Sample Elements for Constructing Survey Questions

Staff	Information Provided
Courteous	Accurate
Enthusiastic	Complete
Friendly	Cost-effective
Giving of their time	Helpful
Helpful	Relevant
Interested	Sufficient (no overload)
Knowledgeable	Timely
Patient	Understandable
Self-confident	

In any survey, staff members should give careful thought to the measurement scale selected, and they should avoid alternating among five-point, seven-point, or other types of point scale. Thus, before settling on a particular scale, they should review works such as Delbert C. Miller's *Handbook of Research Design and Social Measurement.*[15]

Examples

Taking a specific area—a library's networked environment—staff might probe satisfaction with the library's World Wide Web service by asking such questions as:

1. "How satisfied are you with the availability of dial-in connections when you try to connect to the network from off-campus?" (completely satisfied, satisfied, don't know, dissatisfied, completely dissatisfied)

2. "How satisfied are you with the maintenance of the computers?" (completely satisfied, satisfied, don't know, dissatisfied, completely dissatisfied)

3. "What are some of the *best* aspects of the campus computer network?"

4. "What are some improvements that should be made to the campus computer network?"[16]

Library evaluators have a choice: They can approach such questions from a specific use (e.g., today or this week) or globally—all of the customer's uses of the network. They might even include a question such as "Would you recommend the library's WWW service to a friend or colleague?" (yes/no. Discuss) or "Would you use the service again?" (yes/no. Discuss). Willingness to recommend a service or return to use it again are important indicators of satisfaction. The open-ended questions represent a variation of one of the questions in Figure 10.2.

Before settling on an instrument, however, it would be useful to consult Applegate's "Models of User Satisfaction," which reviews satisfaction models and satisfaction "with online searches and other products of information retrieval systems."[17] The staff should ensure that they ask meaningful questions, ones that do not produce "simple and misleading answers." Applegate advocates that staff establish "a real dialogue in which a user's needs, expectations, knowledge, and emotions will be communicated."[18] Thus, she appears to favor the use of in-person interviewing to provide in-depth insights applicable to a few customers. Libraries needing more information that is more cheaply gathered and that applies to a specific population should use a survey, preferably one distributed in person. There is no reason why in-person interviewing might not be used on a selective basis, perhaps with some of the respondents and/or nonrespondents to the general survey, to generate a richer or more in-depth array of data.

Applegate emphasizes that there are different aspects of satisfaction that a study might explore. Furthermore, that study might focus on a material satisfaction model or on an emotional satisfaction model (simple path or multiple path). In the simple path model, customers "are 'happy' or emotionally satisfied when their questions have been answered," whereas with the multiple path model their "happiness depends not only on questions answered (material satisfaction) but also on factors such as setting and expectations."[19] The choice of a model has implications for library services. One of these models might be combined with either service encounter satisfaction or overall service satisfaction.

Figure 10.4, which draws upon Chapter 7 and Figure 7.7, illustrates that library staff can combine questions about service quality with those about satisfaction. With the inclusion of three open-ended questions about satisfaction, it is extremely important that the survey form be short and easy to complete. The staff should have a rationale for the inclusion of each question; why do they want to know about this point over all the other choices they could have made? It is possible that they might tailor separate survey forms to specific services, such as using the online public access catalog, borrowing material, asking an information or reference question, or using the Internet.

Recommendations

A survey such as the one shown in Figure 10.4 should adhere to the data-collection procedures discussed in Chapter 7. Some public libraries might find themselves in the same situation as a number of other government bodies, having to produce valid survey research in which responses come from reasonably representative subsets of given populations. They, as well as any library, should work "toward the goal of service improvement"[20] and:

FIGURE 10.4

Library Customers: A Survey of Expectations and Satisfaction

We ask you to spare about ___ minutes of your time to identify what you think are the most important indicators of high-quality service that you expect a [college, university, public] library to provide. Some indicators are probably more important to you than others. The information that you provide will enable us to understand your service needs and priorities.

For questions 1–6, please circle the number that indicates how important each of the following points is for the *high-quality service* you expect a [college, university, public] library to provide. *(The range is from 1 = of no importance to 7 = of highest importance.)*

If you don't use a particular service, please DO NOT circle a number for that statement.

	No importance					Highest importance	

1. I do not have to wait in line more than three minutes when I ask for assistance at a reference or information desk. 1 2 3 4 5 6 7
2. I do not have to wait in line more than three minutes when I borrow material. 1 2 3 4 5 6 7
3. Library staff are:
   a. Approachable and welcoming. 1 2 3 4 5 6 7
   b. Available when I need them. 1 2 3 4 5 6 7
   c. Courteous and polite. 1 2 3 4 5 6 7
   d. Friendly and easy to talk to. 1 2 3 4 5 6 7
4. Library staff:
   a. Communicate with me using terms I understand. 1 2 3 4 5 6 7
   b. Encourage me to come back to ask for more assistance if I need it. 1 2 3 4 5 6 7
   c. Demonstrate cultural sensitivity. 1 2 3 4 5 6 7
5. Materials are reshelved promptly. 1 2 3 4 5 6 7
6. Equipment is in good working order:
   a. Computer printers 1 2 3 4 5 6 7
   b. Microfilm and microfiche readers 1 2 3 4 5 6 7
   c. Photocopiers 1 2 3 4 5 6 7

The final three questions are open-ended and provide an opportunity for you to comment on library service in general or an aspect of it.

7. Based on all of your experiences in using the library, what are we doing that you particularly like?

8. Based on all of your experiences in using the library, what are we doing that you really don't like?

9. Based on all of your experiences in using the library, if we could do ONE thing to improve, what should it be?

Thank you for your participation.

State clearly what is being measured and how the measure is derived or calculated;

Explain why the measure is relevant to the program or service being provided;

Identify the data source(s) used to calculate the measure and indicate how the data are updated, including basic information on how and when the data were collected and where the data can be obtained;

Include a supplemental attachment with information and explanation of data sources, . . . methodology, and other information required to evaluate . . . data for . . . audit purposes; and

Develop systematic data retention schedules which will allow interested parties to verify and further analyze customer satisfaction data.[21]

And, "in creating performance measures from customer satisfaction surveys, . . . agencies should adhere to guidelines for valid survey research."[22]

Staff should consider standardizing some of the items asked so that there is some consistency, from year to year, about what a library assesses and reports pertaining to customer satisfaction. Some customers might be tracked on a regular basis to ascertain their views on problems and review the impact of corrective actions on resolving the problems.

As noted earlier, the information gathered might be important as part of an audit trail. When libraries, like other organizations, must produce performance reports,

a certain rigor [collecting data generalizable to some population] is necessary since they [the reports] are designed to help improve important public programs, provide accountability to the public and information to policymakers who must decide how to allocate scarce resources. Also, only rigorous methods can provide the quality of information that agencies need to support their claims of good performance. . . . [Nonetheless,] when the best methods are followed some error is inevitable. However, if surveys are properly conducted, they can produce valid, appropriate measures of performance. Otherwise . . . agencies should use customer feedback cautiously, since the results could be misleading.[23]

Figure 10.5 offers an excellent summary of 27 points to address in conducting customer satisfaction surveys. Pat L. Weaver-Meyers and Wilbur A. Stolt, among others, make an exceedingly important point, one that is consistent with the literature on service quality: "Completely satisfied customers are six times more likely to repeat their business than customers who are merely satisfied."[24] As a result, those analyzing and reporting the data might generate an average (mean and/or median), but they should also concentrate on the "very satisfied" or "completely satisfied" category and compare all other responses to it. After all, the question is not "How many customers are satisfied?"; rather, it is "What proportion of the respondents are completely satisfied?" Chapter 11 will amplify on data interpretation and the use of statistics.

FIGURE 10.5
Guidelines for Customer Satisfaction Surveys

Plan

1. Conduct customer satisfaction surveys for purposes that are clearly stated and designed to improve services.

2. Decide the frequency for repeating data collection—use of repeated measures.

3. Decide if focus group interviews will be a follow-up method to expand on the findings.

4. Seek approval from a human subjects committee or other appropriate body.

5. Assign and supervise trained staff to be responsible for the survey.

6. Follow standard, scientifically valid methods to minimize errors and other potential problems.

Identify Customers

7. Decide whether or not to generalize the findings to a population.

8. If generalization is required, develop a list of those who have received services that are the subject of the survey or devise a sampling strategy (e.g., based on time periods). Select customers, perhaps all of them, from the list or select a random sample of customers large enough to provide accurate estimates of satisfaction.

9. Try to obtain responses from the greatest possible percentage of those selected and check to ensure that those who respond are representative of customers receiving services being studied.

Construct and Ask Questions

10. Write clear questions or statements and response options.

11. Allow for various degrees of satisfaction/dissatisfaction, or agreement/disagreement.

12. Be neutral throughout.

13. Ask about several aspects of customer satisfaction during a specific time period.

14. Expect only moderate knowledge and recall of specific services as time goes by.

15. Use efficient, well-established data-collection methods.

16. Treat respondents respectfully.

17. Encourage voluntary participation and remember that you are imposing on the respondents.

18. Confirm that respondents are customers. (Some libraries might house academic departments or other government services. Thus, individuals within the building may not necessarily be library customers.)

Edit and Archive Data

19. Make every attempt to ensure that the data are technically error-free.

20. Justify any changes to original data.

21. Make it possible for others to confirm independently the results later.

Analyze Data and Results

22. Objectively analyze all relevant, usable customer satisfaction data.

23. Attempt to explain unexpected or unusual results.

24. Ensure that published data are consistent with survey results.

25. Interpret results with the appropriate level of precision and express the proper degree of caution about conclusions that can be drawn from the results.

26. Make note of possibly significant problems and limitations.

27. Provide basic descriptive information about how the survey was done.

Adapted from Minnesota Office of the Legislative Auditor, *State Agency Use of Customer Satisfaction Surveys: A Program Evaluation Report* (St. Paul, Minn.: The Office, 1995), xii.

Customer-Related Measures

As presented in Chapters 4 and 7, customer-related measures provide insights into questions of "How well?," "How valuable?," "How reliable?," "How responsive?," and "How satisfied?" Because satisfaction is often measured on a point scale (five-, seven-, or ten-point scale), it is possible to compute the following percentage:

$$\frac{\text{Number of customers expressing some degree of satisfaction}}{\text{Number of responding customers}} = \underline{\quad} \times 100 = \underline{\quad}\%$$

When libraries strive to keep and build their pool of present customers, and aspire to achieve customer loyalty, it becomes essential to seek complete satisfaction for priority services (see Figure 9.1).[25] A relevant measure would be as follows:

$$\frac{\text{Number of customers expressing complete satisfaction}}{\text{Number of customers expressing any degree of satisfaction}} = \underline{\quad} \times 100 = \underline{\quad}\%$$

Or,

$$\frac{\text{Number of customers expressing complete satisfaction}}{\text{Number of customers expressing any degree of satisfaction } or \text{ dissatisfaction}} = \underline{\quad} \times 100 = \underline{\quad}\%$$

For any percentage that emerges, managers need some framework for its interpretation and some plan to raise the percentage over coming years. For instance, they might determine that, in the year 2000, at least 60 percent of the faculty members using interlibrary loan should be "completely satisfied" with that service. At the same time, the managers should set targets, such as to increase the percentage of "completely satisfied" faculty by 3 percent per year for the next five years (beginning in the year 2001). The intended result becomes, for instance, that, by the year 2006, at least 75 percent of the faculty will be "completely satisfied" (60 + 15 = 75). Examples of other areas for setting goals and intended results might be:

The receipt and resolution of complaints (e.g., by the year _____, no more than ____ percent of the people who complain about a particular service will do so again)

Out-of-service conditions (e.g., all equipment needing repair will be reported to the repair shop within 24 hours of breakdown)

In-service conditions (e.g., no photocopier will be out of operation more than ____ days per month).

Measures relating to conditions involve the review and renegotiation of service contracts, and the quality (e.g., durability) of equipment purchased or leased.

Setting targets and intended results ensures that the library engages in regular assessment, consistently uses the same questions or statements, and commits the resources necessary to meet its goals. Failure to meet a target places increased pressure on the organization to analyze and overcome problems. For instance, regarding the complete satisfaction of faculty with interlibrary loan, managers might identify why the library was unable to meet one of the 3 percent targets, and they would have to take corrective action to meet or exceed the next target and to achieve the ultimate result: 15 percent increase after five years. Needless to say, the library needs to use rigorous methods of data collection to ensure that failure to meet a target is not due to mistakes made in conducting the research.

The Customer's Voice

Libraries have options concerning what they investigate regarding customer satisfaction and what types of customer-related measures and research questions they address. They can examine "satisfaction with access, facilities, communications, personnel, types of services provided, service outcomes, and overall satisfaction."[26] They can focus, for example, on content or context (see Figure 10.6), while examining a specific service encounter or encounters in general. Whichever one they choose, it appears that service encounter satisfaction is distinct from overall service satisfaction and service quality.[27] Each provides valuable information; together, they provide a more complete picture of library service. Nonetheless, overall service satisfaction may not provide sufficient in-depth information about problem areas, while the time frame for service encounter satisfaction could be so loosely set that memory or recall presents a problem.

To gain more complete knowledge about customer satisfaction with library services, managers might gauge overall service satisfaction, and then, depending on the findings (where problems are suggested), explore specific services and service encounter satisfaction. When managers determine that such data collection is too costly and time consuming, and that they must settle for less than the complete picture, they need to determine which part of a smaller picture is most important to them and how much time they can devote to data collection.

Summary

This chapter further develops material first presented in Chapter 7, in that the steps in conducting a satisfaction survey mirror those for ascertaining service quality. The emphasis, however, differs. Service quality tends to focus on expectations, whereas satisfaction is more transaction-specific. Still, it should be remembered that, without consistent wording of questions and continual data collection at regular intervals, it is impossible to monitor satisfaction over time.

Satisfaction and Service Quality: Separate but Intertwined

FIGURE 10.6
Satisfaction: Context and Content

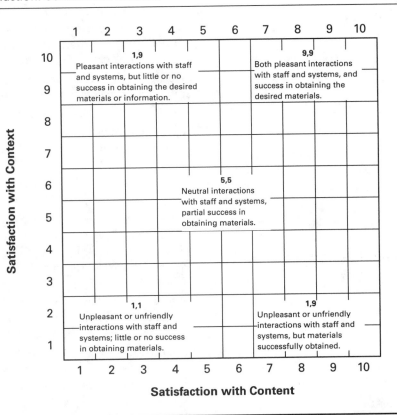

NOTES

1. Michael D. Johnson, *Customer Orientation and Market Action* (Upper Saddle River, N.J.: Prentice-Hall, 1998), 70.

2. Ann M. Turner, "Opinion Polls: A Savvy Tool to Raise Library Value," *Library Journal* 122, no. 17 (October 15, 1997): 41.

3. Rachel Applegate, "Models of Satisfaction," in *Encyclopedia of Library and Information Science* 60, supplement 23, edited by Allen Kent (New York: Marcel Dekker, 1997), 200.

4. Roland T. Rust and Richard L. Oliver, "Service Quality: Insights and Managerial Implications from the Frontier," in *Service Quality: New Directions in Theory and Practice*, edited by Roland T. Rust and Richard L. Oliver (Thousand Oaks, Calif.: Sage, 1994), 3.

5. R. L. Oliver, "A Conceptual Model of Service Quality and Service Satisfaction: Compatible Goals, Different Concepts," in *Advances in Services Marketing and Management: Research and Practice*, vol. 2, edited by T. A. Swartz, D. E. Bowen, and S. W. Brown (Greenwich, Conn.: JAI Press, 1993), 65–85.

6. Rust and Oliver, "Service Quality," 4.

7. Ibid.

8. "A difference between what a person expected to receive . . . and then perceives he or she has received in terms of product performance . . . is called disconfirmation (the expectations have or have not been confirmed by reality)" (Applegate, "Models of Satisfaction," 209).

9. Jagdip Singh, "A Multifacet Typology of Patient Satisfaction with a Hospital," *Journal of Health Care Marketing* 10, no. 4 (1990): 8–21.

10. Applegate, "Models of Satisfaction," 200.

11. Mary Jo Bitner and Amy R. Hubbert, "Encounter Satisfaction versus Overall Satisfaction versus Quality," in Rust and Oliver, *Service Quality*, 76–77.

12. Ibid., 80.

13. Ibid.

14. One source recommends that "respondents should have the opportunity to say that they are uncertain or unable to rate the service in question." See Minnesota Office of the Legislative Auditor, *State Agency Use of Customer Satisfaction Surveys: A Program Evaluation Report* (St. Paul, Minn.: The Office, 1995), 92n. In some instances, library staff might, however, want to force a choice, thereby omitting the neutral category.

15. Delbert C. Miller, *Handbook of Research Design and Social Measurement* (Newbury Park, Calif.: Sage, 1991).

16. Adapted from Charles R. McClure and Cynthia L. Lopata, *Assessing the Academic Networked Environment: Strategies and Options* (Washington, D.C.: Coalition for Networked Information, 1996), 63, 75, 76.

17. Rachel Applegate, "Models of User Satisfaction: Understanding False Positives," *RQ* 32, no. 4 (summer 1993): 525.

18. Ibid., 536.

19. Ibid., 525.

20. Minnesota Office of the Legislative Auditor, *State Agency Use of Customer Satisfaction Surveys*, x.

21. Ibid., 91.

22. Ibid., xv.

23. Ibid., x.

24. Pat L. Weaver-Meyers and Wilbur A. Stolt, "Delivery Speed, Timeliness and Satisfaction: Patrons' Perceptions about ILL Service," *Journal of Library Administration* 23, nos. 1 and 2 (1996): 39.

25. Please note that we prefer the scale for Figure 9.1 to range from "completely dissatisfied" to "completely satisfied."

26. Minnesota Office of the Legislative Auditor, *State Agency Use of Customer Satisfaction Surveys*, 17.

27. Bitner and Hubbert, "Encounter Satisfaction," 92.

11

Interpreting Findings to Improve Customer Service

No single dataset or measure can explain all that the library staff want to know.

—Peter Hernon[1]

Most writings about performance measures and library evaluation do not address the interpretation of the findings. As a result, the use and effect of these measures on library operations and decision making have been more limited than the creators of those measures probably envisioned. Chapters 7 and 10 discuss ways to collect data using quantitative methods, and Chapter 8 explores the use of a qualitative method. As was noted in these chapters, library staff have choices regarding which method of data collection to use and which statements or questions to ask. There are also choices related to the method of data analysis. The method is influenced by several considerations, especially the following:

1. **Level of measurement for the variables studied.** There are four levels of measurement: nominal, ordinal, interval, and ratio. Persons, things, and events characterized by a *nominal* variable are not ranked or ordered by the variable; for example, being female is neither better nor worse than being male. Nominal variables such as gender, therefore, have no inherent order. With an *ordinal* variable, the attrib-

utes are ordered. For instance, observations about the frequency with which customers ask for the assistance of reference librarians might be arrayed into four classifications: "never," "sometimes," "frequently," and "always." Although the ordinal level of measurement yields a ranking of attributes, no assumptions are made about the distance between the classifications. In this example, we do not assume that the difference between persons who "always" request assistance and that between persons who "frequently" request assistance is the same as those who "sometimes" do so. The attributes of an *interval* variable are assumed to be equally spaced, whereas the attributes of a *ratio* variable have equal intervals as well as a true zero point.

A five-point scale for measuring service quality or satisfaction in which the end points are equally anchored (e.g., "completely satisfied" and "completely dissatisfied"), and each number in between (i.e., 2, 3, and 4) has an equal interval from the other numbers, is an interval scale. Depending on the specific variable and the wording of the question, demographic variables might be nominal, ordinal, or interval scale. Frequency of library use might be expressed at the ordinal level, assuming that there are not equal intervals among the response options. Thus, data-collection instruments represent statements and questions involving more than one level of measurement scale.

2. Unit of analysis, or the entity about which we want to say something. Possible units might be customers, never-gained or lost customers, classroom, school, business, city government, residential area, student major, faculty in the humanities, and the institution.

3. Shape of the distribution. A normal distribution is a family of distributions that forms a symmetrical bell shape. This bell-shaped curve extends infinitely in both directions on a continuum close to the horizontal axis or baseline, but never touching it.

4. Study design used to produce the data from populations or probability samples. A population might be depicted in numbers, percentages, and descriptive statistics (e.g., range and average), and findings from a probability sample might be shown in numbers, percentages, descriptive statistics, or inferential statistics—which make inferences back to the population.

5. Completeness of the data. For instance, in a survey, some people may decline to participate and others may not answer certain questionnaire items.

The purpose of this chapter is to identify some general ways to analyze and present study results; it is not intended as an introduction to statistics. Readers wanting that introduction should consult the list of "Selected Sources on Research Methods" beginning on page 128.[2]

Basic Concepts

Presenting Averages

There are two general approaches to describe the average, or measure of central tendency, of a distribution: (1) presenting data through a table or figure, and (2) finding a descriptive statistic that best summarizes the distribution. A descriptive statistic is a number that, in some way, describes the group of cases. Measures of central tendency (mode, mean, and median) form a class of descriptive statistics, each member of which characterizes the typical value of a variable: the central location of a distribution. The mode is the most frequently occurring attribute; although it can be used as a measure of central tendency for any level of measurement, the mode is most commonly used with nominal variables. A distribution can have more than one mode, when two or more attributes tie for the highest frequency.

The mean, or arithmetic average, is calculated by summing the observations and dividing the sum by the number of observations. It is normally used only with interval and ratio-level data. The mean may not, however, be a good indicator if several cases are outliers—extreme values—or if the distribution is notably asymmetric. The reason is that the mean is strongly influenced by the presence of a few extreme values, which may give a distorted view of the average. The median—calculated by determining the midpoint of rank-ordered cases—can be used with ordinal, interval, and ratio-level data, and no assumptions need to be made about the shape of the distribution. Because the median is not greatly affected by changes in a few cases, outliers have less influence on it than on the mean.

Standard Deviation

The standard deviation, which is often used with interval or ratio data, comprises a measure of the spread of scores around the mean, or the extent of variation among cases, when those cases approximate a normal distribution. The greater the scatter of scores, the larger is the standard deviation. For a normal distribution, researchers interpret the standard deviation as the distance measured from the midpoint (the center of the curve) to a point along the baseline. The baseline is divided into standard deviation units. Plus or minus one standard deviation from the center of the curve includes approximately 68 percent of the cases in a sample, and plus or minus two standard deviations accounts for 95 percent of the cases. Thus, studies engaging in gap analysis and using interval-level data might report both the mean and the standard deviation.

Pearson Product-Moment Correlation

Pearson Product-Moment Correlation, commonly called Pearson's *r*, is a measure of linear correlation between two interval-ratio variables; in other words, it indicates the extent to which a straight line best depicts the relationship between the variables. A correlation examines the extent of the relationship between two random variables within specified limits; these limits are stated as correlation coefficients. A correlation coefficient, a number that indicates the degree of relationship between two variables, reflects the extent to which variations in one variable accompany variations in the other variable.

Correlation coefficients range from −1 to +1, with 0 indicating no linear association. Plus 1 indicates that the relationship is a perfect positive one: As one variable changes, the other variable goes through equivalent changes in the same direction. Minus 1 is a perfect negative correlation. A negative (or minus) correlation indicates that changes in one variable are accompanied by equivalent changes in the other variable. The change, however, is in the opposite direction. Consequently, as one variable diminishes, the other increases.

By squaring the r value, it is possible to examine the strength of the overall relationship. The squared value can be converted into a percentage, for instance, when r equals .9, $r^2 \times 100 = 81$ percent.

As shown in this section, survey results might be viewed as numbers and percentages, perhaps displayed in tabular or graphic form. It is also possible to calculate measures of central tendency; the actual one selected depends on the measurement scale and the extent to which the mean or median best depicts the distribution. If the measurement scale is interval or ratio, the standard deviation and perhaps Pearson's r become relevant statistics. Thus, it is possible to display findings in a list ranging from the highest to lowest number of occurrences and percentages, averages, standard deviations, and Pearson's r. Such information becomes useful for interpreting the results. In some instances, library staff might use quadrant analysis.

Quadrant Analysis

Quadrant analysis, a graphic correlation technique, may involve the use of data related to customer expectations to produce "pictorial results that are easy to communicate, understand, and interpret;"[3] those results have value for strategic planning and decision making. As James Lynch, Robert Carver, Jr., and John M. Virgo note, quadrant analysis is useful for "administrators whose skills have progressed beyond simple frequency distributions but who do not have the time, need, nor opportunity to master the intricacies and nuances of advanced statistical methodologies."[4]

Figure 11.1 reflects two dimensions commonly used in quadrant analysis: One dimension (*ideal expectation*) indicates the importance of an expectation to customers, and the other dimension (*actual service*) records the degree to which customers perceive a service as fulfilling the expectation. Quadrant analysis indicates what customers expect from a service (i.e., their ideal) and how they perceive a particular service in re-

FIGURE 11.1
Framework for Quadrant Analysis

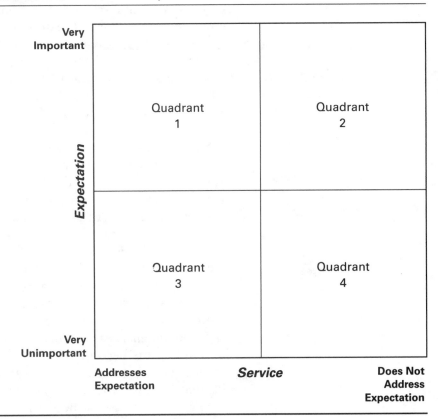

lation to the ideal. Quadrant analysis is *not* appropriate for use in comparing perceived expectations to indicators of the actual service provided, which was discussed in Chapter 7. Rather, it applies to analysis of the gaps between customers' expectations and their perceptions of service (the type of data obtained through the use of SERVQUAL).

A number of expectations can be plotted within the four quadrants if the average responses on both dimensions are known. Customers might be asked to rate the importance of certain service expectations on a five- or seven-point scale. The averages (i.e., means) for the importance of customer expectations are used to locate each expectation's position along the vertical axis. The mean of the perceived service actually provided is subtracted from the mean of the perceived expected measure. In other words, the gap is computed for each expectation. Using both averages as coordinates, the average location of each expectation and perception within the four quadrants can be determined.

The expectations falling into Quadrant 1 are very important to the customers, and they perceive the library as trying to meet those expectations. Librarians would want present and potential customers to be aware that the library places a high value on meeting these fundamental expectations. Over-delivery of services in this quadrant (perceptions of actual service provision exceed expectations), might "represent areas where resources could be saved and reallocated."[5] The expectations that fall into Quadrant 2 are also very important to customers but are not perceived as being prominent features of the service. If the customers' perceptions are correct and service in these areas is in fact not meeting expectations, service changes may be called for. It may be, however, that the service does in fact meet expectations and the customers need to be made aware of this.

Any expectations shown in Quadrant 3 are relatively unimportant to customers, but customers associate those expectations with the service. By trying to elevate the importance of these expectations, library staff seek to enhance the image of a service. Alternatively, the staff might refocus the service so that its image matches the expectations shown in Quadrants 1 or 2, not those depicted in Quadrant 3.

Chapter 12, specifically Figure 12.2, suggests competitors for libraries. By contrasting libraries with their competitors, librarians can view Quadrant 4 as an opportunity to see what expectations their competitors are not meeting that might have some potential to cultivate. Alternatively, because the expectations are unimportant to customers and are not met by either libraries or their competitors, the expectations might be ignored and resources reallocated.

Quadrant analysis contains another element: solid and dashed lines. Thus, quadrants become subdivided. The solid lines, which represent the midpoints on the original ideal and actual scales, indicate the thresholds that separate whether or not an expectation describes the ideal or perceived expectation. The dashed lines are based on averages computed across measurement scales. This approach

> produces quadrants defined by the survey results rather than by question design. This should produce a quadrant configuration that is more reflective of the preferences . . . [of those studied]. It also makes it easier to discuss individual . . . [expectations] since they can be described as being "above average" or "below average".[6]

The solid and dashed lines provide two different ways to view survey results. Most typically, the results fall within midpoint lines—in either Quadrant 1 or 2, since statements of expectation "are only likely to be included in a questionnaire if, *a priori*, there is reason to believe that they are important to the target segment being studied."[7] In contrast, the dashed lines, based on scale averages, provide more "discriminating information."[8] That is, in the idealized version the four squares are of equal size. In reality, once the expectations and gaps are factored in, the quadrants differ in size.

Example

Nicola Harwood and Jillene Bydder examined student expectations and compared the results with perceptions about the service provided. Although their terminology differs from that used here, it is possible to adapt their work to illustrate the use of quadrant analysis.[9]

Harwood and Bydder studied gap analysis at the University of Waikato, Hamilton, New Zealand. One interesting table depicts the gap for 11 statements having a discrepancy of >1 point between expected and actual perceptions (see Figure 11.2). They also note that five questions had the largest gap:

1. Materials in their proper place
2. OPAC accurate and extensive
3. Range of materials in the library
4. Seven-day recall
5. Good order copiers

Figure 11.3 depicts quadrant analysis. Before interpreting the results, let us explain how the data were displayed in the figure. First, drawing on Figure 11.2, the 11 mean scores for expected service are positioned along the vertical axis and the gaps between these scores and the perception of actual service are positioned along the horizontal axis. The midpoint of the seven-point scale is 4, and is represented in Figure 11.1 by solid lines. This represents an idealized situation. In Figure 11.3, however, we plot the means of the actual survey responses, representing them by dashed lines. We add the 11 "expected service" scores and divide the result (69.98) by 11, getting a mean of 6.3618. The mean of the "actual service" scores is 5.0218 (55.24 divided by 11).

FIGURE 11.2
Gap between Expectations and Actual Service Provided

Questions	Mean Score		Gap between the Means
	Expected	Actual	
Materials in proper place	6.68	4.79	1.89
Range of materials in library	6.65	5.16	1.49
Good order copiers	6.59	5.19	1.40
Staff available when needed	6.52	5.28	1.24
OPAC accurate and extensive	6.45	4.92	1.53
Hours open match your schedule and needs	6.33	5.05	1.28
Staff on desks knowledgeable	6.28	5.23	1.06
Seven-day recall	6.28	4.80	1.48
Desk copy available	6.18	5.18	1.00
Knowledgeable staff always available	6.15	4.88	1.27
24 hours from storage	5.87	4.76	1.11

Source: Nicola Harwood and Jillene Bydder, "Student Expectations of, and Satisfaction with, the University Library," *Journal of Academic Librarianship* 24, no. 2 (March 1998), 162.

FIGURE 11.3

Application of Quadrant Analysis

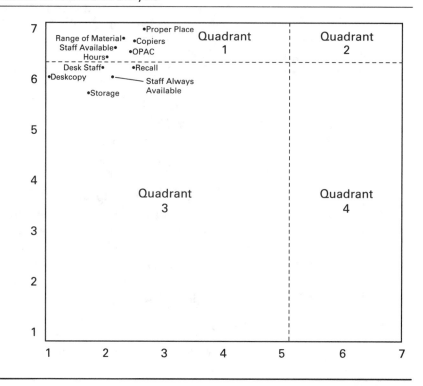

Six statements fall within the newly drawn Quadrant 1, which is now above the dashed lines:

1. Materials in their proper place
2. Range of materials in library
3. Good order copiers
4. Staff available when needed
5. OPAC accurate and extensive
6. Hours open

As such, these statements are important to customers, and they perceive the library as doing these things. The statements tend to focus on and reinforce customer self-sufficiency.

The five other statements collapse into Quadrant 3, as now reconfigured with the dashed lines. They are associated with libraries but are less important to the customers surveyed. Because "knowledgeable staff always available" and "staff on desks knowledgeable" were among the less-important statements, the library staff might use focus group interviews to determine the reasons for this placement and to mount a marketing campaign about the value of knowledgeable staff and their approachability. Clearly, at this university, student customers and the library staff have some differences about the role of, and necessity for, knowledgeable staff.

Survey of Expectations

Figure 11.4 depicts high and low service ratings; the goal is to achieve a high rating for doing something of high importance to customers and, by extension, to meet the mission and goals of the organization. The decision about which statements to include in a survey, as well as the interpretation of study findings should be viewed within the context of Figure 11.4 and the customer service plan.

Librarians might compare external customer perceptions about expectations to staff perceptions about either service expectations or the actual service provided. In both instances, quadrant analysis is appropriate. On the other hand, if staff only elicit perceptions of expectations, then there is no horizontal axis for quadrant analysis. In such instances, there are alternatives for presenting and interpreting the data.

Options include:

1. Calculating both the mean and median, and arraying the statements in descending order for both averages[10]
2. Generating the mean and standard deviation, and arraying the statements in descending order for both values

FIGURE 11.4

Service Rating: Matching Customers to Services

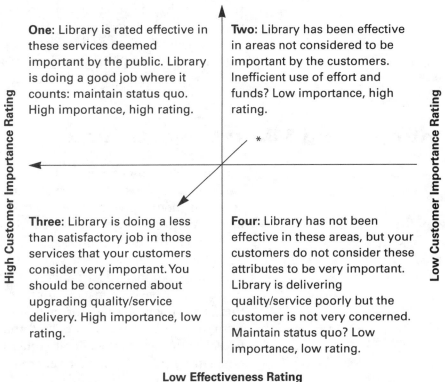

High Effectiveness Rating

One: Library is rated effective in these services deemed important by the public. Library is doing a good job where it counts: maintain status quo. High importance, high rating.

Two: Library has been effective in areas not considered to be important by the customers. Inefficient use of effort and funds? Low importance, high rating.

High Customer Importance Rating

Low Customer Importance Rating

Three: Library is doing a less than satisfactory job in those services that your customers consider very important. You should be concerned about upgrading quality/service delivery. High importance, low rating.

Four: Library has not been effective in these areas, but your customers do not consider these attributes to be very important. Library is delivering quality/service poorly but the customer is not very concerned. Maintain status quo? Low importance, low rating.

Low Effectiveness Rating

*This arrow shows the direction in which to shift resources.

3. Presenting Pearson's r, and arranging the statements in descending order for both values

The third option assumes that the staff survey customers about a vast number of expectations and employ factor analysis[11] to determine groupings among the various statements.[12] Unless the intention is to develop and re-order a far-reaching set of statements (e.g., Figure 7.4), this is the least appropriate option.

The decision about which of the other two options to use might depend on the software available. A number of packages determine an average, but they might not produce the standard deviation. As a result, the second option might not be available. Furthermore, if the staff doubt that their measurement scale is interval-level, they would not need the standard deviation. Instead, they would array the data in descending order of median values. On the other hand, if they are dealing with interval-level measurement and the assumptions of the mean are met, the second option is most appropriate.

Focus Group Interviews

As discussed in Chapter 8, focus group interviews produce qualitative, as opposed to quantitative, data. In other words, the results cannot be reduced to numbers. Rather, the write-up is in narrative form and emphasizes the key points of discussion—probably organized around the research questions discussed. There might, however, be a section comparing general trends among different focus groups. If the participants complete an exit survey eliciting their perceptions, the results (depending on what is asked and as long as there are horizontal and vertical axes) might be summarized by quadrant analysis.

Interpreting Market Penetration

Among public libraries participating in the Public Library Data Service's *Statistical Report '97*, "registrations as a percent of population" averaged about 50 percent for libraries across all the population groupings.[13] Market penetration ranged from a high of 197 percent to a low of 4 percent. Neither figure signifies credibility. The 197 percent raises questions about the currency of the registration file. (How many of these registrations reflect individuals who are no longer in the service area or who have been inactive for many years?) The 4 percent figure either is a typographical error or it reflects a library with weak impact. Both the numbers for volumes held and staff reported by this library are far below the norm in relation to other libraries with comparable service populations. Clearly, market penetration and the building of customer loyalty should be priorities for this library, and, perhaps, improving both might convince local officials to boost the operating budget. Market penetration is a concept that local officials can understand, and one that has meaning for them. Achieving and maintaining market share is a worthwhile goal.

Undergraduate teaching and learning, rather than research, have become top priorities among a number of academic administrators. Therefore, university libraries should shift part of their emphasis from building research collections to showing their involvement in the educational process, especially for undergraduates. The best way to prove involvement is by tying the library to specific courses. A detailed examination of which departments use the library for reserves and presentations, and which do not, allows library managers to pinpoint departments for new educational alliances.

Real and Virtual Visitors

Data on numbers of visitors present another aspect of market penetration. Some public libraries have large numbers of visitors who are not cardholders but who still use library services. In fact, the public library is usually the most visited public facility in most cities. Visitors can create an impression of activity and vibrancy. The widely held stereotype of libraries as dull and quiet places can be dispelled by demonstrating how busy they really are.

The numbers of students who come to the academic library will be reflected in the tallies of visitors. If the door counter can tally the number of persons entering and exiting per hour, the information can be used for staffing public service desks during peak periods.

Virtual visitors should increase within the next few years as more people acquire both the access and the knowledge to go online. If in-person visits to library outlets decline, records of virtual visits offer important information. Virtual visits can be tallied by incoming calls. Such data on calls completed and calls receiving busy signals because of limited ports can be obtained from the local telephone company.

Loyalty and Intensity

In the service business the best measure of quality and value is customer retention. . . . Rather than managing defects in service, one manages defections.

—Fred Reichheld[14]

Two important questions are: Who uses the library?, and To what extent do they use it? Customers who make heavy use of the library are more likely than customers making occasional use to support the library in times of need. Some public librarians are a bit uncomfortable with the oft-repeated statement that 20 percent of the patrons account for 80 percent of the circulation. Although the "80/20 rule" is commonly found in many situations, perhaps it does not apply in some libraries. The point is to check. Even if the rule holds, that in itself is not a problem. With the exception of garbage, water, and sewer, most taxpayers do not use government services to the same extent. Not everyone uses the public golf course, nor the library, nor the services of the police or fire department. People without children do not utilize the school system, and people without automobiles use the roads less than do car owners.

Retention of customers, or holding power, is essential for any successful organization. Figures 9.8 and 9.11 indicate the length and strength of customers' relationship with the library. Librarians can analyze whether or not new borrowers continue as cardholders over time. If they do not, does the drop-off rate, particularly after the first year, represent a large proportion of new cardholders? Unless turnover among the service area population is extremely high, could some aspect within the library cause cardholders not to re-register? Can the library point with pride to long-term relationships with a significant proportion of its cardholders? How many of these customers are active, borrowing at least one item per year?

Libraries might compare the profile of the registered borrowers with the population of the service area. Are certain age groups not well represented among the cardholders? If so, would it be possible to target market to those groups? Do active borrowers tend to come from certain neighborhoods? Do they reflect certain age groupings? At what point does use by schoolchildren seem to decline? Can the library do anything to keep schoolchildren as active customers?

Academic libraries need information on both the status and the subject specialties of borrowers. The staff can look at both borrowers and virtual visitors by status. The campus identification number indicates status in most academic institutions and also serves as the borrower's identification. The numbers represented by each group are easily obtained from central administration. The staff might compare the total in each group with the number of borrowers in that group. It would not be unusual for general staff to be underrepresented as borrowers. Librarians might examine how many lower and upper division undergraduates were active borrowers. How many borrowed nothing? The same questions might be asked of the faculty.

It might be interesting to determine if the nonborrowing students are enrolled in departments whose faculty are nonborrowers or slight borrowers. What do trends in borrowing indicate? Is borrowing declining as the number of electronic resources increases?

To examine borrowing in greater detail, Figures 9.19 and 9.20 can be used for faculty, graduate students, or even undergraduates, if data on their academic majors are available. Such information indicates the intensity of use among different campus groups and disciplines, and presents library administration with the opportunity to investigate the reasons for low use. Is the collection not satisfactory? Are nonbibliographic databases, such as the *Human Genome*, more important resources? Is some aspect of the service not attractive to these groups?

Interpreting Customer Preferences

If the staff believe that the library collection should match the interests of most customers, then the relationship between holdings and circulation is important. The collection can attract new customers and influence retention of existing ones. A new group of customers will be attracted to the public library when it acquires videos. If these customers are valued and their continued patronage desired, then their interests must be satisfied. Some criticize this approach as being like the bookstore. Such criticism implies that bookstores pander to customers' unrefined taste. On the contrary, Baltimore County Public Library staff have found that customers' taste in reading materials is quite diverse. Any library choosing the role of "popular materials center" or the new service response "current topics and titles" has, knowingly or not, opted to let customer preferences guide selection.[15] Preferences are best determined by analyzing circulation patterns and adjusting buying accordingly.

Academic libraries have tended to amass quality collections, containing materials considered the "best"—meaning the most thorough, the most complete, and the most erudite as decided by reviewers or by the reputation of the author. The best in these qualities is not necessarily the best for undergraduates, many of whom would find the text difficult and uninteresting. In fact, there is no "best" without knowing for whom. "Best" is decided by each reader based on his or her interest, knowledge, reading ability, and circumstance. Ranganathan's first law is "Books are for use" and his third "Every reader his [or her] book." Unused books, no matter their critically acclaimed quality, are not meeting customers' requirements. Librarians may decide to acquire what people *should* read, but the customers will do as they please.

Communicating with Stakeholders

By choosing what data to report, librarians have created the standards by which they want to be measured. (No stakeholder ever initiated the category "new serials added per annum.") These self-defined categories emphasize growth, units of work processed, and the need to "keep up" with other libraries or with the publishing output. In essence, the categories have focused on resources. Some stakeholders now use those resources-based categories to question library efficiency and claims for more resources, because so much information on the Internet seems "free."

As a society, we are conditioned to present information in two-dimensional form on paper. This format may not be the best way to get a point across, especially if the paper contains numbers. Consider how many librarians tend to skip over numbers in reports and articles and focus on the text. It is likely that stakeholders and decision makers will do the same.[16] Making sense of a lot of numbers is difficult for most people, especially when they have little time or inclination to spend digesting their import because of the press of other business.

It is not necessary that stakeholders know every number that the library has collected. With the exception of market penetration, we recommend that libraries selectively share the findings from the indicators presented in this book with decision makers. These indicators are intended to assess and improve service quality. Information about activities needed for internal operations, such as cycle times and complaints, should stay internal to the organization. Information likely to create favorable public reaction (e.g., customer recognition programs) should be widely publicized. Compliments, testimonials, and other information about good customer service should be passed along to local officials.

Librarians might consider how to communicate with decision makers in more forceful ways. Unless local officials personally come to the library, their impressions of what goes on are based on library experiences perhaps years out of date, or on a stereotype. Information about the business of the library and the people who use it is best communicated visually. However, getting local officials to schedule visits might be difficult. Videotaping the library during peak periods is an easy and effective way to communicate both vibrancy and activity. Videotaping also shows the diversity of the clientele—another factor important to local officials. Videotaping, however, should be done with caution. Some customers may resent the taping as an intrusion on their privacy and other rights. For example, videotaping individuals using the World Wide Web might be taken as a form of censorship, as some people might alter their search patterns if they believe "big brother" is monitoring them.

Information about library activities should be presented in a form that the community and local officials can clearly understand. Examples include:

- Every minute 12 people come through the doors of the library.
- Every 30 seconds, an item is checked out.
- Every five minutes, someone asks a reference question.
- People from every neighborhood, every age group, etc., are library customers.
- Most customers have been cardholders for more than 10 years.
- The annual per capita cost of library service is about the same as the cost of a movie for two with popcorn and drinks.
- The library provided reserve materials for 193 courses enrolling 2,477 students last academic year.
- Faculty requested 142 class presentations by librarians, last academic year, involving 963 students.
- Circulations to lower division students increased 12 percent over the past year.
- Faculty from 39 of the 41 departments on campus used the library last year by borrowing materials and by requesting reserve collections or presentations.

Summary

No effort has been made to include every possible indicator that might be developed or to count every conceivable use or activity among the measures proposed in this book. Our focus has been on the customer and, to a lesser extent, on factors important to organizational administrators. Most customers do not care about how many "whatevers" the library owns or how many of such "whatevers" the library has processed.

Interpreting Findings to Improve Customer Service

Indicators of "how much" are no substitute for those discussed in this book. Besides, no library can always increase the volume of business. When the volume reaches a plateau or declines (as it will), the library must increase its inputs—including the number of hours open—to reverse the trend. The challenge for libraries is to select from among the various suggestions in this book and to ensure that the mission, vision, goals, and objectives have a customer focus. It should not be assumed that, by addressing the expectations and preferences of customers, the quality of the collection will decline. At the same time, libraries must communicate with their broader community in understandable and meaningful terms.

NOTES

1. Peter Hernon, *Statistics: A Component of the Research Process* (Norwood, N.J.: Ablex, 1994), 207.

2. See also Arthur W. Hafner, *Descriptive Statistical Techniques for Librarians*, 2d ed. (Chicago: American Library Association, 1998).

3. James Lynch, Robert Carver, Jr., and John M. Virgo, "Quadrant Analysis as a Strategic Planning Technique in Curriculum Development and Program Marketing," *Journal of Marketing for Higher Education* 7, no. 2 (1996): 18.

4. Ibid.

5. Ibid., 19.

6. Ibid., 23.

7. Ibid., 25. "Only if the study includes groups that have different priorities (for example, students versus employers), is it likely that a significant number of the . . . [expectations] of high importance to one group will end up in the low importance quadrants for the group (and vice versa)" (p. 25).

8. Ibid.

9. Nicola Harwood and Jillene Bydder, "Student Expectations of, and Satisfaction with, the University Library," *Journal of Academic Librarianship* 24, no. 2 (March 1998), 161–71.

10. See Peter Hernon and Ellen Altman, *Service Quality in Academic Libraries* (Norwood, N.J.: Ablex, 1996), 76–80.

11. "Factor analysis explores the interrelationships and commonalities among a set of variables." See Hernon, *Statistics*, 198–200.

12. See Philip J. Calvert and Peter Hernon, "Surveying Service Quality within University Libraries," *Journal of Academic Librarianship* 23, no. 5 (September 1997): 408–15.

13. Public Library Data Service, *Statistical Report '97* (Chicago: PLA, 1997).

14. Fred Reichheld, Foreward to *Serving Them Right: Innovative and Powerful Customer Retention Strategies* (New York: Harper Business, 1990), x.

15. Baltimore County Public Library's Blue Ribbon Committee, *Give 'Em What They Want! Managing the Public's Library* (Chicago: American Library Association, 1992).

16. See Peter Hernon and Charles R. McClure, *Evaluation and Library Decision Making* (Norwood, N.J.: Ablex, 1990), 199–223.

12

Embracing Change—
Continuous Improvement

Libraries are not "fields of dreams." To build a facility based on the perspectives only of librarians, without accommodating the users' needs, is likely to result in Edsels, not Cadillacs.

—Robert L. Lichter[1]

Public libraries have outlived their usefulness.

—Thomas Peyser[2]

To me a new library is just a $70-million homeless shelter. We don't need it and it is a waste of money.

—Andrew D. Martin[3]

Numerous academic, public, and other libraries must cope, among other things, with such beliefs as those expressed in the three opening quotes and "with the extraordinary changes that are occurring in their environments. It is not simply the complexity of the changes—financial, technological, political, social/demographic, and cultural—but also the accelerated pace of change."[4] Thomas W. Shaughnessy notes that, as a consequence,

> in many research libraries, staff are suffering from mental and physical exhaustion, burnout, frustration, low morale, and other symptoms of stress. In some instances the library's structure adds to the distress by slowing response time, preventing cross-functional solutions to problems, and frustrating efforts to intervene.[5]

To Shaughnessy's list, we might add that a number of research and other libraries are experiencing reductions in operating budgets (e.g., an inability to keep pace with inflation and having to take equipment purchases from the book and periodical acquisitions budget), staff reassignment and downsizing, an increased workload for staff, the consolidation of services, and reconfiguration of the physical plant (including rewiring of part of the building to meet demands for electronic delivery services). Position reductions and the resulting restructuring of services, in some instances, have meant shifting staff from managerial and supervisory ranks to frontline positions, with frontline personnel perhaps assuming some managerial responsibilities.

Complicating matters even more, libraries must improve their access to electronically delivered resources. This places greater pressures on interlibrary loan and document delivery services; on systems, cataloging, and other staff; and on budgets. Libraries are service organizations, and they must balance the demand for electronically delivered resources with that for print resources. Many faculty members and members of the general public are still wedded to print media, and the number of print publications produced annually remains formidable.

As the twenty-first century is about to unfold, there are fewer references in the literature to the library as the "heart" of the college or university, or as the pulse of or lifeline for the community. One academic institution prefers to view the library as the "memory" of the university, and the acquisition, indexing, storage, and retrieval of information as "memory functions."[6] Among other things, such a comparison confuses libraries with records management, archival management, and information resources management, which are more clearly the memory of the organization. Still, the analogy tries to suggest that a decline in financial commitment to the library will have no immediately noticeable impact. Part of the memory might be lost but later regained; however other lost parts might remain so forever, perhaps rightly.

Some academic administrators, members of city government, and others question the role of, and even the need for, a library; after all, they assume everything—or everything worth knowing—is, or will be, available on the information superhighway. Such a belief in virtual library collections reinforces the view of the library as a place—one lacking unique collections and services. Clearly, "improved information technology has made possible new methods of education"[7] and, hence, competition to traditionally delivered higher education from such institutions as the University of Phoenix, Nova University, and Western Governors University, which offer continuing education and degree-granting programs via the Internet.[8] Customers as well as employers will define "both the content and the delivery of education," especially since "lifelong learning is becoming a necessity."[9] Areas where teaching might change include:

Course design—Courses will be developed by professors and technology experts and marketed by traditional universities and publishers.

Lectures—Traditional formats may be replaced by CD-ROM or World Wide Web (WWW) delivery. Scholars worldwide might participate in interactive video recordings.

Discussions—Promoted by professors, these could be face-to-face or delivered online. Relieved of some of their responsibilities, professors would have more time for group discussion and helping students navigate the information superhighway. If students lack a foundation in certain areas, then the professors advise them of relevant hot links to WWW sites or have the links built into the course.

Assessment—Conducted by an independent organization, it might involve grading and course evaluations.[10]

Furthermore, teaching will be separated from degree granting, and content development from content delivery, as there is a movement "away from a campus-centric model of higher education to a consumer-centric model."[11]

Whatever uses they make of the WWW and other information technologies, those designing courses should carefully consider the outcomes they expect from students. Whether the course is delivered electronically or in person, the instructor should discuss course expectations and "acceptable" performance on assignments (e.g., mistakenly using material that, unbeknownst to the student, was fabricated, falsified, or plagiarized),[12] and hold students accountable to these standards. As more instructors teach students "how to read, to take time with language and ideas, to work through arguments, to synthesize disparate sources to come up with the original thought, . . . [and] how to assess sources to determine their credibility," they are trying to teach students "to think in disciplined ways."[13] Such teaching reinforces the point that no list of survey statements reflecting all possible aspects of service quality and satisfaction, now and forever, can be developed. Any list must be fluid and reflect different times and circumstances. The intention of this book is to provide a framework around which others can build as libraries seek to improve service delivery.

Although the concept of virtual universities raises opportunities and alternatives to traditionally delivered education, it also presents problems if people view virtual education in the same way that they do virtual libraries. Higher education administrators tend not to predict the demise of the physical university; rather, they see Internet-delivered courses as complementary. Virtual universities represent an opportunity for the for-profit sector to define a unique role and to deliver courses more accommodating to the schedule of the customer and a diverse workforce. Internet-delivered courses may have an impact on *provider* and *victim* libraries—the institution providing the course and collecting the fee and the nearby institution that the students want to use but that receives no financial reimbursement.[14] In some circumstances, customers who have paid a library for borrowing and other privileges might be denied access to certain products because of the terms of site licensing agreements. Herein lies another set of issues relating to customer service delivery.

Both the library and the larger organization in which the library functions (e.g., the academic institution or city/county/state government) are undergoing change. That larger organization must cope with change while simultaneously dealing with issues of accountability and producing new indicators of quality. A dual expectation may exist: (1) improving productivity (and gaining greater efficiency) and quality, (2) at a reduced cost or with a budget remaining constant or declining. Fiscal stringencies, downsizing, and resource reallocation, as a consequence, might not be limited to the library. Any organization must balance the needs of the library with those of other units, recognizing that budgeting occurs within a political context (competition with academic and other units, and with other government agencies),[15] while addressing issues of "How well?," "How satisfied?," "How productive?," and so forth (see Chapter 4). As a result, organizations change how they do business and how they ensure quality. In fact, the measurement of quality is changing.

Figure 12.1 illustrates the types of questions that the central administration of a college or university, or local government, might ask. These questions focus on assessment and become more complex to answer if the administrators require solid evidence, rather than opinion and "guesstimates."

FIGURE 12.1
Some Critical Questions

---

1. Are library services appropriate considering the needs of the community served?
2. Are the services effectively delivered and are customers satisfied—that is, completely satisfied?
3. Is there an appropriate balance among the services offered?
4. Are there important expectations that the library does not meet?
5. What are the library's strengths and weaknesses?
6. Is the present level of resources adequate to meet the mission, goals, and objectives, considering generally accepted practices in comparable institutions and the environment of resource constraint?
7. Are there adequate and appropriate avenues for customers to communicate their expectations and satisfaction to the library? How well do the library managers and staff listen?
8. Are there healthy and productive relationships with other academic service units on campus or with other government agencies?
9. Does the library effectively utilize information technology?
10. Is the issue of access versus ownership being appropriately defined and addressed?

Competition

Contrary to the assumption of some librarians, libraries do face competition, and the number and diversity of those competitors will increase in an age of electronic information delivery. Figure 12.2 suggests that different competitors already exist, depending on which question the customer asks. For instance, there are:

- Bookstores, including super-bookstores and secondhand bookstores (see, read, or own it)
- CARL UnCover (see, read, or own it)
- CompuServe (see, hear, understand, play with, adapt, and interact with it, as well as look it up)
- Course packets (see, read, understand, and own it, as well as look it up)
- Journal (service) vendors (see, read, and own it, as well as look it up)
- Photocopy services (see, read, own, and interact with it, as well as look it up)
- Term paper services (see, adapt, and own it)[16]
- Video stores and departments (see, hear, understand, play with, and interact with it)
- Virtual universities (see, hear, interact with, and understand it)
- World Wide Web (see, hear, understand, play with, adapt, and interact with it as well as look it up)
- Other libraries (see, read, hear, understand, and own it)

William H. Sanders offers one example of competition:

A working group at a local research university recently discussed ways to characterize the value of its library to students, faculty and staff. The cost of the library actually worked out to be about one dollar per day per

FIGURE 12.2
Library Competitors Depend on the Questions Asked

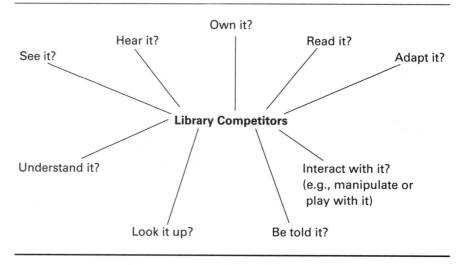

Embracing Change—Continuous Improvement

person. Some saw tremendous value: Access to all that knowledge for only a dollar a day; others saw thirty dollars a month they could use for faster, more direct access to up-to-date information on the Internet.[17]

In such a competitive environment, service performance requires listening to the voice of customers, relating to them on a one-to-one basis, and addressing such questions as:

- "Do you create a learning relationship with your customers?
- Do you keep your customers?
- Do you organize around customers?"[18]
- Do you attract new customers and build loyalty among all (or at least a majority of) customers?

What Is Quality?

As presented in Chapter 1, quality has five dimensions (conformance, expectations, market perception, strategic quality, and excellence), which are interrelated. Conformance quality focuses on reducing errors or mistakes, such as the number of incorrect referrals, and on service delivery time. In filling interlibrary loan requests, what is an acceptable delay or length of time in meeting the request? Furthermore, how can the library initiate practices to ensure that it meets the time limit? The temptation is to say that time boundaries are outside the control of the library initiating the request and, thus, to avoid any time commitment. Alternatively, there might be concern that, by meeting or exceeding expectations, the number of requests will dramatically increase, thereby placing additional pressures on the library to meet these expectations on a recurring basis, without any promise of increased resources to meet the demand. Managers, therefore, link conformance quality with budget priorities.

Quality, when defined in terms of expectations, evaluates performance in terms of customer expectations, and serves as the foundation to this book. It is not sufficient merely to know expectations; that knowledge must be translated into improved service performance and delivery.

Market perceived quality compares performance between or among libraries; how well does one library rank in comparison to its competitors? Of course, there must be a meaningful basis on which to make valid comparisons.

Strategic quality focuses on an organization's strategic position, relative to competitors, expressed in terms of quality and price.

Excellence is an important but elusive dimension of quality. The temptation is to equate excellence with the amount of expenditure, the volume of business, or the meeting of state or national standards. Excellence is intertwined with local, regional, national, and international recognition, but requires new ways of examination and measurement. Nevertheless, a number of academic disciplines still reward the *production* of scholarship more than the *quality* of scholarship. In other words, they focus on the quantity of output, rather than on how the quality is assessed, by whom, and what this indicates.

It is important to validate that we are, indeed, focusing on excellence itself and not on the production of excellence. Toward this end, excellence might be defined in terms of the placement of graduating students in the workforce or graduate programs, student achievement, student retention, meeting enrollment quotas while admitting students with certain qualities (e.g., scores on achievement tests), and the extent of discounting (offering financial aid to attract more students). An important but poorly addressed question is: How can the library provide the institution or local government with performance indicators—meaningful ones—reflecting a contribution to these larger issues of quality? Thus, the intent is to show the library as an integral part of the community and not a support service or mere appendage.

Going beyond "How Much?"

Libraries, when they report measures, most often list those relating to budget allocation (input measures) or turnstile counts or volume of business (output measures). Although such "countables" are easily gathered (e.g., hash mark for each reference question fielded or title processed), they fail to indicate more than "How much?" and to address the questions raised in Chapter 4. The answers to these questions cannot be inferred from "How much?" in part because countables may not deal with what is important to customers or convey organizational effectiveness. Furthermore, they do not address academic success or reflect the outcome of a visit to the library.

Arnold Hirshon issues an important reminder:

Staff may claim that "we know what the customer wants." Staff also may overgeneralize customer behavior based on only those customers they serve. For example, all customers of reference services are customers of the library, but many library customers are not customers of reference services at all.[19]

Hirshon also remarks that "we project on the customer changes that we ourselves do not like"[20] and offers suggestions for change: "changing where we work" and "the way we work."[21] Clearly, the meeting or exceeding of customer expectations has a direct impact on organizational effectiveness, the creation and maintenance of customer loyalty, and customer satisfaction.

Pat L. Weaver-Meyers and Wilbur A. Stolt address a significant question: Why do academic [or public] libraries need loyalty when their services are free?

Such might be the first question posed by academic librarians, who usually run the only library on campus. However, it is an inadequate answer for university administrators looking at options to fund library collection development or purchase document delivery vendor contracts. Without customer loyalty, libraries may see customers defect when vendors become viable alternatives.[22]

Whatever measures libraries develop must reflect what is important to the institution, and there must be a cohesiveness among the measures adopted. One measure or customer-related indicator does not tell the complete story. How many are needed? Which ones? Libraries have choices about what they might assess and report; they should concentrate on those indicators most meaningful to the organization in order to ensure that it maintains and, it is hoped, enhances its strengths, overcomes its weaknesses, and meets the challenges of the future.

Libraries need indicators reflecting the management of the library and how the library serves the broader organization or institution. Those indicators reflecting management should, in part, be customer-focused and lead to improved service performance and delivery, including the promotion of customer self-sufficiency (see Figure 12.3 for

---

FIGURE 12.3
Sample Customer-Related Measures

Attribute

Availability

Staff availability—at service points and to receive telephone calls*

Availability of seating or equipment

Speed

Speed with which items are reshelved (e.g., within a certain time limit):
Reference material
Current periodicals
Backfiles of periodicals
Microforms
Fiction reading
Course reserve material

Number of reference queries received on the WWW site for which a response is given within a specified time frame

Average speed in providing answers to questions

Connectivity (Phone Service)

Encountering busy signal when calling the library

Abandoned call rate

---

*Includes occupancy rate (number of staff answering calls) and agent availability (time answering customer calls and cost per call).

Service level (total calls minus busy signals and abandoned calls)

First call resolution

Queuing

Length of time that customers must wait at service desks to have their information needs met

Satisfaction

Willingness to return to the same library, same service, and same staff member

Operational

Working order of equipment:
Photocopiers
Computer printers
Microform readers and printers
The OPAC

Compliments and Complaints

Promptness with which complaints are handled

Number of signed suggestions responded to within a specified time frame (e.g., two working days)

---

examples). Regarding the broader organization, a typical college would be interested in attracting students (preferably without discounting the cost of tuition); retaining them through graduation and, if appropriate, through graduate study; and assisting them in job placement. A typical university would share the same interest and concerns as a college, but it would also expect the faculty to be active in attracting grants—sizable ones—and sustaining research and scholarship. More than likely, the college and university would be interested in measuring learning, other than subjectively, and faculty productivity, however defined. A number of faculty and others view good teaching, like good coffee, as subjective, and dismiss the validity of these assessments. Nonetheless, subjectivity may produce useful insights.

Higher education is, to some extent, also sensitive to the cost of education and the desire of those paying to receive value for their money. Thus, there is a need for indicators reflecting more than the quantity of teaching (e.g., number of students enrolled in a program or class) and the number of publications produced. Furthermore, the intensity of the competition for students has an impact on programs, departments, and schools. Which ones will be continued, consolidated, or discontinued? Thus, faculty who ignore numbers and resist continuous improvement risk losing competitive advantage to other institutions (e.g., corporate universities) and corporate training programs. As well, university systems may be forced to eliminate some specialties, departmental programs, or entire departments to reduce duplication at each campus.

Figure 12.4 identifies typical areas that the academic institution undoubtedly would appreciate assistance from the library in addressing.

For public libraries, one of the principal factors in the well-being of any community is economic development. Attracting and retaining suc-

FIGURE 12.4
Some Concerns Relevant to Academic Institutions

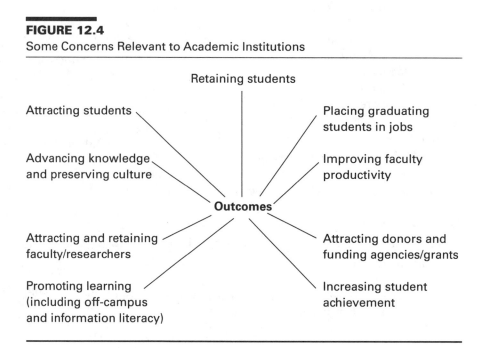

Embracing Change—Continuous Improvement

cessful businesses ensures the continued well-being of the community, not only in the taxes paid by the businesses themselves, but also by the taxes paid by their workers and by the other local jobs generated by the workers' spending. Libraries have been cited as one factor in assessing community attractiveness for businesses contemplating relocation. More recently, the hottest issue between local government and its public library is the library's contribution to the economic life of the community. Research is currently underway seeking to establish how to calculate that contribution in terms of actual dollars spent on and recouped as a result of library service.

Another contribution that local government expects from its library is assistance in preparing an educated workforce. The enhancement of literacy, the improvement of children's reading ability, and help for adults who need to improve their reading or English-language skills are important contributions in achieving a well-educated workforce. The issue of equity deals with the combination of opportunities to improve reading and general access to information and educational materials, regardless of circumstance, race, income, and so forth. Local government, through the library, assumes responsibility for ensuring equal access, regardless of ability to pay.

To a much lesser extent, local government expects that the library will contribute to the cultural life of the community by being a repository for materials of local history, but this is relatively low on the priority scale.

Academic and public libraries should not limit the measures that they report to ones demonstrating their uniqueness within the broader organization (inputs and outputs). Rather, they should address their role, for instance, in attracting and retaining faculty, students, or businesses; advancing learning; educating a workforce to gain local jobs; providing an educational or a cultural facility; and assisting the job placement process. Libraries should be a partner with central administration, with the faculty, and with other community groups in providing those services that customers need and expect.

For example, more academic institutions now expect incoming freshmen to have a certain level of computer literacy, even to have their own computers. Together with the faculty, the library, before the start of the fall term (perhaps during orientation week), might offer a program to provide freshmen with a level of technological literacy (e.g., with Netscape). That literacy might also expose students to evidence-based practice (skepticism concerning the quality of the information publicly available and, thus, a need to validate that information before relying on it) and critical thinking. Of course, meeting such broad goals would require a lot of contact hours with students. At any rate, whatever is done could be converted into such measures as:

$$\frac{\text{Number of students who mastered specific competencies}}{\text{Number of students taking the technological literacy program}} = \underline{\hspace{1cm}} \times 100 = \underline{\hspace{1cm}}\%$$

Such measures can provide useful information for the faculty while, it is hoped, lessening the amount of time that library staff have to spend providing elementary and repetitive instruction to students on a one-to-one basis.

In summary, government and many public institutions are placing greater emphasis on accountability and exploring new ways to assess the extent to which they, and by extension the library, are effective and productive. A number of academic institutions are struggling with how to measure the productivity of faculty members, to determine the effectiveness of academic departments, and to reward good teaching like they do good grantsmanship and good scholarship. Two individuals—one an institutional researcher from the provost's office at a major university, and the other a staff member for a state board of higher education—have suggested that once we solve how to measure faculty and academic departments, there will be a shift of attention to libraries and the extent to which they are accountable. Libraries will have to demonstrate their effectiveness with new measures. Thus, they should not wait the outcome of the debate over academic programs. Their time is coming and they should be preparing.[23]

The primary weakness of the examples given in Figure 12.3 is that they create the impression that the data collected and reported must be presented only in quantitative terms. Qualitative frameworks are needed that complement assessments expressed as ratios and percentages. For example, important issues to examine are the degree to which customers can (and prefer to) be self-sufficient and the extent to which staff feel empowered to resolve problems encountered by customers in their search for information.

Qualitative data collection has an important role to play in representing "subjective reality," "the way things really are rather than . . . such mechanistic elements as data and calculations."[24] Connie Van Fleet and Danny P. Wallace, perhaps in jest, propose *defectiveness* measures, *offput* measures, *how come* measures, and *futility* measures;[25] yet, are not such matters of greater concern to customers than knowing how many titles circulated or how many people were served for the fiscal year? With the increased attention being given to assessment within government, business, and industry, "new generations of measurement philosophies and techniques" will emerge.[26] This is not bad; the key is to select those measures and assessment techniques that have real value to the library and to institutional planning and decision making, taking into account the expectations and satisfaction of library customers with the services provided or planned. After all, the demand for continuous improvement, and for "data-driven decision making" and planning, will only increase.[27]

Staff Development and Training

The skill and ability to communicate with customers, play roles and engage in behaviors desired by customers, and train customers to be coproducers of the product are uniquely required of high-contact workers.

—David A. Tansik[28]

As the Association of Research Libraries (ARL) notes,

> Staff training and development programs [STDPs] maximize the potential and effectiveness of employees in the dramatically changing environment of proliferating electronic resources, budgetary crises, downsizing, outsourcing, restructuring and reorganization.[29]

Thus, improved service delivery and performance are key elements for STDPs. A library must decide which expectations it wants to and is able to meet (long-term resource commitment), and it must learn to look at the organization from the perspective of the customers.

STDPs provide a means to assist staff members in coping with customers—not just so-called problem customers—and their expectations (i.e., with those expectations the library regards as its highest priority to meet). STDPs also afford an excellent opportunity for empowering staff, and for them to see how to deal with and defuse situations involving either priority or nonpriority service expectations. For instance, a person visits the public library 35 minutes before closing requesting information and, within 10 minutes, is shown relevant material on the third floor. The person settles in, but the janitorial staff—members of a powerful union—announce the closing of the library in 15 minutes and begin turning off lights on that floor. The customer is irritated that the closing is early and she cannot see to photocopy the needed material. An STDP might deal with such questions as "How would you handle the complaint?"

Consider the case of an academic library that, in recent years, has encountered drastic budget cuts, staff downsizing, the consolidation of services and departments, an inability to replace librarians who retire (even those taking early retirement packages), and the transfer of technical service staff to public services. The faculty have, to a large extent, been forgiving of what they perceive as a decline in the quality of library collections and services. The students have been less forgiving because faculty expectations concerning course assignments have not declined—in some cases, they have noticeably increased. Thus, some customers might apologize for being critical of the library, whereas others would not. The faculty, especially in the humanities and social sciences, are also concerned about a perceived lack of balance in the collection. They believe that the library stresses access over ownership, and favors use of databases over the availability of physical objects in the collection. As libraries such as this one persist in providing a full array of services, during times of hardship—including the assignment of more responsibilities to a diminishing number of staff—they can only provide a lesser quality of service. Faculty may complain about items not reshelved for a week or more, items misshelved, and students using the library as a study hall and not for research and other purposes. Students complain that they have to

FIGURE 12.5
Satisfied and Dissatisfied Customers

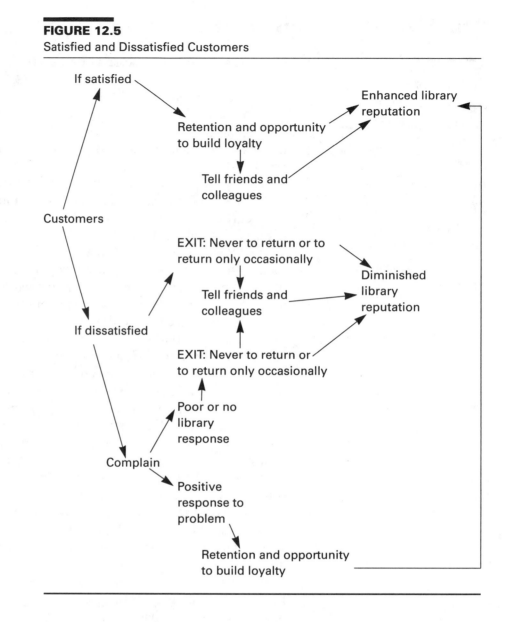

wait long periods of time for access to the Internet and that the library staff do not have a good command of new databases. Again, "How are the complaints handled?" Moreover, complaining customers are offering the library an opportunity to keep them as customers—ones delighted with the service provided (see Figure 12.5).

Figure 12.6 offers other examples for exploration in focus group interviews, role-playing sessions, and so forth, that bring together staff from different units and members of the senior management team and the frontline staff.

FIGURE 12.6

Examples of Discussion Topics for an STDP

1. A person visits the library late Friday afternoon. A stop has been placed on her borrowing card because she owes a sizable amount of money in overdues. She offers to give you cash to cover the costs and clear her record. She desperately needs the materials for a paper due on Monday. You cannot accept the money; the cashier is closed. How do you handle the situation?*

2. A customer asks to check out reserve materials but forgot to bring any identification. He does not have time to walk or drive home and return before the library closes. How do you handle the situation?*

3. A community customer has a borrowing card for which she pays $50 per year and has done so for the past four years. While visiting the library, she discovers a policy change—the need to show photo identification to use a library service. She has, however, neglected to bring such identification and does not understand why she was not informed about the policy change (even through a form letter). The staff members that she first consults will not waive the policy. How would you handle the situation?

4. The library generates a recall notice before a holiday, but the staff neglects to mail the notice to the individual until after the holiday. The person is visiting the library and wants to borrow some books, but the computer says that the overdue material was not returned and the staff want to assess a late fee and to have the item returned before lending new material. How would you handle the situation?

5. Toward the end of the workday, a customer informs the reference staff that the keyboard for the OPAC is very dirty and that there are fingerprints on the screen, making the image difficult to read. In fact, the same condition applies to each terminal and screen. The customer asks if someone can clean the screen and keyboard now. How do you handle the situation?

6. Toward the end of the semester, a faculty member complains that he cannot find the desired book on the shelf and notes that the OPAC lists it as available. Furthermore, he comments that, for days, a number of books have been on tables and carts waiting reshelving. How do you handle the

situation? (Would your answer differ if that person were a dean? An undergraduate student? A graduate student?)

7. One library, every Sunday, employs only the security guard. The OPAC is turned off on the grounds that someone might need help in using it, thus shutting it off to those who already know how to use it. Even though the library acquired a self-issue machine, it allows no circulation on Sunday. The machine is turned off. What might the library do?

8. The façade of the new public library is very pleasing and matches other city buildings in the area. There is a main entrance to the ground floor and an alternate entrance, which leads to the mezzanine level. If someone enters on the mezzanine level, located between floors one and two, he or she must go downstairs before being able to go back up. Once inside the library, customers confront stairways leading in different directions, ramps running up and down, and lots of glass and metal decorative features. No shelves of books are in sight.

The stairways, which have railings and glass siding, are clean and attractive. The marble surface is slippery. To prevent accidents, the marble has nonskid strips affixed to it. When looking out (from the stairway), there is an appearance of open space. Walking up and down the stairway poses an awkward sensation for those afraid of heights.

A customer searching for large print books would find no mention of them on the library map. Now, let's say that an elderly customer could not find a staff member on the first floor who knew the location of these books. The staff on the other floors were unwilling to leave their desks to provide directions, and the customer became confused by their conflicting suggestions. Nevertheless, the person persists and wanders throughout the library. She finally finds the books located next to works for teenagers. Titles on the shelves are arranged alphabetically by author with fiction and nonfiction interfiled. This makes it difficult to locate a biography unless she knows the author's name.

If she had known where the books were located, she would still have had to circumnavigate at least two stairways or use an elevator.

Assuming the customer complains to you about receiving the "runaround," about the difficulty of finding the large print books, and about the layout of an "unfriendly environment," how would you handle the complaint?

*Source: Association of Research Libraries, Office of Management Services, *Staff Training and Development*, SPEC Kit 224 (Washington, D.C.: ARL, 1997), 141.

Service

A service can be defined as a package of explicit and implicit benefits performed with a supporting facility and facilitating goods.

—David A. Collier[30]

Service *drives* the library, not vice versa. Jann E. Freed and Marie R. Klugman visited 10 colleges and universities as part of an investigation into the practice of continuous improvement. They reprint the mission statement for each institution and, within the context of each statement, show how the institutions are engaged in continuous quality improvement. "Areas in which services have been improved include admissions, physical plant, food service, information systems, housing, and purchasing."[31] One of their examples credits improved service to the library:

> "The library has moved to the point now where I can e-mail them and ask for a book and they'll deliver it to my office the same day. They'll do that for an administrator or any faculty member. They'll also do a search, they'll Xerox an article and deliver it to you. The morale up there has gone up tremendously. If you go over there you'll see flowcharts around the wall of processes they're continuing to work on."[32]

This example suggests other statements that might be included in a survey of faculty expectations. Not all libraries would embrace the services suggested by the preceding quotation; that, however, is not the point. Improved customer satisfaction focuses on the services offered to stakeholders, and there may be variations among institutions. "Improvements do not need to be large or costly to produce great benefits. In some cases, small changes lead to significant improvements, large savings of time, and greater stakeholder satisfaction. . . . [T]here may be some simple solutions to problems that really irritate stakeholders."[33]

James G. Neal argues that "a series of radical changes" in 12 areas shape "the organization and delivery of services" in academic libraries. The first area of change or revolution is service quality and accepting users as customers. The other areas include: reengineering ("rethinking of processes and structures in the face of economic trends and expanding, market competition"); demographics (dramatic shifts "in the diversity of the populations and sectors served"); personal computing (expanded "power to access, analyze, and control information individually"); electronics ("producing vast amounts of digital information . . . and software . . . to enable effective search and retrieval"); networks; the multimedia presentation of information, fueled by the MTV generation; values ("growing political schisms in society and the increasing threats to intellectual freedom, privacy, and the open flow of information"); accountability; higher education; partnerships; and the knowledge worker.[34] These revolutions often intertwine and introduce new problems and challenges.

More libraries and other organizations are being held accountable, and accountability may be rigorously defined. Accountability requires the adoption of a multiple stakeholder framework and recognition that librarians are managers of complex service organizations.

Exemplary Service

Attention should shift from the provision of service, or from continuing to be all things to all people, to what libraries can do well or outstandingly. An effort should be made to identify, recognize, encourage, and reward exemplary service. What library has recognized and rewarded (not necessarily financially) the staff member who just served his or her ten thousandth customer, and has maintained a steady commitment to the provision of outstanding service? Librarians should not assume that the service they provide is exemplary, or that they automatically answer more than 55 percent of the reference questions correctly.[35] They should also not assume that they automatically know or can anticipate the expectations of their customers. They should set priorities, goals, and objectives; benchmark performance over time; and commit the resources necessary to maintain levels of exemplary service—that is, service that customers regard as exemplary.

Collections and goals, such as educating students to be intelligent and evaluative consumers of information in libraries and available through the information superhighway, cannot exist outside a service environment and without meeting customer expectations. John M. Budd maintains that "libraries have a history of concern regarding use and users and have tried to structure services, collections, and access to meet user needs."[36] He perpetuates the myth that, because a library exists, customers (in large numbers) will come, be satisfied, be loyal, and be supportive—willing to vote in favor of local propositions providing financial support to the public library. What matters the most to customers, and how can the knowledge gained be applied to improve service delivery? These are the real challenges, and they present an excellent opportunity for libraries to serve their customers better. Service quality, satisfaction, and customer service are not the only issues, but they are fundamental to dealing with other issues and to improving the quality of library services.

Libraries should take the quality journey, meet changing expectations of customers, delight current customers, and seek out new customers. They should learn from their successes and mistakes and believe that everything can be improved. A belief that service is "good enough" does not inspire an organization to improve and to challenge itself. The mission and vision statements become hollow and staff are not empowered and challenged. Continuous improvement is a worthy goal and measures of *how many* or *how much* do not deal with issues central to any service organization at a time of intense competition.

Summary—Time for Action, Not Excuses

Inaction, like action, has consequences.

　　—James R. Lucas[37]

"A lack of resources" is the common response to suggestions that libraries offer new services, change some aspect of the organization, or adopt new indicators, such as those proposed in this book. "A lack of resources" is also the explanation that academic and government managers frequently give to requests for increased library funding. The actual reason is usually an unwillingness to change.

In surveying the landscape of performance measurement over the past 25 years and looking at its actual adoption among libraries, Rowena

Cullen concluded that "as a profession, we have not embraced performance measurement in the decisive way that we have adopted technology."[38] She characterized the adoption of technology as reactive, originated by vendors, while the failure to adopt performance measures is due to lack of incentives and imprecise outcomes/impacts from the present measures. She also proposed a new and innovative model of organizational effectiveness whose dimensions are represented by three separate axes: focus/value/purpose (see Figure 12.7).[39]

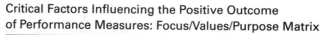

FIGURE 12.7

Critical Factors Influencing the Positive Outcome
of Performance Measures: Focus/Values/Purpose Matrix

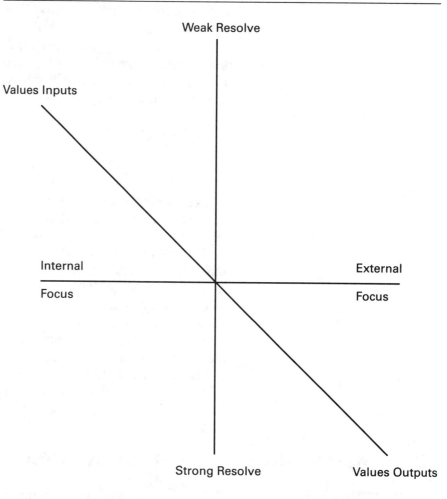

Source: Rowena J. Cullen, "Does Performance Measurement Improve Organisational Effectiveness? A Post-Modern Analysis," in *Proceedings of the 2d Northumbria International Conference on Performance Measurement in Libraries and Information Services* held at Longhirst Management and Training Centre, Longhirst Hall, Northumberland, England, September 1–6, 1997. Published by Information North for the Department of Information and Library Management, University of Northumbria at Newcastle, 1998, 11. Reprinted with permission of the author.

Embracing Change—Continuous Improvement

Focus is a continuum ranging from highly internal (emphasizing staff issues) to highly external (emphasizing customers). *Value* reflects the organization's emphasis on inputs (size, budget, and resources) as compared to its emphasis on outputs (the services provided). *Purpose* refers to "that aspect of organization culture which reflects organizational unity, a sense of common purpose and movement towards that purpose."[40]

Lack of incentives, no pressure to show profit, no shareholders to satisfy, and no need to prove value and worth combine to allow (indeed, to foster) an inward focus. By the same token, traditional measures of library performance—Association of Research Libraries (ARL) rankings, most Public Library Data Service (PLDS) data categories, and those of the National Center for Educational Statistics (NCES), based on state library agency reports—focus heavily on inputs and processes and minimally on outcomes. After all, it is traditional to do so! All these factors combine to lessen any resolve to adopt performance measurement. As a result, most libraries determining their standing on focus/value/purpose would find themselves in the upper left quadrant of Figure 12.7.

The "lack of resources" explanation may be more accurate these days, as both government and education are more financially constrained. Opportunities for either to generate any significant increase in revenue appear limited. Indeed, despite significant and continuing investments in information technology, such as online public access catalogs (OPACs), CD-ROMs, and intranets, in both academic and public libraries, funding has been static or shrinking. Budgets for academic libraries, as a percentage of the institutional budget, decreased from 4.065 percent in 1971 to 3.082 percent in 1990.[41] Over the same period, public library expenditures, as a percentage of local budgets, have fluctuated. Overall public library funding has remained at less than 1 percent of local expenditures.[42] Nevertheless, the principal responsibility of library managers—to optimize the use of resources—has not changed. They try to provide what most people want most of the time, and it is important for them to know:

- The demographic characteristics of customers and the intensity of their relationship to the library
- Customers' preferences for materials, based on their information-gathering behavior—what they actually use
- Customers' assessment of library performance on such factors as timeliness, helpfulness, courtesy, reliability, and responsiveness

With information about customers—their characteristics and preferences—libraries can apply target marketing strategies to such constituencies as students, seniors, or parents. Knowing the types of materials actually borrowed allows for more precise selection of items of interest and the avoidance of likely shelf sitters. The old explanation of "perhaps someday, someone might want . . ." is not acceptable when funds for materials are limited. Customers' assessments help libraries respond so that they can cultivate loyal customers who will rally support for bond issues or actively oppose threatened budget cuts. For a library, the payoff of learning about its customers and their requirements is heavy use of materials and services, and an enhancement of the library's service and resource reputation.

Cullen points out that where an organization sits on any of the axes depicted in Figure 12.7 is "as much a matter of choice as a function of its history and organizational culture."[43] Each library must choose its position on an axis as it reviews the methods discussed in this book, learns about its customers, and translates that knowledge into an action plan. Sponsoring organizations also have choices about which units will be funded and to what extent. According to career city manager Roger L. Kemp, local government officials and administrators now emphasize "programs that improve the management of existing organizations' resources, increase productivity, [and] maintain services without increasing taxes."[44]

Present and potential customers make choices. Ease of use and likelihood of obtaining what is desired, among other factors, drive these choices. The library's value, impact, and benefit can only be experienced and judged by customers. Is it worth the time, money, and staff to find out who they are, what they want in terms of materials and services, and how satisfied they are with those materials and services? We think it is. Now is the time for action: improved customer service linked to the type of framework discussed in this book.

NOTES

1. Robert L. Lichter, "Libraries Must Meet Users' Needs" [letters to editor], *Chronicle of Higher Education* 44, no. 4 (September 19, 1997): B13.

2. English Professor Thomas Peyser, quoted in "Thus Said," *American Libraries* 28, no. 8 (September 1997): 25.

3. Ibid. Quote of Andrew D. Martin, branch manager of an investment firm.

4. Thomas W. Shaughnessy, "Lessons from Restructuring the Library," *Journal of Academic Librarianship* 22, no. 4 (July 1996): 252.

5. Ibid.

6. "Annual Planning Submission for the University of Western Ontario Library System, 1997–1998" (London, Ontario: University of Western Ontario, 1997), 2.

7. Philip H. Abelson, "Editorial: Evolution of Higher Education," *Science* 277, no. 5327 (August 8, 1997): 747.

8. See Dees Stallings, "The Virtual University Is Inevitable: But Will the Model Be Non-profit or Profit? A Speculative Commentary on the Emerging Education Environment," *Journal of Academic Librarianship* 23, no. 4 (July 1997): 271–280.

9. Carol A. Twigg and Diana G. Oblinger, *The Virtual University* (Washington, D.C.: Educom, 1997), 3, 11.

10. Jeffrey R. Young, "Rethinking the Role of the Professor in an Age of High-Tech Tools," *Chronicle of Higher Education* 44, no. 6 (October 3, 1997): A26–A28.

11. Twigg and Oblinger, *The Virtual University*, 2.

12. See Ellen Altman and Peter Hernon, *Research Misconduct: Issues, Implications, and Strategies* (Greenwich, Conn.: Ablex, 1997).

13. Richard Cummings, "To the Editor: The World-Wide Web and the Quality of Students' Research Papers," *Chronicle of Higher Education* 44, no. 7 (October 10, 1997): B3.

14. Robert E. Dugan, "Distance Education: Provider and Victim Libraries," *Journal of Academic Librarianship* 23, no. 4 (July 1997): 315–318.

15. See Douglas G. Birdsall, "The Micropolitics of Budgeting in Universities: Lessons for Library Administrators," *Journal of Academic Librarianship* 21, no. 6 (November 1995): 427–436.

16. Stephen Goode, "Trying to Declaw the Campus Copycats," *Insight* 9, no. 18 (May 3, 1993): 10–13, 36–37.

17. William H. Sanders, "Review," *EDUCOM Review* 32, no. 4 (July/August 1997): 45.

18. "How You Can Help Them," *Fast Company* 11 (October–November 1997): 128.

19. Arnold Hirshon, "Running with the Red Queen: Breaking New Habits to Survive in the Virtual World," in *Advances in Librarianship*, vol. 20, edited by Irene Godden (San Diego: Academic Press, 1996), 9.

20. Ibid.

21. See Ibid., 10–13.

22. Pat L. Weaver-Meyers and Wilbur A. Stolt, "Delivery, Speed, Timeliness and Satisfaction: Patrons' Perceptions about ILL Service," *Journal of Library Administration* 23, nos. 1 and 2 (1996): 39.

23. Comments made to one of the authors at "Evaluating Academic Library Services: The Numbers Game: The Rest of the Story," preconference workshop, Joint Oklahoma Library Association/Mountain Plains Library Association conference, Shangri-La on Grand Lake of the Cherokees, April 30, 1997.

24. Connie Van Fleet and Danny P. Wallace, "Fourth-Generation Measures of Library Products and Services," *RQ* 36, no. 3 (spring 1997): 377.

25. Ibid.

26. Ibid., 376.

27. Jann E. Freed and Marie R. Klugman, *Quality Principles and Practices in Higher Education: Different Questions for Different Times* (Phoenix, Ariz.: Oryx Press, 1997), 175.

28. David A. Tansik, "Managing Human Resource Issues for High-Contact Service Personnel," in *Service Management Effectiveness*, edited by David E. Bowen, Richard B. Chase, Thomas G. Cummings, and associates (San Francisco: Jossey-Bass, 1990), 171.

29. Association of Research Libraries, Office of Management Services, *Staff Training and Development*, SPEC Flyer 224 (Washington, D.C.: ARL, 1997), 1.

30. David A. Collier, "Measuring and Managing Service Quality," in Bowen et al., *Service Management Effectiveness*, 237.

31. Freed and Klugman, *Quality Principles and Practices in Higher Education*, 192.

32. Ibid.

33. Ibid.

34. James G. Neal, "Academic Libraries: 2000 and Beyond," *Library Journal* 121, no. 12 (July 1996): 76.

35. See Peter Hernon and Charles R. McClure, "Unobtrusive Reference Testing: The 55 Percent Rule," *Library Journal* 111, no. 7 (April 15, 1986): 37–41.

36. John M. Budd, "A Critique of Customer and Commodity," *College & Research Libraries* 58, no. 4 (July 1997): 310–21.

37. James R. Lucas, *Fatal Illusions: Shredding a Dozen Unrealities That Can Keep Your Organization from Success* (New York: AMACOM, 1997), 100.

38. Rowena J. Cullen, "Does Performance Measurement Improve Organisational Effectiveness? A Post-Modern Analysis," in *Proceedings of the 2d Northumbria International Conference on Performance Measurement in Libraries and Information Services* (Newcastle on Tyne, England: Information North, 1998), 12.

39. Ibid., p. 11.

40. Ibid., p. 14.

41. National Center for Education Statistics, *The Status of Academic Libraries in the United States: Results from the 1990 and 1992 Academic Library Surveys*, NCES 97-413 (Washington, D.C.: Government Printing Office, 1997), 17–22.

42. Bureau of the Census, *1992 Census of Government. Finances of Municipal and Township Governments*, vol. 4, no. 4 (Washington, D.C.: Government Printing Office, 1997). See also: http://www.census.gov/prod2/gov/gc92-4/gc924-4.pdf.

43. Cullen, "Does Performance Measurement Improve Organisational Effectiveness?" 11.

44. Roger L. Kemp, "The Creative Management of Library Services," *Public Libraries* 34, no. 4 (July/August 1995): 212.

Bibliography

Abelson, Philip H. "Editorial: Evolution of Higher Education." *Science* 277, no. 5327 (August 8, 1997): 747.

Alston, Ruth. "Performance Indicators in Bromley—Purpose and Practice." *Library Management* 16, no. 1 (1995): 18–28.

Altman, Ellen, and Peter Hernon. *Research Misconduct: Issues, Implications, and Strategies*. Greenwich, Conn.: Ablex, 1997.

Anthony, William P. *Practical Strategic Planning*. Westport, Conn.: Quorum Books, 1985.

"Annual Planning Submission for the University of Western Ontario Library System, 1997–1998." Unpublished. London, Ontario: University of Western Ontario, 1997.

Applegate, Rachel. "Models of Satisfaction." In *Encyclopedia of Library and Information Science*. Vol. 60, supplement 23. Edited by Allen Kent, 199–227. New York: Marcel Dekker, 1997.

Applegate, Rachel. "Models of User Satisfaction: Understanding False Positives." *RQ* 32, no. 4 (summer 1993): 525–39.

Association of Research Libraries. Office of Management Services. *Staff Training and Development*, SPEC Flyer 224. Washington, D.C.: ARL, 1997.

Atkins, Stephen. "Mining Automated Systems for Collection Management." *Library Administration & Management* 10, no. 1 (winter 1996): 16–19.

Baltimore County Public Library's Blue Ribbon Committee. *Give 'Em What They Want! Managing the Public's Library*. Chicago: American Library Association, 1992.

Bangert, Stephanie Rogers. "Values in College and University Library Mission Statements: A Search for Distinctive Beliefs, Meaning, and Organizational Culture." *Advances in Librarianship*, edited by Irene Godden, 91–106. Vol. 21. San Diego, Calif.: Academic Press.

Barlow, Janelle, and Claus Moller. *A Complaint Is a Gift: Using Customer Feedback as a Strategic Tool*. San Francisco: Berrett Koehler, 1996.

Bateson, John E. G. "Evaluating the Role and Place of Marketing in Service Firms." In *Service Management Effectiveness*, edited by David E. Bowen, Richard B. Chase, Thomas G. Cummings, and associates, 324–342. San Francisco: Jossey-Bass, 1990.

Benefiel, Candace R., Jeannie P. Miller, and Diana Ramirez. "Baseline Subject Competencies for the Academic Reference Desk." *Reference Services Review* 25, no. 1 (spring 1997): 83–93.

Bertot, John Carlo, Charles R. McClure, William E. Moen, and Jeffrey Rubin. "Web Usage Statistics: Measurement Issues and Analytical Techniques." *Government Information Quarterly* 14, no. 4 (1997): 373–95.

Birdsall, Douglas G. "The Micropolitics of Budgeting in Universities: Lessons for Library Administrators." *Journal of Academic Librarianship* 21, no. 6 (November 1995): 427–36.

Bitner, Mary Jo, and Amy R. Hubbert. "Encounter Satisfaction versus Overall Satisfaction versus Quality." In *Service Quality: New Directions in Theory and Practice*, edited by Roland T. Rust and Richard L. Oliver, 72–94. Thousand Oaks, Calif.: Sage, 1994.

Blake, Robert R., and Anne Adams McCanse. *Leadership Dilemmas—Grid Solutions*. Houston, Tex.: Gulf Publishing Co., 1991.

Boissé, Joseph A. "Adjusting the Horizontal Hold: Flattening the Organization." *Library Administration & Management* 10, no. 2 (spring 1996): 77–81.

Brophy, Peter, and Kate Coulling. *Quality Management for Information and Library Managers*. Hampshire, England: Aslib/Gower, 1996.

Budd, John M. "A Critique of Customer and Commodity." *College & Research Libraries* 58, no. 4 (July 1997): 310–21.

Bureau of the Census. *1992 Census of Government. Finances of Municipal and Township Governments*. Vol. 4, no. 4. Washington, D.C.: Government Printing Office, 1997 (http://www.census.gov/prod2/gov/gc92-4/gc924-4.pdf).

Calvert, Philip J., and Peter Hernon. "Surveying Service Quality within University Libraries." *Journal of Academic Librarianship* 23, no. 5 (September 1997): 408–415.

Camden County Library System. "Our Promise to You . . . from the People of the Camden County Library System." Voorhees, N.J.: August 23, 1994.

Cannie, Joan Koob, with Donald Caplin. *Keeping Customers for Life*. New York: AMACOM, 1991.

Carr, Clay. *Front-line Customer Service: 15 Keys to Customer Satisfaction*. New York: Wiley, 1990.

Carrigan, Dennis P. "Data-Guided Collection Development: A Promise Unfulfilled," *College & Research Libraries* 57, no. 5 (September 1996): 429–37.

Childers, Thomas A., and Nancy Van House. "Dimensions of Public Library Effectiveness," *Library & Information Science Research* 11, no. 3 (1989): 273–301.

Childers, Thomas A., and Nancy A. Van House. *What's Good? Describing Your Public Library's Effectiveness*. Chicago: American Library Association, 1993.

Cipolla, Wilma Reed. "The Mission of a University Undergraduate Library: Draft Model Statement." *College & Research Libraries News* 48, no. 4 (April 1987): 192–94.

Clack, Mary Elizabeth. "Values, a Process of Discovery: The Harvard College Library's Organizational Values Process." *Library Administration & Management* 9, no. 3 (summer 1995): 146–52.

Coleman, Vicki, Yi (Daniel) Xiao, Linda Blair, and Bill Chollett. "Toward a TQM Paradigm: Using SERVQUAL to Measure Library Service Quality." *College & Research Libraries* 58, no. 3 (May 1997): 237–51.

Collier, David A. "Measuring and Managing Service Quality." In *Service Management Effectiveness*, edited by David E. Bowen, Richard B. Chase, Thomas G. Cummings, and associates, 234–65. San Francisco: Jossey-Bass, 1990.

Cullen, Rowena J. "Does Performance Measurement Improve Organisational Effectiveness? A Post-Modern Analysis." In *Proceedings of the 2d Northumbria International Conference on Performance Measurement in Libraries and Information Services*, 3–20. Newcastle upon Tyne, England: Department of Information and Library Management, University of Northumbria at Newcastle, 1998.

Cullen, Rowena J., and Philip J. Calvert. "Stakeholder Perceptions of University Library Effectiveness." *Journal of Academic Librarianship* 21, no. 6 (November 1995): 438–48.

Cummings, Richard. "To the Editor: The World-Wide Web and the Quality of Students' Research Papers." *Chronicle of Higher Education* 44, no. 7 (October 10, 1997): B3.

Curry, Ann. "Managing the Problem Patron." *Public Libraries* 35, no. 3 (May/June 1996): 181–88.

Dart, Jack. "Professional Service Quality: The Practice of the Professional?" *Journal of Customer Service in Marketing and Management* 2, no. 2 (1996): 21–35.

Davis, Annette, and Ian Kirkpatrick. "To Measure Service: Ask the Library User." *Library Association Record* 96, no. 2 (February 1994): 88–89.

De Gennaro, Richard. Foreword to *Gateways to Knowledge: The Role of Academic Librarians in Teaching, Learning and Research*, edited by Lawrence Dowler. Cambridge, Mass.: MIT Press, 1997.

D'Elia, George, and Eleanor Jo Rodger. *Free Library of Philadelphia Patron Survey: Final Report*. Philadelphia, Pa.: Free Library of Philadelphia, 1991.

Department of Commerce. Office of Consumer Affairs. *Managing Consumer Complaints: Responsive Business Approaches to Consumer Needs*. Washington, D.C.: Government Printing Office, 1992.

"Developing Indicators for Academic Library Performance: Ratios from the ARL Statistics, 1993–94 and 1994–95." ARL homepage, http://arl.cni.org/stats/Statistics/arlstat/indi95.html.

Dewdney, Patricia, and Catherine Sheldrick Ross. "Flying a Light Aircraft: Reference Service Evaluation from a User's Viewpoint." *RQ* 34, no. 2 (winter 1994): 217–29.

The Doctor. Directed by Randa Haines. Touchstone Pictures, 1991.

Drucker, Peter. *Managing for the Future: The 1990s and Beyond*. New York: Truman Tally Books, 1992.

Drucker, Peter. *Peter Drucker on the Profession of Management*, edited by Nan Stone. Cambridge: Harvard Business School Press, 1998.

Dugan, Robert E. "Distance Education: Provider and Victim Libraries." *Journal of Academic Librarianship* 23, no. 4 (July 1997): 315–18.

Eccles, Robert G. "The Performance Measurement Manifesto." In *Performance Measurement and Evaluation*, edited by Jacky Holloway, Jenny Lewis, and Geoff Mallory, 5–14. London: Sage, 1995.

Elliott, Kevin M. "A Comparison of Alternative Measures of Service Quality." *Journal of Customer Service in Marketing and Management* 1, no. 1 (1995): 33–44.

Erdos, P. L. *Professional Mail Surveys*. New York: McGraw-Hill, 1970.

"Evaluating Academic Library Services: The Numbers Game: The Rest of the Story." Preconference workshop, Joint Oklahoma Library Association/Mountain Plains Library Association conference, Shangri-La on Grand Lake of the Cherokees, April 30, 1997.

Evans, G. Edward, and Sandra M. Heft. *Introduction to Technical Services*. 6th ed. Littleton, Colo.: Libraries Unlimited, 1995.

Farquhar, Carolyn R. *Focusing on the Customer: A Catalyst for Change in the Public Sector. Lessons from the North American Study Tour on Total Quality in the Public Sector*. Ottawa, Canada: The Conference Board of Canada, 1993.

Florance, Valerie, and Nina W. Matheson. "Health Science Librarian as Knowledge Worker." *Library Trends* 42, no. 1 (summer 1993): 196–219.

Fornell, Claes. "A National Customer Satisfaction Barometer: The Swedish Experience." In *Performance Measurement and Evaluation*, edited by Jacky Holloway, Jenny Lewis, and Geoff Mallory, 95–123. London: Sage, 1995.

Freed, Jann E., and Marie R. Klugman. *Quality Principles and Practices in Higher Education: Different Questions for Different Times*. Phoenix, Ariz.: Oryx Press, 1997.

General Accounting Office. *The Government Performance and Results Act: 1997 Governmentwide Implementation Will Be Uneven*. GAO/GGD-97-109. Washington, D.C.: The Office, 1997.

General Accounting Office. "Statistical Agencies: Collection and Reporting of Race and Ethnicity Data." Statement of Bernard L. Ungar, Associate Director, Federal Management and Workforce Issues, General Government Division, GAO/T-GGD-97-92. Washington, D.C.: The Office, 1997.

General Accounting Office. *Using Statistical Sampling*. Transfer Paper 9. Washington, D.C.: The Office, 1986, 1992.

General Accounting Office. Program Evaluation and Methodology Division. *Case Study Evaluations*. Transfer Paper 9. Washington, D.C.: The Office, 1990.

Goode, Stephen. "Trying to Declaw the Campus Copycats." *Insight* 9, no. 18 (May 3, 1993): 10–13, 36–37.

Griffiths, José-Marie, and Donald W. King. *Increasing the Information Edge*. Washington, D.C.: Special Libraries Association, 1993.

Hafner, Arthur W. *Descriptive Statistical Techniques for Librarians*. 2d ed. Chicago: American Library Association, 1998.

Hardesty, Larry, Jamie Hastreiter, and David Henderson. *Mission Statements for College Libraries*. Chicago: American Library Association, College Libraries Section, College Library Information Packet Committee, 1985.

Harwood, Nicola, and Jillene Bydder, "Student Expectations of, and Satisfaction with, the University Library." *Journal of Academic Librarianship* 24, no. 2 (March 1998), 161–71.

Hawken, Paul. *Growing a Business*. New York: Simon & Schuster, 1987.

Hayes, Bob. *Measuring Customer Satisfaction*. Milwaukee, Wisc.: ASQC Quality Press, 1992.

Hébert, Françoise. "Service Quality: An Unobtrusive Investigation of Interlibrary Loan in Large Public Libraries in Canada." *Library & Information Science Research* 16, no. 1 (1994): 3–21.

Hernon, Peter. *Statistics: A Component of the Research Process*. Rev. ed. Norwood, N.J.: Ablex, 1994.

Hernon, Peter. "Unobtrusive Testing." In *Evaluating Library Programs and Services: TELL IT! Training Manual*, edited by Douglas Zweizig with Michele Besant, 71–80. Madison, Wis.: University of Wisconsin, School of Library and Information Studies, 1993.

Hernon, Peter, and Ellen Altman. *Service Quality in Academic Libraries*. Norwood, N.J.: Ablex, 1996.

Hernon, Peter, and Philip J. Calvert. "Methods for Measuring Service Quality in University Libraries in New Zealand." *Journal of Academic Librarianship* 22, no. 5 (September 1996): 387–91.

Hernon, Peter, and Charles R. McClure. *Evaluation and Library Decision Making*. Norwood, N.J.: Ablex, 1990.

Hernon, Peter, and Charles R. McClure. "Unobtrusive Reference Testing: The 55 Percent Rule." *Library Journal* 111, no. 7 (April 15, 1986): 37–41.

Himmel, Edith, and William J. Wilson, with ReVision Committee of the Public Library Association. *Planning for Results: A Public Library Transformation Process*. Part 1: "How to Manual"; Part 2: "Guidebook." Chicago: American Library Association, 1998.

Hirshon, Arnold. "Running with the Red Queen: Breaking New Habits to Survive in the Virtual World." In *Advances in Librarianship*. Vol. 20, edited by Irene Godden, 1–26. San Diego, Calif.: Academic Press, 1996.

Holt, Glen E. "On Becoming Essential: An Agenda for Quality in Twenty-First Century Public Libraries." *Library Trends* 44, no. 3 (winter 1996): 545–71.

Hope, Tony, and Jeremy Hope. *Transforming the Bottom Line: Managing Performance with the Real Numbers*. Boston: Harvard Business School Press, 1996.

"How You Can Help Them." *Fast Company* 11 (October–November 1997): 128–36.

Ingley, Kathleen. "Pressure's on for Parks to Be Self-Supporting." *Arizona Republic*, August 31, 1991, A1.

Intner, Sheila, and Elizabeth Futas. "Evaluating Public Library Collections." In *The Whole Library Handbook* 2, compiled by George M. Eberhart, 302–6. Chicago: American Library Association, 1995.

Johnson, Michael D. *Customer Orientation and Market Action*. Upper Saddle River, N.J.: Prentice Hall, 1998.

Johnston, Catharine G. *Beyond Customer Satisfaction to Loyalty*. Ottawa, Canada: The Conference Board of Canada, 1996.

Kaplan, Robert S., and David P. Norton. "The Balanced Scorecard—Measures That Drive Performance." *Harvard Business Review* 70, no. 1 (January/February 1992): 71–79.

Kemp, Roger L. "The Creative Management of Library Services," *Public Libraries* 34, no. 4 (July/August 1995): 212–15.

Kroon, George E. "Improving Quality in Services Marketing: Four Important Dimensions." *Journal of Customer Service in Marketing and Management* 1, no. 2 (1995): 13–28.

Lancaster, F. W. *If You Want to Evaluate Your Library*. . . . Champaign, Ill.: University of Illinois, Graduate School of Library and Information Science, 1988.

Lanham, Richard A. "A Computer-Based Harvard Red Book." In *Gateways to Knowledge: The Role of Academic Libraries in Teaching, Learning, and Research*, edited by Lawrence Dowler, 151–67. Cambridge, Mass.: Massachusetts Institute of Technology, 1997.

Larsen, Patricia M. "Mining Your Automated System for Better Management." *Library Administration & Management* 10, no. 1 (winter 1996): 10.

Lenzer, Robert, and Stephen S. Johnson. "Seeing Things as They Really Are: An Interview with Peter Drucker." *Forbes* 159 (March 10, 1997): 122–128.

Lichter, Robert L. "Libraries Must Meet Users' Needs" [letter to the editor]. *Chronicle of Higher Education* 44, no. 4 (September 19, 1997): B13.

Line, Maurice B. "Line's Five Laws of Librarianship . . . and One All Embracing Law." *Library Association Record* 98, no. 3 (March 1996): 144.

Line, Maurice B. "Use of Library Materials" [book review]. *College & Research Libraries* 40, no. 6 (November 1979): 557–58.

Line, Maurice B. "What Do People Need of Libraries, and How Can We Find Out?" *Australian Academic & Research Libraries* 27, no. 2 (June 1996): 77–86.

Liswood, Laura. *Serving Them Right: Innovative and Powerful Customer Retention Strategies*. New York: Harper Business, 1990.

Lubans, John L. "Sherlock's Dog, or Managers and Mess Findings." *Library Administration & Management* 8, no. 3 (summer 1994): 139–49.

Lucas, James R. *Fatal Illusions: Shredding a Dozen Unrealities That Can Keep Your Organization from Success*. New York: AMACOM, 1997.

Lucinao, Lani. "Money Helps: Answers to Your Questions." *Money* 26, no. 4 (April 1997): 175–76.

Lynch, James, Robert Carver, Jr., and John Michael Virgo. "Quadrant Analysis as a Strategic Planning Technique in Curriculum Development and Program Marketing." *Journal of Marketing for Higher Education* 7, no. 2 (1996): 17–32.

Lynch, Richard L., and Kelvin F. Cross. *Measure Up! Yardsticks for Continuous Improvement*. Cambridge, Mass.: Blackwell, 1991.

Mancini, Donna D. "Mining Your Automated System for Systemwide Decision Making." *Library Administration & Management* 10, no. 1 (winter 1996): 11–15.

"Making Team Work Like Roman Orchard Slaves: A Dilbert's-eye View of the Modern Office." *Newsweek* 129, no. 19 (May 6, 1996): 50.

Manolis, Chris, and Scott W. Kelley. "Assessing Service Quality via the Contributions of Service Employees and Customers." *Journal of Customer Service in Marketing and Management* 2, no. 4 (1996): 31–48.

Marco, Guy A. "The Terminology of Planning: Part 1." *Library Management* 17, no. 2 (1996): 17–23.

Marco, Guy A. "The Terminology of Planning: Part 2." *Library Management* 17, no. 7 (1996): 17–24.

Marriott, J. W., Jr., and Kathi Ann Brown. *The Spirit to Serve: Marriott's Way.* New York: HarperCollins, 1997.

Marshall, Joanne. *The Impact of the Special Library on Corporate Decision Making.* Washington, D.C.: Special Libraries Association, 1993.

Martin, Susan K. "The Changing Role of the Library Director: Fund-raising and the Academic Library." *Journal of Academic Librarianship* 24, no. 1 (January 1998): 3–10.

McClure, Charles R., and Peter Hernon. *Users of Academic and Public GPO Depository Libraries.* Washington, D.C.: Government Printing Office, 1989.

McClure, Charles R., and Cynthia L. Lopata. *Assessing the Academic Networked Environment: Strategies and Options.* Washington, D.C.: Coalition for Networked Information, 1996.

McClure, Charles R., Amy Owen, Douglas L. Zweizig, Mary J. Lynch, and Nancy A. Van House. *Planning and Role Setting for Public Libraries: A Manual of Options and Procedures.* 2d ed. Chicago: American Library Association, 1987.

McDonald, Joseph A., and Lynda Basney Micikas. *Academic Libraries: The Dimensions of Their Effectiveness.* Westport, Conn.: Greenwood Press, 1994.

McKenna, Christopher K. "Using Focus Groups to Understand Library Utilization: An Open Systems Perspective." *Journal of Management Science & Policy Analysis* 7 (summer 1990): 316–29.

Miller, Delbert C. *Handbook of Research Design and Social Measurement.* Newbury Park, Calif.: Sage, 1991.

Miller, Glenn. *Customer Service and Innovation in Libraries.* Fort Atkinson, Wis.: Highsmith Press, 1996.

Minnesota Office of the Legislative Auditor. *State Agency Use of Customer Satisfaction Surveys: A Program Evaluation Report.* St. Paul, Minn.: The Office, 1995.

Morgan, Rebecca L. *Calming Upset Customers: Staying Effective during Unpleasant Situations.* Rev. ed. Menlo Park, Calif.: Crisp Publications, 1996.

National Center for Education Statistics. *The Status of Academic Libraries in the United States: Results from the 1990 and 1992 Academic Library Surveys.* NCES 97-413. Washington, D.C.: Government Printing Office, 1997.

National Performance Review. *Serving the American Public: Best Practices in Customer-Driven Strategic Planning.* Federal Benchmarking Consortium Study Report. Washington, D.C.: Government Printing Office, 1997.

National Performance Review. *Serving the American Public: Best Practices in Resolving Customer Complaints.* Federal Benchmarking Consortium Study Report. Washington, D.C.: Government Printing Office, 1996.

Neal, James G. "Academic Libraries: 2000 and Beyond." *Library Journal* 121, no. 12 (July 1996): 74–76.

Nederhof, Anton J. "The Effects of Material Incentives in Mail Surveys: Two Studies." *Public Opinion Quarterly* 47, no. 1 (spring 1983): 103–11.

Nitecki, Danuta A. "An Assessment of the Applicability of SERVQUAL Dimensions as Customer-based Criteria for Evaluating Quality of Services in an Academic Library," Ph.D. dissertation, University of Maryland, 1995.

Nitecki, Danuta A. "Assessment of Service Quality in Academic Libraries: Focus on the Applicability of the SERVQUAL," in *Proceedings of the 2nd Northumbria International Conference on Performance Measurement in Libraries and Information Services,* 181–96. Newcastle upon Tyne, England: Department of Information and Library Management, University of Northumbria at Newcastle, 1998.

Nitecki, Danuta A. "Changing the Concept and Measure of Service Quality in Academic Libraries." *Journal of Academic Librarianship* 22, no. 3 (May 1996): 181–90.

Norman, Ralph. "The Scholarly Journal and the Intellectual Sensorium." In *The Politics and Processes of Scholarship,* edited by Joseph M. Moxley and Lagretta T. Lenker, 77–87. Westport, Conn.: Greenwood Press, 1995.

Oksenberg, Lois, Lerita Coleman, and Charles F. Cannell. "Interviewers' Voices and Refusal Rates in Telephone Surveys." *Public Opinion Quarterly* 50, no. 1 (spring 1986): 97–111.

Oliver, R. L. "A Conceptual Model of Service Quality and Service Satisfaction: Compatible Goals, Different Concepts." In *Advances in Services Marketing and Management: Research and Practice*. Vol. 2, edited by T. A. Swartz, D. E. Bowen, and S. W. Brown, 65–85. Greenwich, Conn.: JAI Press, 1993.

Osborne, David, and Ted Gaebler. *Reinventing Government: How the Entrepreneurial Spirit Is Transforming the Public Sector*. Reading, Mass.: Addison-Wesley, 1992.

"Our Commitment to Excellence." Wright State University Libraries. http://www.libraries.wright.edu./services/Customers_Services.html.

Parasuraman, A., Valarie A. Zeithaml, and Leonard L. Berry. "A Conceptual Model of Service Quality and Its Implications for Future Research." *Journal of Marketing* 49, no. 4 (fall 1985): 41–50.

Poll, Roswitha, and Peter te Boekhorst. *Measuring Quality: International Guidelines for Performance Measurement in Academic Libraries*. IFLA Publication 76. New Providence, N.J.: K.G. Saur/Reed Publishing, 1996.

Pratt, Allan D., and Ellen Altman. "Live by the Numbers; Die by the Numbers." *Library Journal* 122, no. 7 (April 15, 1997): 48–49.

Public Library Data Service. *Statistical Report '95*. Chicago: Public Library Association, 1995.

Public Library Data Service. *Statistical Report '97*. Chicago: Public Library Association, 1997.

Quinn, Brian. "Adopting Service Quality Concepts to Academic Libraries." *Journal of Academic Librarianship* 23, no. 5 (September 1997): 359–69.

Radford, Marie L., and Gary P. Radford. "Power, Knowledge, and Fear: Feminism, Foucault, and the Stereotype of the Female Librarian." *Library Quarterly* 67, no. 3 (July 1997): 250–66.

Reference and Adult Services Division. Ad Hoc Committee on Behavioral Guidelines for Reference and Information Services. "Guidelines for Behavorial Performance of Reference and Information Services Professionals." *RQ* 36, no. 2 (winter 1996): 200–203.

Reichheld, Fred. Foreward to *Serving Them Right: Innovative and Powerful Customer Retention Strategies*. New York: Harper Business, 1990.

Roberts, Harry V., and Bernard E. Sergesketter. *Quality Is Personal: A Foundation for Total Quality Management*. New York: Free Press, 1992.

Rosenbaum, Ed. *A Taste of My Own Medicine*. New York: Ballantine Books, 1991.

Ross, Catherine Sheldrick, and Patricia Dewdney. "Best Practices: An Analysis of the Best (and Worst) in Fifty-Two Public Library Reference Transactions." *Public Libraries* 33, no. 5 (September/October 1994): 261–66.

Rossi, Peter H., and Howard E. Freeman. *Evaluation: A Systematic Approach*. 5th ed. Newbury Park, Calif.: Sage, 1993.

Rubin, Howard A. "In Search of the Business Value of Information Technology." *Application Development Trends* 1, no. 2 (November 1994): 23–27.

Rust, Roland T., and Richard L. Oliver. *Service Quality: New Directions in Theory and Practice*. Thousand Oaks, Calif.: Sage, 1994.

Sampson, Scott E. "Ramifications of Monitoring Service Quality through Passively Solicited Customer Feedback." *Decision Sciences* 27, no. 4 (fall 1996): 601–21.

Sanders, Betsy. *Fabled Service: Ordinary Acts, Extraordinary Outcomes*. San Diego, Calif.: Pfeiffer, 1995.

Sanders, William H. "Review." *EDUCOM Review* 32, no. 4 (July/August 1997): 45.

Sandy, John H. "By Any Other Name, They're Still Our Customers." *American Libraries* 28, no. 7 (August 1997): 43–45.

Saracevic, Tefko, and Paul B. Kantor. "Studying the Value of Library and Information Services. Part II. Methodology and Taxonomy." *Journal of the American Society for Information Science* 48, no. 6 (1997): 543–63.

Schneider, Benjamin, and David E. Brown. *Winning the Service Game*. Boston: Harvard Business School Press, 1995.

Schwarzwalder, Robert. "Building the Digital Sci/Tech Library. Part 1: The Revolutionaries' Handbook." *Database* 20, no. 3 (June/July 1997): 63–65.

Seay, Thomas, Sheila Seaman, and David Cohen. "Measuring and Improving the Quality of Public Services: A Hybrid Approach." *Library Trends* 44, no. 3 (winter 1996): 464–90.

Shaughnessy, Thomas W. "Lessons from Restructuring the Library." *Journal of Academic Librarianship* 22, no. 4 (July 1996): 251–56.

Singh, Jagdip. "A Multifacet Typology of Patient Satisfaction with a Hospital." *Journal of Health Care Marketing* 10, no. 4 (1990): 8–21.

Smith, Mark, and Gerry Rowland. "To Boldly Go: Searching for Output Measures for Electronic Services." *Public Libraries* 36, no. 3 (May/June 1997): 168–71.

Smith, Nathan. "Active Listening: Alleviating Patron Problems through Communication." In *Patron Behavior in Libraries: A Handbook of Positive Approaches to Negative Situations*, edited by Beth McNeil and Denise J. Johnson, 127–34. Chicago: American Library Association, 1996.

Spector, Robert. *The Nordstrom Way: The Inside Story of America's #1 Customer Service Company*. New York: Wiley, 1995.

St. Clair, Guy. *Customer Service in the Information Environment*. London: Bowker Saur, 1993.

Stallings, Dees. "The Virtual University Is Inevitable: But Will the Model Be Non-profit or Profit? A Speculative Commentary on the Emerging Education Environment." *Journal of Academic Librarianship* 23, no. 4 (July 1997): 271–80.

Stein, Joan. "Feedback from a Captive Audience: Reflections on the Results of a SERVQUAL Survey of Interlibrary Loan Services at Carnegie Mellon University Libraries," in *Proceedings of the 2nd Northumbria International Conference on Performance Measurement in Libraries and Information Services*, 207–22. Newcastle upon Tyne, England: Department of Information and Library Management, University of Northumbria at Newcastle, 1998.

Tansik, David A. "Managing Human Resource Issues for High-Contact Service Personnel." In *Service Management Effectiveness*, edited by David E. Bowen, Richard B. Chase, Thomas G. Cummings, and Associates, 152–76. San Francisco: Jossey-Bass, 1990.

"Thus Said." *American Libraries* 28, no. 8 (September 1997): 25.

Tillotson, Joy, Janice Adlington, and Cynthia Holt. "Benchmarking Waiting Times." *College & Research Libraries News* 58, no. 10 (November 1997): 693–94, 700.

Turner, Ann M. "Opinion Polls: A Savvy Tool to Raise Library Value." *Library Journal* 122, no. 17 (October 15, 1997): 40–41.

Twigg, Carol A., and Diana G. Oblinger. *The Virtual University*. Washington, D.C.: Educom, 1997.

U.S. Office of Management and Budget. "Primer on Performance Measurement." Revised February 28, 1995. ftp://ftp.fedworld.gov/pub/results/primer0.1txt.

Van Fleet, Connie, and Danny P. Wallace. "Fourth-Generation Measures of Library Products and Services." *RQ* 36, no. 3 (spring 1997): 376–80.

Van House, Nancy A., and Thomas A. Childers. "Dimensions of Public Library Effectiveness II." *Library & Information Science Research* 12, no. 2 (1990): 131–52.

Van House, Nancy A., Beth T. Weil, and Charles R. McClure. *Measuring Academic Library Performance: A Practical Approach*. Chicago: American Library Association, 1990.

Van House, Nancy A., Mary Jo Lynch, Charles R. McClure, Douglas L. Zweizig, and Eleanor Jo Rodger. *Output Measures for Public Libraries*. Chicago: American Library Association, 1987.

Weaver-Meyers, Pat L., and Wilbur A. Stolt. "Delivery Speed, Timeliness, and Satisfaction: Patrons' Perceptions about ILL Service." *Journal of Library Administration* 23, nos. 1 and 2 (1996): 23–42.

Wehmeyer, Susan, Dorothy Auchter, and Arnold Hirshon. "Saying What We Will Do, and Doing What We Say: Implementing a Customer Service Plan." *Journal of Academic Librarianship* 22, no. 3 (May 1996): 173–80.

Weingand, Darlene E. *Customer Service Excellence: A Concise Guide for Librarians*. Chicago: American Library Association, 1997.

Wilson, Lizabeth A. "Glacier or Avalanche? Shifts in the Electronic, Education, and Library Landscape." In *LOEX of the West: Teaching and Learning in a "Climate of Change,"* edited by Thomas W. Leonhardt, 1–18. Greenwich, Conn.: JAI Press, 1996.

Wilson, Patrick. "Unused Relevant Information in Research and Development." *Journal of the American Society for Information Science* 46, no. 1 (1996): 45–51.

Young, Jeffrey R. "Rethinking the Role of the Professor in an Age of High-Tech Tools." *Chronicle of Higher Education* 44, no. 6 (October 3, 1997): A26–A28.

Zammuto, Raymond F., Susan M. Keaveney, and Edward J. O'Connor. "Rethinking Student Services: Assessing and Improving Service Quality." *Journal of Marketing for Higher Education* 7, no. 1 (1996): 45–70.

Zeithaml, Valarie A., A. Parasuraman, and Leonard L. Berry. *Delivering Quality Service: Balancing Customer Perceptions and Expectations*. New York: The Free Press, 1990.

Index

Ellen Altman was Visiting Professor, Department of Library and Information Studies, Victoria University of Wellington, New Zealand, until July 1997. She has been a faculty member at the Universities of Kentucky and Toronto, and Indiana University. She was Professor and Director of the Graduate Library School at the University of Arizona. She has been Feature Editor of *Public Libraries*, the official publication of the Public Library Association of the United States, since 1992. Dr. Altman is co-editor of "The JAL Guide to the Professional Literature" in the *Journal of Academic Librarianship* and a member of *Library Quarterly*'s Editorial Board. Professor Altman was one of the coauthors of *Performance Measures for Public Libraries* published in 1973. She has served on many professional and governmental committees. She received the Distinguished Alumni Award from Rutgers School of Communication, Information and Library Studies in 1983, and has been included in *Who's Who in America* since 1981.

Peter Hernon is Professor, Graduate School of Library and Information Science, Simmons College, Boston, where he teaches courses related to research methods, evaluation of library services, statistics, and government information. Dr. Hernon received his Ph.D. degree from Indiana University, Bloomington, in 1978. He is the editor-in-chief of the *Journal of Academic Librarianship*, founding editor of *Government Information Quarterly*, and co-editor of *Library & Information Science Research*. Professor Hernon is the author or editor of 33 books and more than 120 articles, and he has received a number of awards for his research and professional contributions.